Italy

120th anniversary

Berlitz

- A in the text denotes a highly recommended sight
- A complete A–Z of practical information starts on p.219
- Extensive mapping throughout

Berlitz Publishing Company, Inc.

Princeton   Mexico City   Dublin   Eschborn   Singapore

Text:	Jack Altman
Editors:	Christina Jackson
Photography:	Daniel Vittet, Walter Imber, PRISMA/Schuster GmbH, Jean Mohr, Claude Huber, Kurt Ammann, and Jean - Claude Vieillefond
Cover photo:	© Michael Simpson/FPG International
Layout:	Media Content Marketing, Inc.
Cartography:	Falk - Verlag Munich GeoSystems Global Corp.

Thanks to Adrienne Farrell, Francesca Rahimi, Don Larrimore and Lyon Benzimra for their invaluable help in the preparation of this guide.

Found an error we should know about? Our editor would be happy to hear from you, and a postcard would do. Although we make every effort to ensure the accuracy of all the information in this book, changes do occur.

ISBN 2-8315-6308-9
Revised 1998 – Second Printing May 1998

Printed in Switzerland by Weber SA, Bienne
029/805 RP

CONTENTS

ITALY

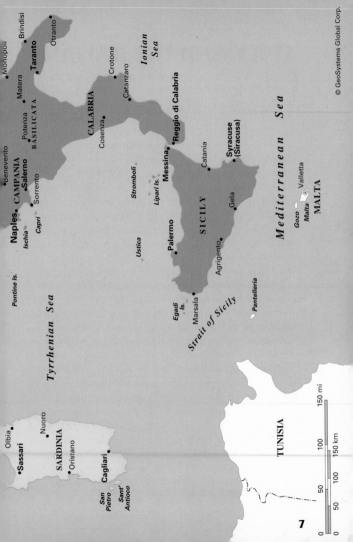

© GeoSystems Global Corp.

Brindisi
Monopoli
Otranto
Taranto
Matera
Ionian Sea
Benevento
Potenza
CAMPANIA
Crotone
BASILICATA
Salerno
CALABRIA
Catanzaro
Naples
Sorrento
Cosenza
Capri
Ischia
Reggio di Calabria
Messina
Syracuse
(Siracusa)
Stromboli
Catania
Lipari Is.
Pontine Is.
Ustica
SICILY
Gela
Tyrrhenian Sea
Palermo
Agrigento
Mediterranean Sea
Valletta
Gozo
Malta
MALTA
Egadi Is.
Marsala
Pantelleria
Strait of Sicily

Olbia
Nuoro
Sassari
SARDINIA
Oristano
Cagliari
San Pietro
Sant' Antioco

TUNISIA

0   50   100   150 mi
0   50 100 150 km

7

ITALY AND THE ITALIANS

From the Alps right down to the southern tip of Sicily, Italy provides the most tangible proof that the world indeed is a stage. Architects and sculptors treat the myriad parks and gardens as set designs, and nature itself turns the landscapes, with their characteristic statuesque cypresses, tortuous olive and fig trees, or chorus rows of vineyards, into just so many artful backdrops for the daily histrionics of Italian life.

In the cities, the cathedrals, palaces, or town halls are planned as harmonious elements in stagesets for the streets and the all-important piazzas, just as much monuments in their own right. In Venice, dazzling as the basilica, Doges' Palace, and Marciana Library may be, the focus of life is in the Piazza San Marco and the Piazzetta beyond. The same is true of Rome's piazzas—Navona, del Popolo, or di Spagna; Siena's Campo; Turin's Piazza San Carlo. Conceived as a theatre emphasizing the decorative space more than the buildings around it, the piazza satisfies the need of Mediterranean peoples to conduct their lives in the open air.

For we mustn't forget the players. In each town, at that magic moment at the end of the afternoon, they stroll across the piazza, find themselves a well-placed seat at their favourite café or stand in groups to argue business, politics, or football—more often football than politics—and never merely discuss when it's possible to argue. Their celebrated gift for gesticulation has not deserted them nor that keen look that reassures them of the appreciation of their audience. No people more joyfully lives up to its legendary image than the Italians. As Orson Welles put it, all 58-odd million of them are actors, with only a few bad ones, and those, he added most unfairly, are on the stage and in films.

The gondolier rests his vocal chords before serenading the afternoon's passengers.

Watch them at the wheel of a car: every time they stop, reluctantly, at a traffic light, the men, even more than the women, check their looks in the rear-view mirror and comb their hair —ever ready to go on stage. Driving, of course, has become a major opportunity to display their dramatic talents. An Italian designer observed that a nation's cars are like its people: Scandinavian and German models are solid, strong, and reliable, built to resist an accident; Italian cars tend to be more fragile, but slick and spirited, built to *avoid* an accident.

Built, above all, to indulge the national sense of style. The imaginative flair of Neapolitans zig-zagging out of a traffic jam forces the admiration of the most nerve-shattered onlooker. In the purely visual sphere, style has been a national preoccupation from the Golden Age of Michelangelo or Leonardo da

The Dukes of Milan built Pavia's Charterhouse as a flamboyant family mausoleum.

10

Vinci in the Renaissance to the grandiose cinematographic fantasies of Fellini or Visconti in the modern era. It is there not only in the splendour of the frescoes and monumental fountains but also in the dazzling design of a scarlet Ferrari, a coffee pot, or a fountain pen. The smart international man-about-town insists that good "English" tailoring is now only to be found in the meticulous workshops of Milan or Rome. And he is Italianized by such national quirks as the overcoat almost invariably draped over the shoulders like a cloak or, in the summer, the sleek leather moccasins imperatively worn *without* socks.

> **Fuel types for cars/trucks:**
> Unleaded *(sensa piombo)*,
> regular *(normale)*,
> premium *(super)*,
> diesel *(gasolio)*

In 1401, a cool French scholar told his Milan colleagues: "Art without science is nothing." The Italians replied: "Science without art is nothing," and today, pasta manufacturers employ designers to invent new forms for noodles.

In the simplest *trattoria* or most elegant of restaurants, your choice of a meal begins before you sit down. Not with the menu, but with yet more theatre décor, sprawling across a long table as you enter: plates of pink scampi and purple squid, stuffed eggplant and zucchini, red, yellow, and green peppers, cascades of grapes and figs.

And if you take a plane or train the length of the peninsula, Italy offers itself as another long table of delights spilling out into the Mediterranean. In the north, the snowcapped Alps and jagged pink rocks of the Dolomites; the gleaming lakes of Como, Garda, and Maggiore; the fertile and industrial plain of the Po stretching from Turin and Milan across to ancient Verona, the hills of Vicenza, and lagoons of Venice.

On the west coast, the Italian Riviera curves from San Remo to Viareggio on either side of the venerable port city of Genoa. Behind the sandy beaches, from the marble quarries of Carrara, the mountain chain of the Apennines climbs into Tuscany—where lie the

A bambino enjoys an elevated view of the processions on the Piazza del Duomo in Florence.

ageless beauties of Pisa, Lucca, Florence, and Siena and the magical hill towns of Montepulciano, Volterra, and San Gimignano.

Umbria's rich green countryside surrounds a golden triangle of historic cities, the Assisi of St. Francis, the noble university town of Perugia, and medieval Gubbio. To the east, the grand Byzantine citadel of Ravenna dominates the seaside resorts of the Adriatic.

And, half way down the west coast, the unique golden universe of Rome, witnessing countless declines, falls, and rebirths, resists all the assaults of brutal modernity.

In another world unto itself, the exhilarating chaos of Naples commands a magnificent bay, the isles of Ischia and Capri, and the ruins of Pompeii in the shadow of the Vesuvius volcano. To the south, the fishing villages of Sorrento and Positano spill down the craggy cliffs of the Amalfi coast. Meanwhile, on the other side of the peninsula, well off the beaten tourist track, are the strange prehistoric landscapes of Puglia and the medieval fortresses of the German emperors.

Italy's western approaches are guarded by the islands of Sardinia and Sicily, rugged, mysterious, at once bright and sombre.

The Italian people, with Latins and Etruscans mixing over the centuries with Greeks, Lombards, Normans, and Spaniards, are as diverse as this panoply of landscapes. Each region sustains a solid and pugnacious local pride from historic division into the city-states, duchies, kingdoms, and republics of Florence, Naples, Venice, Lombardy, Piedmont, and Sicily. Nurtured within the geographical separations of the Alps, the Po valley, and the coasts on either side of the Apennines, it was this very diversity that created the richness of Italian art with its competing regional schools of painting and architecture. Significantly, the move towards national unity in the 19th century coincided with a dramatic artistic decline from which the country is only now recovering.

Given its short history as a unified nation, Italy's patriotic sense is invested almost exclusively in the national football team. After the devastating experience of Mussolini's fascism, national government is rarely regarded as an obvious solution to the people's daily problems. If some form of government proves necessary, they prefer the local town hall to the parliament in Rome.

Most Italians are naturally cheerful and friendly towards foreigners, with an almost total absence of "racist" terms. They reserve their scorn for each other—Venetians and Romans or Milanese and Neapolitans.

Over and above the regional identifications, the country remains divided culturally, economically, and psychologically between the prosperous, industrial North and relatively backward South, the *Mezzogiorno* ("Midday"). This division was perpetuated by centuries of feudal rule in Naples and Sicily while the North developed more progressive forms of economy and government, almost to the point of regarding the South as Italy's own Third World, offering a supply of cheap migrant labour.

But at the personal level, the warm-hearted, high-spirited Neapolitans, for instance, in no way feel themselves inferior to the cool, pragmatic "manager" types of the big northern cities. Italy's two halves come face to face in Turin, where Fiat's automobile factories have attracted thousands of workers from the *Mezzogiorno*. Sociologists have noted that the transplanted southerners tend to support the populist Juventus football team, owned by Fiat's Agnelli family, while the other, more bourgeois local team, Torino, is favoured by the longer-established Turin citizenry.

Foreign visitors are not obliged to take sides. We can fall in love with the whole country.

It's the children who lend colour to a greystone village in the Abruzzi mountains.

FACTS AND FIGURES

Geography: The Italian landmass covers 301,245 square km (116,228 square miles). The familiar boot-like silhouette stretches 1,200 km (850 miles) from the northwest Alpine frontier with France to the southeast "heel" of Puglia. Below the three great lakes, Maggiore, Como, and Garda, the fertile plain of the Po river separates the Alps from the rugged chain of the Apennines running like a wall down the middle of the peninsula to the arid and poorer south. Other major rivers are the Tiber at Rome, Arno in Tuscany, and Adige in the Tyrolean Dolomites. Across the Adriatic to the east lies the rocky coastline of Yugoslavia. Off the Tyrrhenian (west) coast are the mountainous islands of Sardinia (south of France's Corsica) and Sicily (off the boot's "toe"), largest of the Mediterranean islands. Three major volcanoes in the south, Vesuvius, Stromboli, and Sicily's Etna, are still active. Highest point: on Mont Blanc (Monte Bianco) 4,760 metres (15,616 ft.).

Population: 58 million

Capital: Rome (pop. 2,830,000)

Major cities: Milan (1,500,000), Naples (1,200,000), Turin (1,000,000), Genoa (700,000), Palermo (700,000), Bologna (400,000), Florence (400,000), Catania (380,000), Bari (370,000), Venice (340,000).

Government: By its constitution of 1948, Italy is a republic of provinces grouped into 20 regions. A President with honorary rather than political powers is chosen by an Electoral Assembly of parliamentary and regional representatives. Government is in the hands of a Prime Minister and his cabinet selected from among the parliament's Senate of 322 members and more powerful 630-strong Chamber of Deputies. A parliamentary mandate is 5 years.

Religion: 99% Catholic, 1% Protestant, Greek Orthodox, and Jewish.

HISTORY

I taly as a nation has existed only since 1871. Before then, despite the peninsula's obvious geographical unity bounded by the Alps and the Mediterranean, its story is a fragmented tale of independent-minded cities, provinces, and islands.

We have abundant evidence of the ancient Etruscan, Greek, and Roman communities in Italy, but know very little of the country's earlier, prehistoric settlers. Vestiges of dwellings survive—cabins on stilts in the frequently flooded Po valley, larger clay houses on the western marshlands of Tuscany, and Sardinia's still visible domed dry-stone *nuraghi*. But the inhabitants? Perhaps North Africans and eastern Europeans peopled the Ligurian coast, while the Adriatic and south may have been settled from the Balkans and Asia Minor.

Nobody knows where the Etruscans came from. During the millennium before the Christian era, their civilization reached beyond Tuscany north to the Po valley and south towards Naples. At a time when Roman and other Latin tribes were still primitive, Etruscan society was aristocratic and highly sophisticated. Gold and other metal ornaments showed Greek influence, but the Etruscans' vaulted architecture was indigenous, as were their roads, canals, and sewers.

Arriving in the eighth century B.C., the Greeks set up city-states in eastern and southern Sicily, dominated by Syracuse, and others on the Italian mainland, at Naples, Paestum, and Taranto. Pythagoras squared his hypotenuse in Calabria, and it was at Agrigento on Sicily that Empedocles concluded the world was divided into four elements—fire, air, earth, and water.

After defeats by Greeks in the south, Latins in the centre, and Gallic invaders in the north, the Etruscan empire ended in the fourth century B.C. As Greek colonial power weakened through Athens-Sparta rivalry back home and pressure from Phoenicians in Sicily,

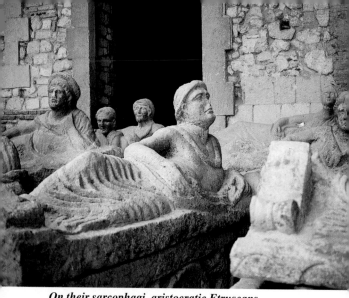

On their sarcophagi, aristocratic Etruscans recline in dignified repose.

the vacuum was filled by an uppity confederation of Latin and Sabine tribes living on seven hills known collectively as Rome.

The Romans

Legend says Rome was founded by Romulus, sired with twin brother Remus by Mars of a Vestal Virgin and abandoned on the Palatine Hill to be suckled by a she-wolf. Historians agree that the site and traditional founding date of 753 B.C. are just about right.

Under Etruscan domination, Rome had been a monarchy until a revolt in 510 B.C. established a patrician republic, which lasted five centuries. In contrast to other Italian cities weakened by internal rivalries and unstable government, Rome drew strength from a solid aristocracy of consuls and senate ruling over plebeians proud of their Roman citizenship and only rarely rebellious.

Recovering quickly from the Gallic invasion of 390 B.C., the Romans took effective control of the peninsula by a military conquest reinforced by a network of roads with names that exist to this day: Via Appia, Flaminia, Aurelia. From chariots to Ferraris, Italians have always liked careering across the country on wheels.

Roman power extended around the Mediterranean with victory in the Punic Wars against Carthage and conquests in Macedonia, Asia Minor, Spain, and southern France. The rest of Italy participated only by tax contributions to the war effort and minor involvement in commerce and colonization. Resentment surfaced when former Etruscan or Greek cities such as Capua, Syracuse, and Taranto supported Hannibal's invasion in 218 B.C. Rome followed up defeat of the Carthaginians with large-scale massacres and enslavement of their Italian supporters. National solidarity was still a long way off.

Under Julius Caesar, provincial towns won the privileges of Roman citizenship. His reformist dictatorship, bypassing the senate to combat unemployment and ease the tax burden, made dangerous enemies. His assassination on the Ides of March, 44 B.C., led to civil war and the despotic rule of his adopted son Octavian, who, as Augustus, consolidated the empire.

Conquest of the Greeks accelerated rather than halted the influence of their culture in Italy. Romans infused Greek refinement with their own energy to create that unique mixture of elegance and realism, delicacy and strength that have remained the essence of Italian life and art.

In architecture, the Romans made a great leap forward from the Greek structures of columns and beams by developing the arch, vault, and dome, well suited to the needs of empire—basilicas for public administration, the new engineering of aqueducts and bridges, and triumphal arches for victorious armies. If they adopted the Greeks' gods, turning Zeus into Jupiter, Aphrodite into Venus, the cult placing the emperor at the apex of the gods served the interests of the Roman state.

In the centuries of imperial expansion, decline, and fall, Italy took a back seat as power moved with the armies away from Rome east to Byzantium and north to Gaul or Germany.

Despite persecution under Nero in the first century A.D., Christianity spread from Rome through southern Italy, later to the north. With Constantine (306–337) in Byzantium, Milan and then Ravenna became the capital of Italy. Christianity was made the state religion. At the end of the fourth century, Emperor Theodosius organised the Church into dioceses and declared paganism and heresy a crime. He himself was excommunicated by St. Ambrose, Bishop of Milan, for massacring 7,000 rebels in Thessalonica. The position of Bishop of Rome as primate of the Western Church was asserted by Pope Leo I (440–461), tracing the succession back to St. Peter.

The invasion of Attila's Huns and the sacking of Rome by Goths and Vandals brought an end to the Western Empire in 476.

After the Empire

Wars between the Goths and Byzantines and new waves of invasions made Italian unity impossible.

The dual influence of Greek and Latin culture persisted. In the sixth century, Justinian reannexed Italy to his Byzantine Empire and codified Roman law as the state's legal system. Under Heraclius (610–641), Greek was extended to Italy as its official language.

Hellenistic and Oriental influences were most evident in religion. Byzantine ritual coloured the Roman liturgy. The Roman basilica's long colonnaded nave leading to an apse gave way to the Greek cross with a central space surrounded by arches and topped by a dome. Sculptural reliefs flattened out to symbolic decorative, non-human forms, and painting and mosaics were high in colour, but more rigid and formal. Spiritual preoccupations turned away from the world's few joys and many woes in the present to mystic contemplation of the ineffable hereafter.

Much too ineffable for Italian tastes. The monastic movement founded by St. Benedict in the sixth century reasserted involvement in the realities of social life. The Benedictine order emphasized moderation in the austerity of its food, clothing, and sleep, not unlike the habits of any peasant of the times. Flagellation and similar rigours introduced into other Italian monasteries by the Irish monk Columbanus were soon modified by the gentler Benedictine rule.

Monasteries in Italy remained modest affairs as bishops moved faster than abbots to take over lands laid waste by barbarian invasions. The Church ordered monasteries to forget secular matters and devote themselves to liturgy.

By the eighth century, the Byzantines held the balance of power with the Lombards (a Germanic tribe), who had invaded Italy in 568 and set up their capital at Pavia four years later. The Lombards controlled the interior in a loose confederation of fiercely independent duchies. Lombard territory split Byzantine Italy up into segments ruled from the coasts—Veneto (Venice and its hinterland), Emilia (between Ravenna and Modena), and Pentapolo (between Rimini and Perugia), plus Rome and Naples (with Sicily and Calabria).

> Last names began to be used towards the end of the ninth century. Many last names were descriptive, based on specific characteristics and personal history.

In Rome, the highly political popes played the Lombard duchies off against those of the Byzantine Empire. They cited a forged document, the *Donation of Constantine*, supposedly bequeathing them political authority over all Italy. Seeking the powerful support of the Franks, Pope Leo III crowned their king, Charlemagne, ruler of the Holy Roman (in fact, mostly German) Empire, in 800.

But the pope had in turn to kneel in allegiance, and this exchange of spiritual blessing for military protection laid the seeds of future conflict between the papacy and the German emperors.

Venice, founded on its lagoons in the sixth century by refugees from Lombard raiders, prospered from a privileged relationship with Byzantium and uninhibited readiness to trade with Muslims and other infidels farther east. The merchants of Venice were only too happy to bring a little Oriental spice and colour into the dour lives of Lombards in the Po valley and beyond the Alps to northern Europe.

Naples held on to its autonomy by prudently combining links with Rome and Constantinople. When Arabs conquered Sicily in the ninth century and turned to the mainland, Naples at first sought an alliance. But as the invaders advanced towards Rome, Naples successfully linked up with neighbouring Amalfi. Despite military expeditions by the Franks and Byzantines, however, the Arabs remained on the Italian scene for two centuries.

The Middle Ages

In the 11th century, the adventurous Normans put an end to Arab control of Sicily and southern Italy. Exploiting a natural genius for assimilating the useful elements of the local culture rather than indiscriminately imposing their own, they adopted Arab-style tax collectors and customs officials and Byzantine fleet-admirals for their navy. In Palermo, churches and mosques stood side by side, feudal castles next to Oriental palaces.

The Crusades against the Islamic threat to Christendom brought great prosperity to Italy's port cities. Pisa sided with the Normans in Sicily and profits from its new commercial empire in the western Mediterranean paid for its cathedral, baptistery, and Leaning Tower. Genoa's merchant empire spread from Algeria to Syria.

Supreme master of the art of playing all sides, Venice stayed out of the First Crusade to expand its trade with the East while ferrying pilgrims to Palestine. Later, when Byzantium threatened its eastern trading privileges, Venice persuaded crusading armies to attack Constantinople in 1204, thereby strengthening its position even more.

The Po valley's economic expansion through land clearance and new irrigation works brought a rapid decline of feudalism. Dukes, administrators, and clergy lived in towns rather than isolated castles, absorbing the hinterland into communes, forerunners of the city-states.

The communes were strong enough to confine German Emperor Frederick Barbarossa's Italian ambitions to the south, where he secured Sicily for his Hohenstaufen heirs by marrying his son into the Norman royal family. Ruling from Palermo, Barbarossa's cultured but brutal grandson Frederick II (1194–1250) was a prototype for the future Renaissance prince.

Food with a view — Romans enjoying lunch on the Piazza della Rotunda.

His power struggle with the papacy divided the country into two highly volatile camps—Guelfs supporting the pope and Ghibellines supporting the emperor. The backbone of the Guelfs was in communes such as Florence and Genoa. In 1266, they financed the mercenary army of Charles d'Anjou to defeat the imperial forces—and take the Sicilian throne. But Palermo rose up against the French in the murderous Sicilian Vespers

The basilica of San Francesco—before the earthquake of 1997 struck Assisi and surrounding areas.

of 1282, when the locals massacred everyone who spoke Italian with a French accent and forced Charles to move his capital to Naples. The Sicilians offered their crown to the Spanish house of Aragon.

The Guelf-Ghibelline conflict became a pretext for settling family feuds (such as the one in Shakespeare's *Romeo and Juliet*) or communal rivalries from which Genoa and Florence emerged stronger than ever. In Rome, the dissolute popes repeatedly switched factions for temporary advantage and lost all political and moral authority in the process.

After two centuries of religious heresy, the Church needed a spiritual renewal, finding the perfect ally in Francis of Assisi (1182–1226), pious without being troublesomely militant (see page 110).

His sermons had immense popular appeal. He chose not to attack Church corruption but to preach instead the values of a Christly life. By involving religion in a love of nature, preaching even to sparrows, he appealed to an old pagan Italian tradition. The Franciscan order provided a much needed manageable revival. The architecture of the church built in his name at Assisi contradicted Francis's humble testament denouncing "temples of great dimension and rich ornament." But Assisi's frescoes of the saint's life, painted by Cimabue and disciples of Giotto, proved an immensely effective act of artistic propaganda against the prevalent libertinism and heresy.

The City-States

By the end of the 13th century, with the independent-minded communes growing into fully fledged city-states, Italy was clearly not to be subjugated to the will of one ruler.

The Middle Ages in Italy were far from being the murky era that many humanist scholars liked to contrast with the brilliance of the Renaissance. Bologna had founded Europe's first university, famous above all for its law studies, in the 11th century, followed by Padua, Naples, Modena, Siena, Salerno, and Palermo. Unlike other Church-dominated European universities, Italian universities emphasized sciences, medicine, and law over theology.

In the absence of political unification, it was the universities that awakened the national consciousness. Scholars travelling across the country needed a common tongue beyond the elitist Latin to break through the barriers of regional dialects. It had been a foreigner, German Emperor Frederick II, who launched the movement for a national language at his court in Palermo, but

The local dialect of Tuscany served as the basis of modern literary Italian, which came into being in the 14th century.

Dante Alighieri (1265–1321) provided the ardour, moral leadership, and literary example to bring it to fruition.

Genoa rose to challenge Venice's supremacy. It dislodged Pisa in the western Mediterranean, whittled away at Venice's hold on eastern ports, and set up colonies on the Black Sea for trade with Russia and the Far East. But Genoa's 1381 participation in the ruinous Chioggia war on the Venetian lagoon exhausted its resources. Its newly formed Bank of St. George had to sell off overseas colonies and ran the town like a private company for the benefit of a local oligarchy seeking future prosperity as international financiers for the kings of Spain or France.

Venice rebounded to turn to the mainland, extending its Veneto territory from Padua across the Po valley as far as Bergamo. After relying exclusively on overseas trade, Venice created a new land-owning aristocracy through this expansion.

In its fertile Po valley, Milan prospered from trade with Germany, principally in textiles and armour. Escaping unscathed from the Great Plague of 1348 and subsequent epidemics, it built up a sound economic base and maintained a strong army with its plentiful manpower.

Florence was the first Italian town to mint its own gold coin (*fiorino* or florin), a prestigious instrument for trade in European markets, and organized textile manufacture on a large-scale industrial basis. Although outside troops were called in to crush an uprising of the Ciompi (wool-workers), the people of Florence were well-fed and highly literate compared with the rest of the country. The Medici emerged as the dominant merchant family, with Cosimo becoming the city's ruler in 1434. A building boom underlined the prosperity: Giotto's Campanile was at last completed, as were Ghiberti's great baptistery doors, Brunelleschi's dome on the cathedral, and palaces by Alberti and Michelozzo.

Divided in the 14th century between the Spanish in Sicily and the French in Naples, southern Italy remained solidly feudal. Its almost exclusively agricultural economy suffered much more than the north from plague and famine. Landlords resorted to banditry to replenish their treasury. If Palermo was in decline, Naples flour-ished as a brilliant cosmopolitan capital. In 1443, it was reunited in one kingdom with Sicily, under Alfonso of Aragon.

With the papacy in comfortable exile in Avignon since 1309, the brutal rule of the Orsini and Colonna families reduced Rome to a half-urban, half-rural backwater. Self-educated visionary Cola di Rienzo governed briefly in 1347 until the nobles drove him out. Thirty years later, the papacy returned.

The Renaissance

A new national fraternity of scholars with multiple expertise in the arts, sciences, and law emerged as itinerant consultants to rulers eager to make their city states centres of cultural prestige and political propaganda.

Bust of Lorenzo de Medici, patron of such artists as Leonardo and Michelangelo.

Men like Leon Battista Alberti, architect-mathematician-poet, brought a new spirit of inquiry and scepticism. From their detailed study and translation of the Greek philosophers, they developed principles of objective scientific research, independent of all the political, religious, or emotional bias characterizing medieval scholarship. The emphasis switched from heaven to earth.

Leonardo da Vinci eagerly applied the new method to architecture, civil and military engineering, urban planning, geography, and map-making. It was Giorgio Vasari, facile artist but first-rate chronicler of this cultural explosion, who dubbed it a *rinascita,* or rebirth, of the glories of Italy's Greco-Roman past. But even more, it proved, with the humanism of Leonardo and Michelangelo and the political realism of Machiavelli, to be the birth of our modern age.

For the creative ferment by no means precluded new horrors of war, assassination, persecution, plunder, and rape. It was the heyday of the brilliant but lethal Spanish-Italian Borgias: lecherous Rodrigo, who became Pope Alexander VI, and treacherous son Cesare, who stopped at nothing to control and expand the papal lands. (His sister Lucrezia, forever smeared by anti-Spanish propaganda of the day as mistress of both her father and brother, was in fact, as Duchess of Ferrara, a generous patroness of the arts and benefactress of the poor.)

In Florence, where his family had to fight tooth and nail to hold on to their supremacy, Lorenzo de' Medici also found time to encourage the art of Perugino, Ghirlandaio, Botticelli, the young Leonardo, and tempestuous Michelangelo. But decadence set in and Dominican preacher Girolamo Savonarola denounced the corruption of a Church

and society more devoted to pagan classics than to the Christian gospel. At the Carnival of 1494, he shamed the Florentines into throwing their "vanities"— clothes, jewellery, and cosmetics, but also books and paintings, with Botticelli contributing some of his own—onto a giant fire on the Piazza della Signoria. Four years later, when Savonarola declined to test the validity of his apocalyptic prophesies with an ordeal by fire, he was arrested, hanged, and burned anyway, on the Piazza della Signoria.

On the international scene, the Turkish conquest of Constantinople in 1453 closed Genoa's Black Sea markets, but Venice worked

The Sistine Chapel's new brilliance startles those used to the pre restoration grime.

out a new deal in Cyprus and even a *modus vivendi* in Constantinople itself. But the Venetians' empire declined as they lost their taste for the adventure of commerce in favour of the safety of their landholdings. From 1494 to 1530, the Spanish Habsburgs and the French turned Italy into a battleground for the Kingdom of Naples and the Duchy of Milan. Genoa threw in with the Spanish to give Emperor Charles V access, via Milan, to his German territories, and later became a lucrative clearing-house for Spain's American silver. Rome was plundered by imperial armies in 1527; the Medici were driven out of Florence and returned to power under tutelage of the Spanish, who won effective control of the whole country.

Dusk is the perfect time to enjoy the Palazzo Vecchio in Florence.

But when the dust of war settled it was the dazzling cultural achievements that left their mark on the age. True father of Rome's High Renaissance, Pope Julius II (1503–1513) began the new St. Peter's, and commissioned Michelangelo to paint the ceiling of the Vatican's Sistine Chapel and Raphael to decorate the Stanze. Architect Donato Bramante was nicknamed *maestro ruinante* because of all the ancient monuments he dismantled to make way for the pope's megalomaniac building plans. With the treasures uncovered in the process, Julius founded the Vatican's magnificent collection of ancient sculpture.

Counter-Reformation

Badly shaken by the Protestant Reformation, the Church convoked the Council of Trent (north of Lake Garda) in 1545. Non-Italian bishops urged the Church to carry out its own reform, hoping to democratize relations with the pope. But the threat of Lutherans, Calvinists, and other heretics shifted the emphasis to repression, culminating in the Counter-Reformation formally proclaimed in 1563. The Church reinforced the Holy Office's Inquisition and the Index to censor the arts. The Jesuits, founded in 1534, quickly became an army of theologians to combat heresy. Italian Protestants fled and Jews in Rome were shut up in a ghetto (50 years later than in Venice) and expelled from Genoa and Lucca.

Cardinal Carlo Borromeo, nephew of Pope Pius IV and Archbishop of Milan (1565–1584), was the exemplary spiritual leader of Italy's Counter-Reformation. In alliance with the Jesuits, he weeded out corrupt clerics and the, for him, too soft Umiliati order of Catholic laymen. As a symbol of his crusading spirit, he consecrated the new Flamboyant Gothic cathedral, which took centuries to complete.

Art proved a major instrument of Counter-Reformation propaganda, but it had to undergo some important changes. The vigour and intellectual integrity of the High Renaissance had softened into Mannerism's stylized sophistication. Condemning the preoccupation with pagan gods and worldly decadence, the Church urged artists to deliver a strong, clear message to bring the troubled flock back to the fold. The Madonna and saints of Annibale Carracci attracted the faithful with a sensuous image of ideal beauty, while Caravaggio made a more brutal, but no less effective, appeal with a proletarian Mary and barefoot Apostles. As the Church regained ground, it promoted a more triumphant image, epitomized by Bernini's grandiose Baroque altar in St. Peter's.

But the self-confidence had its limits, as when, in 1633, the Vatican ordered Galileo to deny the evidence of his own eyes, through the new telescope he had designed, and stop teaching that God's earth was only one of many planets in orbit around the sun.

After a 16th century in which Naples had become the largest town in Europe—and one of the liveliest—the south was increasingly oppressed and impoverished. The army had to crush revolts in Sicily and Naples against heavy taxes and conscription for Spain's wars in northern Europe.

Towards Nationhood

Lacking the solidarity to unite and too weak to resist by themselves, Italian kingdoms and duchies were reduced to convenient pawns in Europe's 18th-century dynastic power plays. At the end of the Wars of Spanish, Austrian, and Polish Succession, the Austrians had taken over northern Italy from the Spanish. The Age of Enlightenment engendered a new cultural ferment. The theatre of La Scala opened in Milan and La Fenice in Venice. Stimulated by the ideas of Voltaire, Rousseau, and Diderot, intellectuals were more keenly aware of being Europeans, but also *Italians*, a national consciousness they promoted in the Milan magazine, *Il Caffè*.

The hopes of progressives were raised by Austrian reforms in Lombardy and Tuscany (where the Medici dynasty ended in 1737): fairer taxes, less Church influence in schools, more public education, removal of the Inquisition, Jesuits, the death penalty, and instruments of torture. Outside the Austrian sphere of influence, Italy remained stolidly conservative. Venice stagnated under the rule of a small entrenched élite, drawing nostalgic comfort from the city's petrified beauty as painted in the *vedute* of Guardi and Canaletto. The papacy in Rome had lost prestige with the dissolution of the Jesuits and the crippling loss of revenue from the Habsburg Church reforms. The south's aristocracy resisted all significant social reforms proposed by the Spanish. Don Carlos, descendant of Louis XIV who saw himself as a southern Sun King—with Caserta Palace as his Versailles—is best remembered for launching the excavations of Pompeii in 1748.

On the northeastern Alpine frontier, a new state had appeared on the scene, destined to lead the movement to a united Italy. With Savoy split in the 16th century between France and Switzerland, its foothill region southeast of the Alps, Piedmont, had come into the Italian orbit. Sidestepping the stagnant economic burden of Spanish domination, the sparsely populated duchy expanded quickly. Turin was little more than a fortified village of 40,000 inhabitants in 1600, but it rose to 93,000 a century later. The pragmatic dukes of Piedmont liked French-style absolutist monarchy but tempered it with a parliament to bypass local fiefdoms. They copied Louis XIV's centralized administration and tax-collection and, by the 18th century, Turin was a sparkling royal capital built, quite unlike any other Italian city, in classical French manner.

Napoleon Bonaparte, with his seductive ideas of Italian "independence," was welcomed after driving out the Austrians and Spanish in 1797. But the French soon proved just as great a burden on Italian treasuries to support their war effort and the Bonaparte family. If Napoleon did not exactly "liberate" Italy, he did shake up the old conservatism from Lombardy to Naples by creating new universities and high schools, streamlining the bureaucracy, creating a new legal system with his Napoleonic Code, and generally awakening the forces of Italian nationalism. Clandestine political clubs like the *Carbonari* sprang up around the country.

Caution was the watchword among Italian rulers restored to their lands after Napoleon's defeat. Austria seized the occasion to add the Veneto to its Lombardy territories. The 1823 conclave of *zelanti* (zealot) cardinals elected arch-conservative Leo XII to help the papacy recover from its Napoleonic shock. On the lookout for any contagiously progressive movement, the Austrians helped Bourbon King Ferdinand of Naples crush an 1821 revolt for constitutional monarchy and foiled a similar uprising in Piedmont. The danger became clear in 1831 when insurrection spread through Bologna, Modena, and Parma to the Papal States of central Italy. But the Aus-

Republican guards leaving the Quirinal Palace in Rome.

trians defeated a rebel government of "united Italian provinces," weakened by regional rivalries and conflicting personal ambitions.

The Risorgimento, the "resurrection" of national identity, took two conflicting paths. Genoese-born Giuseppe Mazzini's *Giovine Italia* (Young Italy) movement sought national unity by popular-based insurrection. He opposed Piedmontese patricians and intellectuals of the Moderates party seeking reform through a privilege-conscious confederation of Italian princes blessed by the papacy, with Piedmont providing the military muscle. The moderates feared a new proletarian militancy among factory workers. Landowners bringing in cheap migrant day-labour faced mounting peasant resentment. Food riots broke out in Lombardy, revolts in Tuscany, and southern peasants demanded a share of common land.

Composer Giuseppe Verdi was the Risorgimento's towering artist. His operas' romantic humanism inspired fellow patriots, who saw in the *Nabucco* Freedom Chorus a positive call to action.

Outright rebellion erupted in Milan on March 18, 1848, year of revolution all over Europe. Emissaries flew by balloon to nearby cities for reinforcements that freed Milan from the 14,000-strong Austrian garrison. The Venetians restored their republic, a Piedmontese army joined up with troops from Tuscany, the Papal States, and Naples, and a new democratic Roman Republic was proclaimed. But the hesitant Carlo Alberto of Piedmont gave the Austrians time to recover and Italian gains toppled like dominoes. National unity was again sabotaged by provincial rivalries.

Conceding the need for more reform, the new king of Piedmont, Vittorio Emanuele II, became a constitutional monarch with a moderate-dominated parliament. Prime Minister Count Camillo Benso di Cavour, a hard-nosed political realist, won over moderate left-wing support for a programme of free-trade capitalism and large-scale public works construction. Among the political exiles flocking to Piedmont was a veteran of the earlier revolts, Giuseppe Garibaldi.

With their French allies, Piedmont defeated Austria at Magenta and Solferino to secure Lombardy in 1859. A year later, Cavour negotiated the handover of Emilia and Tuscany. But it was the adventure of Garibaldi's Red Shirts that imposed the unification of the peninsula in 1860. With two steamers, antiquated artillery, and 94,000 lire in funds, Garibaldi set sail from Genoa with his "Expedition of the Thousand." The heroic Red Shirts seized Bourbon Sicily and crossed to the mainland. At Teano, outside Naples, they met up with Vittorio Emanuele, who was proclaimed King of Italy. National unity was completed with the annexation of Veneto in 1866 and Rome, the new capital, in 1871.

The Modern Era

Despite its extraordinary fragmented history, unified Italy took its place among modern nations as an unexceptional centralized state, careful to protect the interests of its industrial and financial establishment and granting reforms to the working classes only under the pressure of their united action.

From migrant labour in France and Germany, where they were known as Europe's Chinamen, factory and farm workers brought back expert knowledge of union organization and strikes. But in keeping with the Italians' traditional local attachments, their first unions were *camere del lavoro*, regionally based chambers of labour linking workers to their town or commune rather than their individual trade.

Both left and right wanted Italy to join the European race for colonies—their eyes fixed on Ethiopia and Libya. Conservatives supported expansion for reasons of national prestige. Socialists talked of Italy's "civilizing mission" in the Mediterranean, seeking to divert the flow of emigrants (heading increasingly to the Americas) to experimental collective land management in new African colonies in Tripoli and Cyrenaica.

At home, in addition to traditional textiles, industry was expanding fast in metallurgy, chemicals, and machinery. The national love affair with cars had begun—from seven produced in 1900 and 70 in 1907, there were 9,200 rolling out of the factories by 1914, most of them from Fiat, founded in 1899.

With wily Prime Minister Giovanni Giolitti manoeuvring the forces of capital and labour, Italy began its 20th century in a blithe state of calm and prosperity known as *Italietta:* holidays by the sea or in the mountains, soothing operas like Puccini's *La Bohème* and *Madame Butterfly*, the first silent-movie extravaganzas of *The Last Days of Pompeii* and *Quo Vadis*, relaxed conversations in city squares at the hour of the *passeggiata*, the evening walk. Avant-garde artists enraged by the smug bourgeoisie seemed harmless enough—futurists declaring war on spaghetti and preferring the beauty of Maseratis and Alfa Romeos to that of Greek statues.

They were less amusing when hailing World War I as the "world's hygiene." Previously committed to a Triple Alliance with Austria and Germany, Italy remained neutral in 1914. The following year, acting with what Prime Minister Antonio Salandra acknowledged to be "sacro egoismo," Italy signed a secret treaty to enter the war on the side of Britain, France, and Russia in exchange for the post-war annexation of Austrian-held Trento, South Tyrol (now Alto Adige), and Trieste.

The people were at first cool to the war, despite the jingoism of flashy aristocratic aesthete Gabriele D'Annunzio and his friend, an ex-socialist newspaperman named Benito Mussolini. The Italian Army was the least well prepared of the combatants, lacking artillery, machine guns, trucks, and properly trained officers, but the infantry showed remarkable courage in the trenches. After the disaster at Caporetto, the Austro-German 1917 advance across the Veneto plain was held until the Italian counterattack of October–November 1918 permitted a triumphant entry into Trento and Trieste.

For the peasant, worker, and petit bourgeois, war in uniform was their first real experience of Italian nationality. Enthusiastic war-supporters like D'Annunzio, who captured the popular imagination by flying over Vienna to drop propaganda leaflets, were acclaimed as patriots, while democrats and pacifist republicans were dismissed as defeatists. Parliament, which was denied knowledge of the secret war treaty till the Peace Conference of 1919, was exposed as impotent.

The left was in disarray. The Socialists won the elections but split over support for the Russian Revolution, leading to the formation in 1921 of the Italian Communist Party. In an atmosphere of economic crisis—stagnant productivity, bank closures, and rising unemployment—conservatives wanted somebody tougher, more dynamic than eternally compromising old-style politicians. With black-shirted *Fasci Italiani di Combattimento* (Italian combat groups) beating up Slavs in Trieste and union workers in Bologna, Mussolini filled the bill. Threatened by the Fascists' March on Rome in 1922, King Vittorio Emanuele III invited Mussolini, *il Duce*, to form a government.

The now all-too familiar process of totalitarianism set in: opposition leaders assassinated, their parties, free unions, and free press all abolished. The Vatican did not complain, though it was upset when the fascist youth movement dissolved the Catholic Boy Scouts. After the Lateran Treaty of 1929 had created a separate Vatican state and perpetuated Catholicism as Italy's national religion with guaranteed religious education in the schools, Pope Pius XI described Mussolini as a man sent by Providence.

Italian fascism remained a style rather than a coherent ideology, typified by the raised-arm salute replacing the "weakling" handshake, bombastic architecture, and Mussolini's arrogant harangues from the Palazzo Venezia's "heroic balcony" in Rome. The Duce's motto of "Better to live one day as a lion than 100 years as a sheep" contrasted with the one he gave the country: "Believe, obey, fight." Neither lions nor sheep, most Italians survived with lip-service and good humour, while communists re-allied with socialists in the anti-fascist underground whose partisans linked up with the Allies during World War II.

In 1936, Mussolini diverted attention from the worsening economic climate at home with an invasion of Ethiopia and proclamation of the Italian Empire. With the Vatican's enthusiastic support, Italian war planes joined Hitler's Luftwaffe on General Franco's side in the Spanish Civil War (5,000 Italian communists and socialists fought on the Republican side). In 1938, German-style racist legislation was introduced against the country's 57,000 Jews. The next year, Italy invaded Albania and, after France's collapse in June 1940, plunged with Germany into World War II. Its poorly equipped armies were defeated by the British in the African desert and by the mountain snows in the Balkans. The Allies landed in Sicily in June, 1943, and liberated Rome one year later. Mussolini, toppled soon after the Allied landings and re-instated briefly as a German puppet in the north, was caught fleeing in German uniform to the Swiss border and executed in April 1945.

The sordid hardships of post-war Italy—unemployment, the black market, and prostitution—have been made graphically familiar through the brilliant neo-realist cinema of Rossellini, de Sica, and Fellini. Today, the remarkable economic recovery has silenced the old condescension about Italy's technological and managerial talents. In the European Union, Italy has more than held its own in heavy industry, agribusiness, and the new electronics. A specifically Italian ingredient has come from the highly productive clandestine—and so untaxable—manufacturing and other activity parallel to the open market.

Movie poster for "La Dolce Vita," directed by Fellini, whose films captured the spirit of post-Mussolini Italy.

Italians didn't take easily to national government. They had gone most of their history without it and Mussolini had spoiled their appetite. Now, fatigued by his excesses, they rejected the militant left for a little *dolce vita* with the less adventurous but less disturbing Christian Democrats. Their perpetually changing coalitions hardly constituted real national government, but the people seemed to function quite well anyway. In the 1980s, a pragmatic socialist coalition government with the Christian Democrats brought a few years of unusual stability. Corruption, *combinazione*, and tax-evasion continued, but police clamped down on the political terrorism of the Red Brigades and neo-Fascists and the age-old criminality of the Mafia.

In Tuscany, the cypresses recover from their blight. As Fellini puts it, "*E la nave va*" (And the ship sails on).

HISTORICAL LANDMARKS

Early Settlements

9th c B.C.	Etruscans settle in Italy
8th c B.C.	Greeks in Sicily and south

Roman Era

753 B.C.	Rome founded
510	Establishment of Roman Republic
202	Rome defeats Carthage
44	Julius Caesar assassinated
27	Augustus installs empire
64 A.D.	Christian persecutions in Rome
79	Vesuvius volcano buries Pompeii
312	Constantine becomes Christian
410	Visigoths sack Rome

Invasions

6th c A.D.	Lombards invade Milan; Venice founded on lagoon
800	Pope crowns Charlemagne
827	Arabs invade Sicily
1000–1100	Normans conquer south

Middle Ages

1182–1226	St. Francis of Assisi
1198–1250	Frederick II's court in Palermo
1271–95	Marco Polo in Far East
1305	Giotto paints Padua Chapel
1309–77	Popes exiled to Avignon
1312	Dante writes *Inferno*
1347	Cola di Rienzo rules Rome
1378–1381	Venice and Genoa fight for supremacy

Renaissance

1434	Cosimo begins Medici rule in Florence
1442	Spanish rule Naples and Sicily
1494–1559	Spanish and French fight over Naples and Milan
1497	Leonardo da Vinci's *Last Supper*

1498	Savonarola burned in Florence
1508–12	Michelangelo paints Sistine Chapel ceiling
1527	Sack of Rome by imperial troops

Counter-Reformation and Enlightenment

1545–63	Council of Trent
1633	Trial of Galileo
1748	Excavations of Pompeii begin
1778	La Scala theatre opens in Milan
1796	Napoleon invades north

Risorgimento

1821	Austrians crush insurrection
1831	Mazzini founds *La Giovine Italia*
1848–49	Abortive countrywide revolts
1859	Franco-Piedmontese alliance takes Lombardy
1860	Garibaldi's Expedition of 1,000
1861	Kingdom of Italy proclaimed; capital Turin
1871	Rome capital of unified Italy

Modern Era

1915	Italy joins British, French, and Russians in World War I
1919	Trento, South Tyrol (Alto Adige), and Trieste acquired from Austria
1921	Italian Communist Party founded.
1922	Mussolini begins Fascist regime with March on Rome
1929	Lateran Treaty establishes separate Vatican state
1936	Italy invades Abyssinia, bombs Republican Spain
1940	Italy joins Germany in World War II
1943–44	Allies liberate Sicily, then Rome
1945	Mussolini caught and executed
1945	Post-war years bring prosperity and many changes in government to Italy

WHERE TO GO

Not an easy decision. "Doing" Italy is a lifetime job, and many devotees are so in love with the place that they don't even think of any other holiday destination. After a first romance with, say, Rome, Venice, or Florence, they spend the rest of their lives systematically working their way through the country, region by region, year after year. But if this is your first trip, without being too ambitious, you might like to get at least a first overall impression. If the seduction works, and it usually does, you'll want to come back for more, to fill in the gaps. If that's not possible, what we propose here will still give you a feel for Italy and things Italian.

The book includes all the most important towns and regions to help you make your choice. We've divided the country up into five areas, each with a principal city as a focus or starting point: *Rome* for central Italy, plus Sardinia; *Florence* for Tuscany, Umbria, and the Adriatic seaside resorts; *Venice* for Veneto, the Dolomites, and Emilia's historic towns from Parma to Ravenna; *Milan* for Lombardy, Piedmont, and the Italian Riviera; and *Naples* for the south and Sicily.

As always, we try to be representative rather than encyclopedic in our coverage of the country. Given the sheer richness of Italy, our selection of places within those five areas is not in any way exhaustive (nor, by the same token, exhausting). Those who know something of Italy already will inevitably feel that a few of their favourite spots have been neglected (though they may also be grateful we've kept their secret), while they'll find others they never dreamed of. Newcomers will have more than enough to choose from.

Depending on how much time you have for that all-important first taste, we suggest you try to visit at least two, even three of the regions.

Loafers, workers, tourists, and pigeons convene
on Milan's Piazza del Duomo.

Those with a passion for the big city can combine Rome or Milan with the artistic delights of Florence and Tuscany or the romance of Venice. But for many, the key to Italy's Mediterranean soul is to be found in Naples and the south. After the intense emotion, you can always cool off at the seaside resorts on the Riviera or the Adriatic.

The trick is in the mix. Not just geographically, in exploring the variety and contrasts of north and south, but in combining the attractions of town and country and the different facets of Italy's daily life. Nowhere is it easier to overdose on museums and monuments than in Italy. A dear old lady returned from her first visit with the observation: "Italy's very nice, very nice indeed, but for my taste, too much history." While it would be a crime to ignore the churches, palaces, and museums chronicling the glories of Italy's history, the best way to enjoy them is also to spend plenty of time lazing around in cafés or on the beach or just sleeping under an olive tree out in the country. The siesta is one of the greatest of all Latin institutions, and the most important Italian expression you may ever learn is *dolce far niente* (how sweet to do nothing).

Many people cannot manage to go to Italy outside the major holiday periods — Easter, July, and August. But if your options are more flexible, the most enjoyable months are May, June, September, and October, especially for Rome, Venice, and Tuscany. Certainly, July and August can be almost unbearably hot and humid in the big cities, but some find a perverse ghostly pleasure in being in Rome on Ferragosto (on and around August 15) when the city is abandoned to the cats and the crazy. And remember, Italians make no bones about public holidays (see page 238); they just close the country down.

Getting Around

Even the most free-spirited traveller can use a little help occasionally. With the tourist industry such a vital factor in the economy, Italy has an elaborate network of information offices. Bureaucrats being bureaucrats, efficiency and amiability vary from place to place, but the offices all provide useful maps and brochures.

For general information, the state tourist office ENIT (*Ente Nazionale Italiano per il Turismo*) has offices in major foreign cities as well as regional capitals. APT (*Azienda di Promozione Turistica*) gives more detailed regional sightseeing information and can also help with hotel and camping accommodation. CIT (*Compagnia Italiana di Turismo*) is a national travel agency for transportation, excursions, and hotel bookings.

The Travel Tips section at the back of the book (pages 219–246) gives detailed practical guidance on the technicalities of travel through Italy, but here are some general thoughts to help you plan your trip.

Except for a major journey from one part of the country to another, say, from Milan to Rome or down to Naples, touring by train,

---

Not Too Much

Museum-going in Italy is not always simple. Even the local tourist office cannot always keep up with the changes in opening hours. Some museums are closed temporarily, for days, months, or even years, for *restauro* (restoration). This is a blanket term covering budgetary problems for museum staff and modern security systems or genuine, long overdue programmes of renovation of the buildings and restoration of the paintings. Many ancient Roman monuments may also go into prolonged hiding under protective scaffolding.

When you do go to one of the really big museums like the Uffizi in Florence, the Vatican in Rome, or Milan's Brera, treat it like Italy itself: unless you're a museum-fiend, don't try to do it all. Before you go in, look at the guide, study the museum plan in the lobby, and head for the things you really want to see. Or, if you prefer the serendipity of coming across beautiful surprises, just wander around, but not for much more than an hour. Otherwise, you may get a sharp attack of visual overload and won't be able to tell the difference between a Fra Angelico and the sign for the fire extinguisher.

---

given the uncertainties of schedules and frequency of strike action, is best reserved for train buffs with plenty of time, timetables, and patience. If you are making a long rail journey, don't rely on the generally dreary dining-car service. Make up your own picnic hamper of cold meats, salad, cheese, fruit, and Chianti from the local market before you get aboard. Very often, you end up sharing it with Italian passengers who offer their own local delicacies.

But the great breathtaking Italian adventure remains the road. The *autostrada* (toll motorway or expressway) runs the length and breadth of the peninsula, a challenge to the imagination and survival instincts of Western civilization. Only to the uninitiated do Italian drivers seem dangerous. Most of them are highly skillful—they have to be—and proud of their reflexes. Two attitudes to avoid: recklessness and excessive caution. Don't try to match their improvisations, you will only raise their competitive spirit into the realm of high risk. They may be similarly provoked by indecisive slow coaches.

Full tank please!
Il peno, per favore.
(eel peeainoa pair fahvoaray)

Keep your car for use on the open road. In the overcrowded cities, just drop your bags off at the hotel, park your car, and walk, take a bus, or rent a bike. Most big towns have solved the problem for you by closing off their old centre (*centre storico*) to private cars.

Try to vary the kind of places you stay in. Little old hostelries and country inns are charming, but, depending of course on your budget, it's worth indulging for at least one night on the special comforts and pampering of the great hotels. Look out, too, for converted monasteries: the frugality has long gone, the heating is modern, and the medieval well has been replaced by a swimming pool, but the setting is still conductive to meditation.

One last tip: even if you're a linguistic dud, do speak a couple of Italian words. The pronunciation is remarkably easy. Italians are usually delighted by anyone making the effort. A cheerful *buon giorno* (good day) or *buona sera* (good evening) can work wonders when coming into a shop. In a land where politeness is much more important than you might imagine, *per favore* (please), *grazie* (thank you), *prego* (don't mention it), and, when pushing through a bus, *permesso* (excuse me) will be greatly appreciated. You'll find some further simple phrases on page 245. Now enjoy it, *buon viaggio*!

Stylish cyclist—a man rides through the Piazza in Florence.

CENTRAL ITALY

The centre of Italy is the cradle of Latin civilization, administrative headquarters of that ancient conglomerate known as the Roman Empire. Immediately surrounding Rome, Lazio is the old province of Latium. On the eastern flank of the Apennines, the Abruzzi region, of which the province of Molise is a recently created offshoot, came under Roman domination in the third century B.C. While first-time visitors will want to spend most of their time around Rome, the wilderness of the Abruzzi National Park makes a pleasant excursion within fairly easy reach of Rome.

The rugged island of Sardinia deserves at least a week to do it any kind of justice, but you may want to spend just a long weekend at one of its attractive little seaside resorts.

Rome

Within and beyond its seven hills and along the winding banks of the River Tiber, Rome has four or five different personalities: ancient Rome of the imperial ruins; Catholic Rome of the Vatican and churches; the Renaissance city of Michelangelo and Raphael or the Baroque of Bernini and Borromini; and a modern metropolis of interminable traffic jams, fashionable boutiques, and cafés, but also factories and high-rises in the industrial suburbs.

You may choose one, two, or all of them, but none is easily separable from the others. Churches are built on the ruins of Roman baths or pagan temples. The flights of fancy of the T-shirted, designer-jeaned café crowd on Piazza Navona draw natural inspiration from Bernini's grandiose 17th-century fountain. The secret of the Eternal City is that it has lived all its ages simultaneously. The road-building Caesars *knew* their descendants would be obsessed with cars.

Park yours, get into some comfortable walking shoes, and ease yourself into the city gently. Before you face the daunting challenge of the ancient city around the Colosseum or the Vatican's formidable complex, we suggest you get to know the modern Romans' town.

The Centre

Make an early start with breakfast on **Piazza del Popolo** at a veritable Roman institution, meeting-place of the city's brighter spirits, the **Caffè Rosati** (and come back for an evening apéritif). Its terrace is a perfect vantage point for admiring the gracefully curving piazza as an exemplary piece of open-air urban theatre, designed in 1816 by Giuseppe Valadier, architect to Napoleon.

On the north side, the **Santa Maria del Popolo** is important for Raphael's Chigi Chapel, exquisite frescoes by Pincturicchio, and, above all, two profoundly disturbing early 17th-century paintings by Caravaggio, the *Conversion of St. Paul* and *Crucifixion of St. Peter,* in the Cerasi Chapel left of the choir.

Next to the church, an arched gateway marks what was the entrance to ancient Rome along the Via Flaminia, leading from Rimini on the Adriatic coast.

The **obelisk** in the centre, dating from the Egypt of Rameses II (13th century B.C.), was brought here from the Circus Maximus and re-erected by Pope Sixtus V in 1589. Rounding off the south side are the twin Baroque churches, **Santa Maria dei Miracoli** and **Santa Maria in Montesanto**, completed by the 17th-century masters Gianlorenzo Bernini and Carlo Fontana.

Above the piazza to the east, the **Pincio** gardens offer a magical view of the city, especially at sunset. (For the great art museum in the Villa Borghese behind the Pincio, see page 67.) The Pincio promenade lined with pine trees and open-air restaurants takes you past the **Villa Medici**, home of many French artists visiting on national scholarships, to the 16th-century French church, **Trinità dei Monti**.

Bernini's fountain of the Four Rivers on Rome's Piazza Navona.

Its twin belfries loom over the **Spanish Steps** (*Scalinata della Trinità dei Monti*), eternal hang-out of guitar-playing youths, lovers, and peddlers of trinkets and flowers. The pleasant daze induced on the three-tiered travertine staircase, festooned in spring with pink azaleas, was celebrated by John Keats as a "blissful cloud of summer indolence" before he died here in 1821. His house at the bottom of the steps has been preserved as a museum.

Named after a palace used as the Spanish Embassy, the steps and the Piazza di Spagna are the heart of the city's most fashionable shopping area, leading over to the Via del Corso. The piazza's 17th-century boat-shaped marble fountain, Fontana della Barcaccia, is by the great Bernini's father. The venerable Babington's Tea Rooms are a relic of the days when Romans called the piazza the "English ghetto." More quintessentially Roman, on nearby Via Condotti, is the city's oldest coffee house, the 18th-century Caffè Greco, popular, as you'll see from pictures, busts, and autographs, with Goethe, Byron, Baudelaire, Liszt, Gogol, and Fellini.

The **Trevi Fountain** (*Fontana di Trevi*) benefited from Fellini's keen sense of Baroque aesthetics when he dipped the sumptuous Anita Ekberg in its legendarily purifying waters for his film *La Dolce Vita*. Most people are content just to toss in a coin over their shoulder—causing daily fights between street urchins and the municipality for the considerable revenues in high season. Nicola Salvi's astounding 18th-century fountain is in fact a triumphal arch and palace façade (to the old Palazzo Poli) framing mythic creatures in a riot of rocks and pools, with a rearing horse symbolizing the ocean's turmoil and a calmer steed its tranquillity. Tucked away behind narrow alleys, this extravaganza is out of all proportion to its tiny piazza and no amount of signposts leading to it can prepare you for the marvellous shock of discovery. Romantics go at the dead of night, to be alone with its illumination.

That other symbol of the *dolce vita,* the **Via Veneto**, has been deserted by its starlets and *paparazzi* and only the expensive cafés, shops, and hotels remain.

On one of the seven hills of ancient Rome, the fortress-like **Palazzo del Quirinale**, once residence to popes fleeing the malarial swamps of the Vatican down by the Tiber, housed the king of Italy after 1870, and is now the presidential palace. The only embellishment on its formidable façade is Bernini's graceful porch, but its piazza is worth the climb for the view over the city and the Vatican.

You couldn't miss **Piazza Venezia** if you tried—and many do try, because of its endless traffic jams and the grotesque **Vittorio**

Emanuele Monument, celebrating the first king of unified Italy with inimitable 19th-century pomposity. Northwest of the monument, the 15th-century **Palazzo Venezia** is a fine example of severe but elegant early Renaissance architecture, now containing a museum of medieval and Renaissance arms, furniture, and sculpture. Mussolini had his office there and harangued his followers from the balcony.

Behind the Piazza Venezia, one staircase leads steeply up to the austere 13th-century **Santa Maria in Aracoeli**, while another, more graceful and gradual, takes you up between statues of Castor and Pollux to Michelangelo's beautifully cambered square of the **Campidoglio** (Capitoline Hill). This haven of quiet, away from the traffic, forges a superb link between the Renaissance and ancient Rome's most sacred site, where sacrifices were made to Jupiter and Juno. The grand central bronze equestrian **statue of Marcus Aurelius** (undergoing prolonged restoration) is to be sheltered in a museum and replaced by a copy. At the rear of the square is the handsome 16th-century façade of the **Palazzo Senatorio** (now the City Hall), flanked by the **Palazzo Nuovo** and **Palazzo dei Conservatori**.

Dental Surgery

Few edifices have known such universal hostility as the Vittorio Emanuele Monument, or "Vittoriano." Popularly known as the "wedding cake" or "Rome's false teeth," the bombastic colonnade with its pedestrian equestrian bronzes and almost unclimbable steps are a true monument of urban catastrophe. Begun in 1885, the 40-year construction entailed the demolition of a piece of the ancient Capitoline Hill. Parts of the Palazzo Venezia were dismantled for a clearer view. The gigantic proportions completely dwarf the surrounding splendours of ancient Rome and the dazzling white Brescia marble clashes with the city's preference for gentle amber, ochre, or pink travertine. In 1944, art historians pleaded with the Allies to suspend Rome's status as an open city—protecting it against bombardment—just long enough to destroy the Vittoriano.

These last two house the Capitoline Museums (see page 67), whose Greek and Roman collections provide an excellent introduction to the Forum.

The church of the **Gesù**, severe and relatively discreet on its own square west of the Piazza Venezia, was a major element in the Jesuits' Counter-Reformation campaign. Begun as their Roman "headquarters" in 1568, its open ground plan was the model for the Congregational churches that were to regain popular support from the Protestant faith. While its façade is more sober than the exultant Baroque churches put up as the movement gained momentum, the interior glorifies the new militancy in gleaming bronze, gold, marble, and precious stones. Perhaps inevitably, the church's richest, almost overwhelming ornament is the **altar of St. Ignatius Loyola**, covering the tomb of the Jesuits' founder (this can be found in the left transept) with a profusion of lapis lazuli. The globe at the top is said to be the largest piece of this stone in the world.

In gentler contrast, the church of **Sant'Ignazio** stands in an enchanting Rococo stage-set of 18th-century houses. Inside, Andrea Pozzo (himself a Jesuit priest and designer of the saint's tomb at the Gesù) has painted a superb *trompe l'oeil* ceiling fresco (1685) depicting St. Ignatius' entry into paradise. Stand on a buff stone disk in the nave's centre aisle for the full effect of the celestial dome apparently rising above the transept.

The circular **Pantheon** (Piazza della Rotonda) is the best-preserved monument of ancient Rome and rivals the Colosseum in its combination of quiet elegance and sheer massive power. Emperor Hadrian, its builder (around A.D. 120), achieved a marvel of engineering with its magnificent coffered dome, over 43 metres (141 feet) in interior diameter (larger than St. Peter's). Bronze that once embellished the entrance was taken away to make Bernini's canopy for the high altar in St. Peter's. This "Temple of all the Gods" today contains the tombs of Renaissance deities such as Raphael and architect Baldassare Peruzzi and of kings Vittorio Emanuele II and Umberto I.

Caravaggio admirers will find some of his greatest master-pieces right in the neighbourhood: the *St. Matthew* trilogy in the fine Baroque church of **San Luigi dei Francesi**, and the moving *Madonna of the Pilgrims* in the Renaissance church of **Sant'Agostino**.

Pause now at a café in that most serene of city squares, the **Piazza Navona**. Nowhere in Rome is the spectacle of Italian street life more pleasantly indulged, thanks to an inspired collaboration of Roman genius across the ages. The elongated piazza was laid out around A.D. 90 by Emperor Domitian as an athletics stadium, *Circus Agonalis*—a sporting tradition continued in the Renaissance with jousting tournaments. The 17th century contributed its sublime Baroque décor, and today, sages on the city council safeguard it as a pedestrian zone. In the centre, Berni-ni's **Fountain of the Four Rivers** *(Fontana dei Fiumi)* cel-ebrates the great rivers of south America (Río de la Plata), Eu-rope (Danube), Asia (Ganges), and Africa (Nile). Romans who delight in Bernini's scorn for his rivals suggest that the Nile god covers his head rather than look at Borromini's church of **Sant' Agnese in Agone** and the river god of the Americas is poised to catch it in case it collapses. In fact, the fountain was completed several years *before* Borromini's splendid—and structurally im-peccable—façade and dome. Popular tradition suggests the

Dizzying heights—interior of the Pantheon, the "Temple of all the Gods."

Behind Campo dei Fiori, artisans will fix anything.

church was built on the ruins of a Roman brothel where St. Agnes was stripped before being martyred.

The boisterous fruit and vegetable market on the **Campo dei Fiori** gives way in the afternoons to political meetings, admonished by the statue of philosopher Giordano Bruno. The Inquisition burned him alive here in 1600 for his preposterous idea that the universe was infinite, with many more galaxies than ours. An even more famous death occurred at the nearby Piazza del Biscione, more precisely the restaurant Da Pancrazio, whose cellar shelters ruins of Pompey's Theatre where Julius Caesar was assassinated.

Only with a special appointment can you visit the glorious **Palazzo Farnese**, built by Antonio da Sangallo the Younger, Michelangelo, and Giacomo della Porta, which is now the French Embassy. Only the inner courtyard of Rome's finest Renaissance palace is accessible to the public, but its grand portico and the handsome stuccoed vestibule leading to it make it well worth while. A privileged few get in to see the ceremonial dining room's fabulous frescoes by Annibale Carracci. Since 1870, the French pay a rent of one lira every year and provide a palace in Paris as Italy's embassy — very nice, too, but not exactly Michelangelo.

Narrow streets southeast of the Campo de' Fiori take you to the **Jewish Ghetto** near the ruins of the ancient Roman Theatre of Marcellus (*Teatro di Marcello*), architectural model for the Colosseum. Jews have been a permanent feature of Roman life for over 2,500 years but forced into a ghetto only in the 16th century; a small Jewish community still lives nearby around the Via del Portico d'Ottavia. The hefty neo-Babylonian synagogue (inaugurated in 1904), with a small museum of Jewish history next door, is down by the river.

Classical Rome

The nucleus of classical Rome is around the Colosseum, with the Forum to the northwest and the Baths of Caracalla to the south. Don't be daunted—even the best-informed scholars find the monumental relics difficult to decipher—the mystery itself is more than half the charm of these vestiges of a vanished world. Take them in your stride, slower and more relaxed than ever when it comes to walking the ruins. Avoid the midday sun in the shadeless Forum and finish your visit with a picnic and siesta on the Palatine. Even if you're not an archaeology buff who wants to understand the meaning of every stone, it's worth at least an hour or two to stand among the debris of empire and wonder whether Fifth Avenue, Piccadilly, the Champs-Elysées, or Red Square will look any better 2,000 years from now.

It says something about Rome's essential earthiness that, more than any inspirational church or palace, it's the **Colosseum**—what Byron called "the gladiator's bloody circus"—that is the symbol of the city's eternity. Built in A.D. 80 by 20,000 slaves and prisoners, the four-tiered elliptical amphitheatre seated 50,000 spectators. Flowing in and out of 80 arched passageways known as *vomitoria*, aristocrat and plebs alike came to see blood: bears, lions, tigers, and leopards starved into fighting each other and against criminals, war captives, and Christians. Gladiators butchered one another to the crowds' cries of *Jugula!* ("Slit his throat!")

For their churches and palaces, popes and princes have stripped the Colosseum of its precious marble, travertine, and metal. They have left in the arena's basin a ruined maze of cells and corridors that funnelled men and beasts to the slaughter. The horror has disappeared beneath the moss and what remains is the thrill of the monument's endurance. As an old Anglo-Saxon prophecy goes: "While stands the Colosseum, Rome shall stand; when falls the Colosseum, Rome shall fall; and when Rome falls, with it shall fall the world."

The nearby **Arch of Constantine** celebrates the fourth-century emperor's battlefield conversion to Christianity. Unperturbed by their depiction of pagan rituals and sacrifices, a cost-conscious Senate took fragments from monuments of earlier rulers, Trajan, Hadrian, and Marcus Aurelius. Only a few reliefs, over the two outer arches, show the newly Christian Constantine.

With an exhilarating leap of the imagination, you can stand among the columns, arches, and porticoes of the **Roman Forum** (see map pg 58) and picture the hub of the great city, the first in Europe to house a million inhabitants. Earthquake, fire, flood, and the plunder of barbarians and Renaissance architects reduced the area to a muddy cow pasture until the excavations of the 19th century. Today, a detailed plan and the sound-guide rented at the entrance (on the Via dei Fori Imperiali) will make sense of the apparent confusion and help you trace the layout of palaces, temples, and market halls.

Part of the **Curia**, home of the Roman Senate, still stands. Steps nearby lead underground to the **Lapis Niger**, a black marble pavement laid by Julius Caesar over the presumed grave of Romulus, the city's founder. To the south of it are remains of the Basilica Julia law court and the **Rostra** orators' platform from which Mark Antony informed the people of Caesar's assassination. Countless Renaissance

*Rome's Colosseum—built in A.D. 80—
is a symbol of the city's eternity.*

and Baroque sculptors have drawn inspiration from the friezes on the **Arch of Septimius Severus** (honouring a third-century emperor who died in York, England).

The **Temple of Saturn** doubled as state treasury and centre of the merry December debauchery known as the Saturnalia, pagan precursor of Christmas. In the circular **Temple of Vesta**, the sacred flame perpetuating the Roman state was tended by six Vestal Virgins who, from childhood, observed a 30-year vow of chastity on pain of being buried alive if they broke it. At the end of the Via Sacra, the **Arch of Titus** commemorates the sack of Jerusalem in A.D. 70.

Most impressive monument of the Imperial Forums, built as an adjunct to the Roman Forum in honour of Julius Caesar, Augustus, Trajan, Vespasian, and Domitian, is the 30-metre- (98-foot-) high **Trajan's Column** (A.D. 113). Celebrating Trajan's campaigns

The once great Roman Forum was reduced to a cow pasture, before 19th-century excavations.

against the Dacians in what is today Romania, the minutely detailed friezes spiralling around the column constitute a veritable textbook of Roman warfare. St. Peter's statue replaced the emperor's in 1587.

South of the Roman Forum, the **Palatine Hill** is Rome's legendary birthplace and today its most romantic garden, dotted with toppled columns among the wild flowers and spiny acanthus shrubs. Only rows of cypress trees and summer pavilions remain from the more formal botanical gardens laid out here in the 16th century by the Farnese family. From grassy knolls, enjoy the fine view back over the Colosseum or southward over the great **Circus Maximus**, where chariot races were held for crowds of up to 200,000.

A kilometre (about half a mile) south of the Colosseum, the huge third-century **Baths of Caracalla** (*Terme di Caracalla*) were built for 1,600 people to bathe in considerable style and luxury. Imagine the still impressive brick walls covered in coloured marble, some of which you can see today adorning the fountain basins of the Piazza Farnese in front of the French Embassy (see page 54). The baths and gymnasia were of alabaster and granite, decorated with statues and frescoes. Public bathing was a prolonged social event as merchants and senators passed from the *calidarium* hot room to cool down in the *tepidarium* and *frigidarium*. Now the stage for spectacular open-air operas in the summer, the *calidarium* is vast enough for processions of elephants, camels, and four-horse chariots.

South of the baths begins the **Old Appian Way** (*Via Appia Antica*), over which the Roman legions marched on their way to Brindisi to set sail for the Levant and North Africa. On either side lie the ruins of sepulchres of 20 generations of patrician families. The chapel of Domine Quo Vadis marks the site where St. Peter, fleeing Nero's persecution in Rome, is said to have encountered Christ. Farther along the Via Appia are the **Catacombs of St. Callisto**, a vast underground Christian cemetery, notably containing graves of third-century popes.

The Vatican

The power of Rome endures both in the spirituality evoked by every stone of St. Peter's Basilica and in the almost physical awe inspired by the splendours of the Vatican palace. At their best, the popes and cardinals replaced military conquest by moral leadership and persuasion; at their worst, they could show the same hunger for political power and worldly wealth as any Caesar. A visit to the Vatican is an object lesson for faithful and sceptic alike.

Named after the hill on which it stands and which in the Middle Ages was surrounded by a malarial swamp, the Vatican has been a papal residence for over 600 years, but a sovereign state independent of Italy only since the Lateran Treaty of 1929.

If you have the time, try to visit St. Peter's and the museums of the Vatican palace on separate days. The riches here pose the city's biggest threat of fatigue and visual overload. In any case, it's a good idea to divide your visit in two with a relaxed lunch. But check opening times: the Vatican museums are usually open all day around Easter and in the summer months, but close at 1:00 P.M. the rest of the year.

Best of all, have a picnic and siesta in the nearby gardens of the **Janiculum Hill** (*Gianicolo*) where, in the stormy times of the Risorgimento, as an equestrian statue proclaims, Garibaldi fought one of his fiercest battles.

To appreciate the unique panorama of St. Peter's and its square, take your courage in both feet and walk. Start out by crossing the Tiber to the **Castel Sant'Angelo**, which was originally Hadrian's mausoleum built in A.D. 139. Its name derives from Pope Gregory's vision of the Archangel Michael—now represented by a statue on top—heralding the end of a plague in 590. (If you're walking *all* the way, take the pretty Sant'Angelo Bridge, adorned by ten Bernini angels.) It was sixth-century barbarians who commandeered the massive round pile as a fortress, using ancient statues as missiles to hurl on the heads of their enemies below. Linked to the Vatican by a thick-walled passage, it served as a hideout for popes in times of danger, notably Pope Clement VII, who holed up here for a month during the sack of Rome by Habsburg troops in 1527 (see page 30). Philosopher Giordano Bruno and sculptor-goldsmith Benvenuto Cellini were imprisoned in the dungeons, which can be visited on a guided tour of what is now a museum of Renaissance art, furnishings, and weapons.

In **St. Peter's Square** (*Piazza San Pietro*), his greatest creation, Bernini has performed one of the world's most exciting pieces of architectural orchestration. The sweeping curves of the colonnades reach out to the unending stream of pilgrims from Rome itself and the whole world, *urbi et orbi*, to take them into the bosom of the church beyond. In a rare opportunity for concentrated effort by one man on such a gigantic project, Bernini completed the 284 travertine columns, 88 pilasters, and 140 statues of the saints in just 11 years, from 1656 to 1667. Stand on either of the circular paving stones set

St. Peter's Basilica—the largest of all Catholic churches—
is the product of various Renaissance architects.

between the square's twin 17th-century fountains and the red granite Egyptian obelisk to appreciate the harmony of the quadruple rows of Doric columns, so perfectly aligned that they seem like a single row. The purity of Bernini's work here refutes the popular conception of Baroque as being nothing but overblown extravagance.

The great risk of the Renaissance lay in what would happen if too many of those geniuses got involved in the same project. For instance, **St. Peter's Basilica**. Largest of all Catholic churches and by any standards a grandiose achievement, it inevitably suffers from the competing visions of all the architects called in to collaborate — Bramante, Giuliano da Sangallo, Raphael, Baldassare Peruzzi, Michelangelo, Giacomo Della Porta, Domenico Fontana, and Carlo Maderno, each adding, subtracting, and modifying, often with a pope looking over his shoulder.

From 1506 to 1626, it changed from the simple ground plan of a Greek cross, with four arms of equal length, as favoured by Bramante and his arch-enemy Michelangelo, to the final form of Maderno's Latin cross extended by a long nave, as demanded by the popes of the Counter-Reformation. One result is that Maderno's porticoed

---

Seeing the Pope

When he's not in Bogotá or Bangkok, it is possible to see the pope in person at the Vatican. He normally holds a public audience every Wednesday at 11 a.m. (5 p.m. in summer) down in St. Peter's Square. An invitation to the Papal Audience Hall may be obtained from the Pontifical Prefect's Office (open Tuesday and Wednesday mornings) through the bronze gates in St. Peter's Square. A visitor's bishop at home can arrange a private audience.

On Sundays at noon, the pope appears at the window of his apartments in the Apostolic Palace (right of the basilica, overlooking the square), delivers a brief homily, says the Angelus and blesses the crowd below. On a few major holy days, the pontiff celebrates high mass in St. Peter's.

---

façade and nave obstruct a clear view of Michelangelo's dome from the square.

The church's dimensions are impressive: 212 metres (695 feet) exterior length, 187 metres (613 feet) inside length; 132.5 metres (435 feet) to the tip of the dome (diameter 42.45 metres/139 feet).

As you go in, notice the keys of St. Peter inlaid in the doorway paving. Set in the floor by the centre door is the large round slab of red porphyry where Charlemagne knelt for his coronation as Holy Roman Emperor in the year 800 (see page 21).

You'll find the basilica's most treasured work of art, Michelangelo's sublime **Pietá**—Mary with the dead Jesus on her lap—in its own chapel to the right of the entrance. The artist was 25, young and justly proud enough to append his signature (the only surviving example), visible on the Madonna's sash. Since a religious fanatic attacked it with a hammer, the statue is protected by bullet-proof glass.

But reverence can also cause damage: on a 13th-century blackened bronze **statue of St. Peter**, attributed to Florentine architect-sculptor Arnolfo di Cambio, the lips and fingers of countless pilgrims have worn away its toes.

Beneath the dome, Bernini's great **baldacchino** (canopy), cast out of bronze beams taken from the Pantheon's porch (see page 52), protects the high altar, built right over St. Peter's tomb and reserved for the pope's mass. In the apse beyond, the Baroque master gives full vent to his exuberance with his bronze and marble **Cathedral of St. Peter**, throne of the apostle's successors. It is crowned by a *gloria* in which the dove of the Holy Spirit is lit up on sunny days from a window at the back.

It should come as no surprise that, as the greatest patron that painters, sculptors, and architects have ever known, the Catholic Church should house in its "headquarters," one of the world's richest collections of art. The **Vatican Palace** contains eight museums, five galleries, the Apostolic Library, the Borgia Apartments, the Raphael

Bernini's great baldacchino, beneath the dome of St. Peter's Basilica, was cast out of bronze beams taken from the Pantheon's porch.

Rooms, and the Sistine Chapel. Shuttle buses run regularly from St. Peter's Square to the museum entrance.

If you want at all costs to avoid the Sistine's day-long crowds, go straight there first thing in the morning (don't forget your binoculars for details on the ceiling). In any case, you can't miss it—arrows point the way. But there are many marvels to see en route.

With the booty from the ruthless dismantling of ancient monuments to make way for the Renaissance city in the 16th century, the **Pio-Clementino Museum** has assembled a wonderful collection of Roman and Greek art. Most celebrated is the tortured *Laocoön* group (from Rhodes, first century B.C.–first century A.D.), only recently returned more closely to its pristine state by the removal of one son's pathetically outstretched arm added by over-zealous 16th-century "restorers."

Pope Julius II took a calculated risk in 1508 when he called in a relatively untried 25-year-old to do the interior decoration of his new apartments. The result was the four **Raphael Rooms** (*Stanze di Raffaello*). In the central Stanza della Segnatura are the two masterly frescoes, *Disputation over the Holy Sacrament* and the *School of Athens*, confronting theological with philosophical wisdom. The *Disputation* unites biblical figures with historical pillars of the faith such as Pope Gregory and Thomas Aquinas, but also painter Fra Angelico and the divine Dante. At the centre of the *School*, Raphael is believed to have given the red-coated Plato the features of Leonardo da Vinci, while portraying Michelangelo as the thoughtful Heraclitus, seated in the foreground.

In stark contrast to Raphael's grand manner, look out for the gentle beauty of Fra Angelico's frescoes in the **Chapel of Nicholas V** (signposted as *Cappella del Beato Angelico*). The lives of saints Lawrence and Stephen are depicted in delicately subdued pinks and blues.

The richly decorated **Borgia Apartments** contain, in addition to Pinturicchio's frescoes with portraits of lusty Pope Alexander VI and his notorious son Cesare and daughter Lucrezia, the modern religious art collection of Paul VI. The latter includes Rodin bronzes, Picasso ceramics, Matisse's Madonna sketches, and designs for ecclesiastical robes and, perhaps unexpectedly, a grotesque Francis Bacon pope.

Nothing can prepare you for the visual shock of the **Sistine Chapel** (*Cappella Sistina*), built for Sixtus IV in the 15th century. Even the discomfort of the throngs of visitors (silence requested) seems to yield to the power of Michelangelo's ceiling, his *Last Judgement*, and the other wall frescoes of Botticelli, Pinturicchio, Ghirlandaio, and Signorelli. In this private chapel of popes, where the cardinals hold their conclave to elect a new pope, the glory of the Catholic Church achieves its finest artistic expression.

The chapel portrays nothing less than the story of man, in three parts: from Adam to Noah; the giving of the Law to Moses; and from the birth of Jesus to the Last Judgment. On Michelangelo's **ceiling**, you'll make out the celebrated outstretched finger of man's creation, the drunkenness of Noah, the turmoil of the Flood, but most overwhelming of all is the impression of the whole—best appreciated looking back from the bench by the chapel's exit.

On the chapel's altar wall is Michelangelo's tempestuous **Last Judgment**, begun 23 years after the ceiling, when he was 60 and imbued with deep religious soul-searching. An almost naked Jesus dispenses justice more like a stern, even fierce classical god-hero than the conventionally gentle biblical figure. The artist's agonizing self-portrait can be made out in the flayed skin of St. Bartholomew, to the right below Jesus.

Amid all the Vatican's treasures, the 15 rooms of the **Picture Gallery** (*Pinacoteca Vaticana*), in a separate wing of the palace, sometimes get short shrift. This collection of ten centuries of paintings should not be overlooked, and art-lovers may even want to devote a separate visit. Among the most important are works by Giotto, Fra Angelico, Perugino, Raphael's *Transfiguration* (his last great work), Leonardo da Vinci's unfinished *St. Jerome*, Bellini's *Pietà*, and Caravaggio's D*escent from the Cross*.

The neighbourhood south of the Vatican, **Trastevere**, literally "across the Tiber," has long been renowned as the most popular quarter of Rome. Here, ordinary people who, like the Cockneys in London, consider themselves the original citizens uphold ancient traditions and customs. It is good to wander among the narrow streets and markets to sample the authentic life of the city, highlighted by the July *Noantri* ("We Others") street festival of music and fireworks down by the river. Another sort of festival atmosphere prevails every Sunday, when the Porta Portese section of Trastevere hosts Rome's liveliest flea market. The stalls are filled with everything from vintage clothing to valuable antiques.

Inevitably, "popular" and "authentic" became chic and the ambience is now somewhat diluted by a certain smart set moving in—

and raising the rents. But the true Trasteverini hang on, mainly in the area immediately around **Santa Maria in Trastevere**, reputedly the oldest church in the city. Its foundation may date back to the third century, but the present structure is the work of Pope Innocent II, himself a Trasteverino, around 1140. A wonderful Byzantine-influenced **mosaic** of Mary enthroned with Jesus decorates the domed ceiling of the apse. The liveliest fruit and vegetable market is to be found on **Piazza di San Cosimato**.

Other Museums

The **Borghese Gallery**, open again after extensive renovations, is housed in a handsome Baroque villa inspired originally by Hadrian's Villa at Tivoli (see page 69), but with its Italian formal gardens now transformed into an English-style landscaped park. This great collection includes outstanding sculptures by Bernini and paintings by Raphael, Correggio, Titian, Caravaggio, Botticelli, Rubens, Dürer, and Cranach.

The **Capitoline Museums**, in the palaces of the Campidoglio, have extensive collections of sculpture excavated from ancient Rome. In the

---

Man at Work

As might be imagined, painting the Sistine ceiling wasn't easy. Michelangelo, a sculptor in marble with only a little oil painting behind him, had never before done a fresco (wall-painting on damp plaster). Preferring his inexperience to their incompetence, he fired his seven assistants in the first couple of weeks and continued alone for four years, from 1508 to 1512. Contrary to legend, he did not lie on his back, but painted erect on tiptoe, bent backwards "like a Syrian bow," with Pope Julius II climbing the scaffolding to check on progress and threatening to throw him off his platform if he didn't hurry up.

"I'm not in a good place," he wrote to a friend, "and I'm no painter."

Palazzo dei Conservatori is the most celebrated piece, the superb Etruscan bronze **She-Wolf** (*Lupa Capitolina*), symbol of the city. The wolf dates from around the fifth century B.C., but the little Romulus and Remus that she is suckling are Renaissance additions by Pollaiuolo. The **Picture Gallery** (*Pinacoteca Capitolina*) has important Venetian works by Bellini, Titian, Tintoretto, Lotto, and Veronese, as well as a fine Rubens *Romulus and Remus* and Caravaggio's *St. John the Baptist*.

The **Palazzo Barberini** (Via delle Quattro Fontane), another architectural battleground for arch-rivals Borromini and Bernini, is worth a visit as much for its splendid Baroque décor as for its collection of paintings. They come together in the palace's Great Hall with Pietro da Cortona's dazzling ceiling fresco, *Triumph of Divine Providence*. Notable in the collections are a Fra Angelico triptych, Raphael's *La Fornarina* (though his authorship is disputed), and works by Titian, Tintoretto, and El Greco.

Other Churches

It's impossible even to count all the churches worth visiting in Rome, many of which it's most enjoyable to stumble on by accident. We suggest just three in easy reach of the Via Cavour thoroughfare leading from the main railway station (*Stazione Termini*).

Originally built in the fourth century on the Esquiline Hill site of a Roman temple to the goddess Juno, **Santa Maria Maggiore** is the largest of the churches dedicated to the Virgin Mary and a great favourite with pilgrims. They come, especially at Christmas time, to admire relics of the **holy crib** from Bethlehem. In the Oratory of the Crib (*Oratorio del Presepio*) are the moving 13th-century sculptures of Joseph, the Three Kings, the ox, and the ass, by Arnolfo di Cambio (Mary and the child Jesus are 16th-century additions). The most spectacular art treasure of the church, one of its gorgeous fifth-century **mosaics**, 36 Old Testament scenes high on the walls (don't forget the binoculars), and a triumphant Mary and Jesus enthroned over the high altar. The coffered Renaissance ceiling glitters with the gold of the first shipments from the Americas.

In a nearby side street, **Santa Prassede** is unprepossessing from the outside but enchanting in the intimacy of its interior. The delicate ninth-century mosaics of Jesus and four angels make the *Chapel of St. Zeno* the city's most important Byzantine monument. To the right of the chapel is a fragment of rare jasper said to come from the column to which Jesus was tied for his flagellation. Notice, too, the fine mosaic of Jesus and the New Jerusalem over the chancel.

San Pietro in Vincoli (St. Peter in Chains) might not attract a second look (and might even prefer it that way, given the hordes of visitors) if it didn't contain one of the greatest of Michelangelo's sculptures, his formidable **Moses**. Intended for St. Peter's Basilica as part of Michelangelo's botched project for Julius II's tomb, the statue of the great biblical figure sits in awesome majesty at the centre of the monument. You can imagine how grandiose the original plan must have been when you realize from his sideward stare that Moses was supposed to be just a corner figure facing the centre.

> **When visiting churches, shorts, backless dresses, and tank tops should not be worn.**

The horns on his head continue a traditional medieval mistranslation of the Hebrew for halo-like rays of light. On each side, the comparatively passive figures of Jacob's wives, a prayerful Rachel and melancholy Leah, were Michelangelo's last completed sculptures.

Lazio

The excursions to be made today into the Lazio hinterland around Rome are those that ancient Romans themselves made to vacation homes by the sea or nearby lakes.

Tivoli

Follow the old Roman chariot road (repaved) of Via Tiburtina 30 km (19 miles) east of the capital to the haunting ruins of **Hadrian's Villa** (*Villa Adriana*), near the picturesque town of Tivoli, at the foot of the Sabine Hills. Sprawling across 70 hectares (173 acres), this retirement hideaway of the great emperor-builder was designed to recapture some of the architectural marvels of his empire, especially the Greece he loved above all else — a travel notebook for his old age. Barbarians and museum curators have removed most of the villa's treasures, but a stroll through the remaining pillars, arches, and mosaic fragments in gardens running wild among the olive trees, cypresses, and pines can be marvellously evocative of a lost world. To get a clear sense of the original, start with the villa's excellent scale model. The monumental baths, separate Latin and Greek libraries, Greek theatre, temples, and pavilions together make up the home of a man who drew no distinction between the pleasures of mind and body. In the centre, the enchanting **Villa dell'Isola,** a pavilion surrounded by a little reflecting pool and circular portico, epitomizes all the magic of the place.

In Tivoli itself, overlooking the Roman plain, the **Villa d'Este** is a 16th-century counterpart, celebrating all the extravagance of the late Renaissance. The house, home of Cardinal Ippolito d'Este, plays second fiddle to the joyous theatre of its gardens: alleys of cypresses and soaring fountains (500 in all, including Bernini's *Bicchierone*), grottoes, waterfalls, and reflecting pools.

Alban Hills and Castel Gandolfo

The region immediately southeast of Rome is known locally as the Castelli Romani (Roman Castles) for the fortified hilltop refuges built during the medieval civil wars. Today it's just the summer heat that drives the Romans out on day-trips to the vineyards of the Alban hills and lakes. The country villages of Frascati, Grottaferrata, Marino, and Rocca di Papa make delightful stops, not least of all for a cool glass of their estimable white wine, especially during the autumn grape-harvest festivals.

The pope has his summer palace at **Castel Gandolfo**, on the shores of Lake Albano. He holds audience here on Wednesdays from

Cooling off is a special joy behind the fountains of the Villa d'Este, a celebration of late Renaissance extravagance.

mid-July to early September and blesses the thousands of pilgrims on Sundays at noon. In the mellow microclimate of the nearby **Lake Nemi**, strawberries are grown all year round, served—with cream or lemon juice—in Nemi's village park.

The Beaches

For a swim in the Mediterranean or to nurture a suntan, Rome's closest beaches are **Ostia** and **Fregene**, the latter cleaner and more pleasant. But **Ostia** has the added attraction of the ruins of ancient Rome's seaport, set among lovely pine forests on the coastal plain.

Strawberries are served all year round at Nemi.

North of Rome, off the Via Claudia, a cooler, more secluded swim is to be had in the crystal-clear waters of **Lake Bracciano**, which is surrounded by olive groves and relatively clean beaches of reeds and black volcanic sand.

Tarquinia and Northern Lazio

The A12 *autostrada* and the old Via Aurelia (which ends up in Arles in French Provence) take you to **Tarquinia**. Most important of the original 12 towns of the Etruscan confederation, the town dominated Rome in its heyday of the seventh and sixth centuries B.C. Today, the paintings and sculptures found in its **necropolis** of over 5,700 tombs provide fascinating evidence of the brilliant Etruscan civilization. Visits to the tombs, outside town, are organized from the **National Museum**, housed in the fine 15th-century Gothic-Renaissance Palazzo Vitelleschi as you enter Tarquinia. The museum exhibits sarcophagi, Etruscan and imported Greek vases, and some of the best wall-paintings, in reconstructed tombs. Displayed in a room by itself, the prize of the collection is the **Winged Horses** sculpture from Tarquinia's Ara della Regina Temple.

Tuscania is a quiet little fortified town, recovering now from an earthquake in 1971 which luckily did not harm its two Romanesque churches on the eastern outskirts (the tourist office on Piazza Basile will get you the keys). Built from the eighth to the 12th centuries, **San Pietro** stands at the back of a grassy courtyard with Etruscan sarcophagi, beside two crumbling medieval towers. The sober interior has Byzantine-style frescoes, an 11th-century altar canopy, and a **crypt** built on Etruscan and ancient Roman pillars. The Romanesque tower and rose window of **Santa Maria Maggiore's** façade have a similar simple beauty.

Drive up to **Montefiascone** for the lovely view from its Rocca dei Papi gardens over Lake Bolsena. The church of San Flaviano at the bottom of the town's hill has some richly sculpted capitals on its massive columns.

In the restful charm of its medieval quarters, **Viterbo** makes a good overnight stop. The oldest neighbourhood, with narrow streets and little market squares, is around the Via San Pellegrino. On the equally attractive Piazza San Lorenzo, the Palazzo Papale has an impressive 13th-century Gothic loggia, opposite the Cathedral's intriguing mixture of Gothic campanile (bell tower) and Renaissance façade with a Romanesque interior.

Abruzzi National Park

As a tonic for polluted lungs and street-weary limbs, plunge into the cool fresh air and mountain greenery of this exhilarating nature reserve (via the Pescina exit on the A25 *autostrada*). The Abruzzi plateau is the highest in the Apennines, excellent for climbers and hikers, and the national park protects magnificent forests of beech, maple, and silver birch trees. Wildlife is abundant: brown bear, wolves, rare Abruzzi chamois, foxes, badgers, and red squirrels. Bird-watchers can see golden eagles, yellow-billed Alpine choughs and little firecrests, while even the most cloth-eared city-slicker might catch the drumming of a woodpecker.

Enter the park near the wild 1,400-metre- (4,600-feet-) high **Passo del Diavolo** (Devil's Pass) overlooking the Fucino valley and, to the north, affording a spectacular panorama of the Gran Sasso d'Italia plateau, the Apennines' rooftop. Nine km (6 miles) south at **Pescasseroli** is the park administration Visitor's Centre, at which you can get camping permits and maps for hiking. A ski resort in winter, the town also has a nature museum, botanical garden, and small zoo. Drive east to **Villetta Barrea** with its attractive villas bordering the lake.

Outside the park lie the pretty lake and popular summer resort of Scanno, where the village women still wear the handsome but rather austere regional costume.

Sardinia (Sardegna)

The Mediterranean's second largest island (Sicily being the largest) is worth a holiday all to itself—and much more detailed treatment than we give it here. But for those who have just a few days to get a feel for its atmosphere as part of a first-time visit to Italy, we suggest some seaside resorts, trips along the coast, and a couple of excursions into the hinterland.

Prehistoric man dotted the island with his mysterious cone-shaped *nuraghi* houses and watchtowers before it was colonized by Cretans, Phoenicians, Carthaginians, and Romans. Later, the island became part of the commercial empires of Pisa, Genoa, and the Spanish, and was annexed in 1718 by the dukes of Savoy. Malarial mosquitoes and repressive feudalism restrained the island's development until the 19th century, since then it has undergone a rapid industrialization balanced today by renewal of its cattle farming.

Cagliari

The island's capital and main port is a largely modern city, but with a Spanish flavour to its older quarters up on the hill. The **Archaeo-**

After a ramble in the Abruzzi, relax on Lake Scanno.

logical Museum includes important bronze statues of warriors and priests found in prehistoric tombs. The much renovated cathedral has two superbly carved 12th-century pulpits, originally commissioned for the cathedral in Pisa. Before heading for the open road, try the savoury local cuisine, combining Spanish-style fish stews and Genoese pasta dishes.

The winding **Cagliari-Muravera** road across the plunging ravines of the Sarrabus mountains to the coast is one of the most spectacular drives on the whole island.

Continue up the coast to Lanusei and head inland across the rugged **Gennargentu mountains**, covered with dense forests of cork oak and chestnut trees. Another regional delicacy: hot melted cheese with honey.

Farther north, just off the Nuoro-Dorgali road is the secluded site of **Serra Orrios**, a well-preserved prehistoric village (signposted *Villaggio Nuragico*). A short walk along a marked path through the fields takes you to a group of drystone houses with two temples and

The backstreets of Porto Cervo, Costa Smeralda's fashionable centre.

circular ramparts in a lovely setting of eucalyptus and olive trees. Archaeologists have located some 7,000 of these *nuraghi* structures around the island, most of them flattened cone towers believed to be parts of fortified citadels.

Costa Smeralda

The glittering Emerald Coast on the northeast tip of the island is one of Italy's smartest resort areas, with beautiful beaches, grand hotels, sports complexes, and marinas for yachts and motor launches. It stretches round bays and rocky inlets from Olbia in the east to the promontory of La Maddalena.

Porto Cervo is the coast's fashionable centre, but **Baia Sardinia** competes with its craggy coastline. More exclusive is the little luxury resort island and fishing village of **La Maddalena**, a 15-minute ferry-ride from Palau. It is in fact the principal island of an archipelago of 14, most of them little more than a pile of rocks.

Linked to **La Maddalena** by a 7–km- (4–mile-) long causeway, the isle of **Caprera** was the last home of Giuseppe Garibaldi, military leader of the Risorgimento movement for Italian unity (see page 35). The house where he died in 1882 (his tomb is nearby) is now a **museum**, practically a sanctuary, where devout patriots refer to him not by name, but as "the Hero," *l'Eroe*.

The north coast road makes an enjoyable excursion along the dunes and pine groves lining the Gulf of Asinara. The fortress-town of **Castelsardo** stands high on a spectacular promontory overlooking the gulf. Inside its 16th-century cathedral, you hear the sea crashing on the rocks directly below the foundations. At **Porto Torres**, visit the important 11th-century Pisan Romanesque church of San Gavino. It has no façade, but its interior has a noble simplicity. Some of the pillars come from an ancient Roman temple, with two Corinthian capitals serving as a lectern.

Alghero

This quiet little seaside resort on the northwest coast has a pleasant Catalan flavour to its older quarters around the cathedral. Take a sunset stroll along the 16th-century Spanish ramparts.

There's good fishing to be had in the nearby bay of Porto Conte, and the Palmavera **nuraghi** citadel is well worth a visit. On the bay's southwestern promontory is the fascinating **Grotta di Nettuno** (Neptune's Grotto). Guided tours of these subterranean caverns with their dramatic stalactites and stalagmites are organized by boat from Alghero or on foot directly at the site, down a steep stairway in the cliffs. It's a freshwater grotto fed by an underground river. The stalactites grow down at the rate of one centimetre every 100 years, faster than the stalagmites rising to meet them from the cave floor.

TUSCANY AND UMBRIA

Light is the secret of the region's magic. In that apparently miraculous collision of imagination and intellect that sparked the Renaissance in 15th-century Florence, its painters and architects had the constant inspiration of the dramatic changes in Tuscan light from dawn to dusk. And more than anywhere else in the country, Tuscany and Umbria present that ideal green Italian landscape, dotted with pink stone hilltop towns, where cypress-tree sentinels watch over the olive groves and vineyards.

Florence lies at the heart of the northern Apennines, in a basin of the Arno river which runs out to Pisa. Siena, its proud historic rival, dominates the Tuscan hill towns to the south, while the university town of Perugia and the Assisi of St. Francis are the keys to Umbria's luminous beauty.

With some careful timing, modern visitors can capture a glimpse of that miracle of light. Arrive early in the morning for your first look across the hills to the grey-stone towers of San Gimignano, but come to Siena's Piazza del Campo at sunset. Pisa's dazzling white marble is at its best in the noonday sun, but late afternoon is the blessed moment for the brilliant façade of Orvieto's cathedral.

Florence *(Firenze)*

First-time visitors may want to stay in the thick of the fray, but veterans often prefer to enjoy the treasures of Florence by driving in from a vantage-point like Fiesole (see page 98) or other nearby hill-towns. Despite the magnificence of its monuments and museums, the city, in the heat of summer, is less amenable to "hanging around" in than Venice, and the people are more reserved and less seductive than Romans or Neapolitans.

Our itineraries divide the city's heart into four quarters: from the Duomo north to San Marco; from the Piazza della Signoria, the Palazzo Vecchio, and the Uffizi east to Santa Croce; from Mercato Nuovo west to Santa Maria Novella; and south of the Arno around the Pitti Palace and the Piazzale Michelangelo.

From the Duomo to San Marco

The **Duomo** (cathedral), officially Santa Maria del Fiore, proclaims the inordinate but certainly justified civic pride of the Florentines. It was started in 1296 and the imposing green, white, and rose marble façade was completed only six centuries later.

The first of its glories is the free-standing **campanile**, based on a design by Giotto. The 85-metre- (267-foot-) tall bell-tower is deco-

rated on its lower sections by hexagonal bas-reliefs sculpted by Andrea Pisano and Luca della Robbia from Giotto's drawings. Characteristic of the city's civic consciousness, they portray the Life of Man
from Adam's creation to the rise of civilization through the arts and
sciences—music, architecture, metallurgy, and the like—pursued so
earnestly by the Florentine guilds that commissioned the work. Originals of Donatello's sculpture for the third-storey niches are kept in
the cathedral museum, **Museo dell'Opera del Duomo** (Piazza del
Duomo, 9), most notably statues of the prophet Habakkuk and Abraham with Isaac. Also in the museum, Michelangelo's unfinished
Pietà of the dead Jesus in his
mother's arms emphasizes the
agony rather than the pathos
portrayed by the Pietà in St.
Peter's in Rome (see page 63).
Michelangelo originally conceived the group for his tomb
and represented himself in the
figure of Nicodemus. Flaws in
the marble so enraged the artist
that he hurled a hammer at it,
destroying Christ's left leg—
the left arm has been restored
and the rather insipid Mary
Magdalen was added by a pupil.

Brunelleschi's masterpiece,
the cathedral's grandiose red-
brick **cupola**, with its eight white
stone ribs curving to the marble
lantern at the top, is the city's
symbol, visible not only all over
Florence but also from far beyond in the Tuscan hills. Com-

*Florence's cathedral
is ever the central focus
of city life.*

Detail of bas-reliefs on the celebrated bronze doors of the baptistery of San Giovanni.

pleted in 1434, it measures 45.5 metres (149 feet) in diameter. The 463 steps to its top (entrance inside the church, in the north aisle) climb in comfortable stages to reveal glimpses of the surrounding city, different views of the cathedral's interior, and fascinating close-ups of the dome's structure. (Brunelleschi's original wooden model is displayed in the cathedral museum.) Look out, too, for Ghiberti's **bronze shrine** below the high altar.

In the third bay on the north aisle is Paolo Uccello's statuelike equestrian painting of the 14th-century English mercenary Sir John Hawkwood (unpronounceable for Italians, so known as Giovanni Acuto). After brilliant performances in the Hundred Years' War in France, Sir John obtained what modern-day footballers would call an "independent transfer" to Florence as a condottiere. His "fee" included tax-exemption, state funeral, and cathedral monument.

The octagonal 12th-century Romanesque **baptistery** of San Giovanni (St. John) is celebrated for the magnificent bas-reliefs of its **bronze doors**. The oldest, facing south and telling the story of John the Baptist, were designed by Andrea Pisano in 1330. A century later, Lorenzo Ghiberti won the competition to design the great north and east doors, devoted respectively to the life of Jesus and scenes from the Old Testament. Michelangelo said the latter, facing the Duomo, were good enough to adorn the entrance to heaven and they have been known ever since as the *Doors of Paradise*. Among the losing candidates was Filippo Brunelleschi, who thereafter devoted himself entirely to architecture. (In the Bargello, pages 89–90, you can compare his bronze model with Ghiberti's.) Byzantine-style **mosaics** inside the cupola include scenes from the *Creation, Life of St. John,* and a *Last Judgment.*

Something of the might of the Medici family can be sensed in their massive palace, northwest of the cathedral, the 15th-century **Palazzo Medici-Riccardi**. Now Florence's prefecture offices, the formidable edifice, with its rough ashlar stone façade smoothing out in the upper storeys, set the style for the city's Renaissance palaces. The ground floor originally had an open loggia at the corner for the family banking business. After a rest in the quiet little garden of orange trees beyond the main courtyard, visit the upstairs chapel for Benozzo Gozzoli's 15th-century **fresco** of the *Journey of the Magi to Bethlehem*. It portrays the Medici clan led by Lorenzo the Magnificent in what is in fact an allegory of the Greek patriarchs' procession to an ecumenical council with Pope Pius II in Florence.

Just across the square is the family church of **San Lorenzo** designed by Brunelleschi. Funds ran out before Michelangelo's planned façade could embellish the austere barn-like exterior. Inside, you'll see the Medici family arms set in the floor in front of the altar. Brunelleschi is at his most elegant in the **Old Sacristy** at the end of the left transept, decorated with four Donatello wall-medallions.

Adjoining the church but with a separate entrance are the **Medici Chapels** (*Cappelle Medicee*), monuments to the splendour and decadence of the dynasty. The **Princes' Chapel** (*Cappella dei Principi*) is a piece of 17th-century Baroque bombast in oppressive dark marble, for which the altar was not completed, appropriately enough, till 1939. At the end of a corridor, the summit of Medici power is celebrated in Michelangelo's superb **New Sacristy**, conceived as a pendant to Brunelleschi's in the church. Lorenzo the Magnificent and brother Giuliano lie in simple tombs beneath the sculptor's *Madonna and Child,* flanked by lesser artists' statues of the family saints Cosmas and Damian. Michelangelo's greatest work here is reserved for two minor members of the family, Lorenzo's grandson, the Duke of Urbino, portrayed as a pensive Roman soldier above two allegorical figures of Twilight and Dawn, and his son, the Duke of Nemours, more warrior-like above figures of Night and Day.

For a moment of peace, wander through the handsome **Laurentian Library** (*Biblioteca Medicca Laurenziana*) to the left of the church entrance. Michelangelo designed the wooden desks displaying illuminated manuscripts in a collection ranging from Egyptian papyri to manuscripts of Napoleon.

The Dominican **Monastery of San Marco** provides the exquisite setting for a museum largely devoted to the paintings of Fra Angelico (1387–1455), who lived here as a monk. Off the cloister, with its ancient cedar tree, are some of his finest works, notably a *Descent from the Cross* altar-piece from the church of Santa Trinità and miniatures of the life of Jesus. In the small refectory is a stately Ghirlandaio mural of the *Last Supper*, a popular subject for monastic dining rooms. In the monks' cells upstairs, the frescoes of the man Italians call Beato (Blessed) Angelico were intended to be inspirational rather than decorative. His celebrated *Annunciation* faces the top of the stairs—compare the simpler version in cell 3—while other outstanding works include the mystic *Transfiguration* in cell 6 and *Jesus Mocked* in cell 7. The Prior's Quarters in the second dormitory (cells 12, 13, and 14) were the home of fire-and-brimstone preacher Giro-

---

Keeping the Gods Safe

Almost as beautiful as the statue of Perseus are the little figures of Jupiter, Minerva, Mercury, and Danae around the base. To keep Duke Cosimo's wife, Eleonora of Toledo, from taking them for her private apartments—"they'll risk being spoilt down in the piazza," she said—Cellini soldered them firmly to the pedestal. But the art custodians of Florence have now decided the Duchess was right, replaced them with copies, and put Cellini's originals in the Bargello.

lamo Savonarola from 1481 till his death in 1498 (see page 29). You
can see some of his belongings, a portrait by fellow-monk Fra Bartolomeo, and the picture of his burning at the stake.

As a museum conceived primarily for students of Florentine
painting from the 13th to 16th centuries, the **Accademia Gallery**
(Via Ricasoli, 60) is an important adjunct to the Uffizi (see pages 86
-88). But the major interest is in the seven statues of the **Michelangelo sculpture hall**. Six of them are unfinished—four *Prisoners, St.
Matthew*, and a *Pietà*—but each is a fascinating revelation of how
Michelangelo releases their power from the marble. At the end of
the hall, the great *David* (of which a mediocre copy stands in the Piazza della Signoria) provides the perfect object lesson of the finished product, a hero infused with all the contained energy needed to
hurl that stone at Goliath.

In the Piazza Santissima Annunziata, Brunelleschi produced a
consummate piece of Renaissance urban planning, a pioneering example of the piazza as stage-set. He designed the graceful colonnade
of nine arches for the **Ospedale degli Innocenti**, hospital for
foundlings, symbolized by the charming little babes in Andrea della
Robbia's roundels above the arches. Michelozzo's later Santissima
Annunziata church, together with the 17th-century fountains and
equestrian statue of Grand Duke Ferdinando, preserve the har-
monies of the master's overall design.

Piazza della Signoria to Santa Croce

Flanked by the city's most elegant shoe shops, the quarter's main
street retains the tradition of its medieval name, Via de' Calzaiuoli
(stocking- and shoe-makers).

If the tall rectangular block of **Orsanmichele** looks to you more
like a grain-silo than the church it's supposed to be, that's because it
was once both. Florentines always liked combining faith and business
and rebuilt the oratory to St. Michael in the 14th century to house a
wheat exchange, with arches in place of the present ground-floor win-

The shadow of David—tourists take a break at the Palazzo Vecchio.

dows and a granary upstairs. For 14 niches overlooking the streets, the guilds commissioned **statues** of patron saints from Florence's greatest talents, a landmark in Renaissance sculpture. Look out for Ghiberti's vigorous bronze of the city's patron *St. John* (east wall, on the Via de' Calzaiuoli) and *St. Matthew,* the bankers' tax-collector turned Apostle (west); Donatello's *St. George*, the armourers' dragon-killer (north, a bronze cast of a marble original in the Bargello) and *St. Mark,* whose vividly sculpted robes do credit to the linen-drapers he protects (south); and Nanni di Banco's outstanding conspiratorial group of *Four Crowned Martyrs* for the sculptors' own guild of stonemasons and wood-workers (north). In the interior is Andrea Orcagna's elaborate 14th-century Gothic **tabernacle** with a *Madonna* painted by Bernardo Daddi.

Piazza della Signoria is Florence's civic centre. Site of the town hall (*Palazzo Vecchio* or *della Signoria*) since 1299, the square bustles in all seasons, not least because it leads to the richest of Italy's art museums, the Uffizi. At the south end of the square is the 14th-century arcaded **Loggia della Signoria** or **dei Lanzi**, transformed from the city fathers' ceremonial grandstand into a guardroom for Swiss mercenary *Landsknechte*. It shelters Benvenuto Cellini's bronze masterpiece, **Perseus**

brandishing the severed head of Medusa. In one inspired moment, the Renaissance braggart has combined the legendary technical wizardry he loved to show off as a goldsmith with undeniable sculptural beauty.

Also in the Loggia, the spiralling *Rape of the Sabines* of Giambologna (actually a Flemish artist named Jean de Boulogne) is another piece of dazzling virtuosity.

In a piazza that is a veritable sculpture garden, more statuary graces the orator's platform along the town hall's sober façade. To the left is a copy of Donatello's *Marzocco*, Florence's heraldic lion, next to his bronze of *Judith and Holofernes,* which always made the Medici uneasy with its theme of a tyrant decapitated. Directly beneath the palace tower, as a counterpart to Bandinelli's clumsy *Hercules and Cacus,* is a copy of Michelangelo's *David.* Standing against a hostile world of cruel Philistines, Florentines loved to identify with the beauty and courage of the poetic young giant-killer.

A commemorative stone (near the Baroque fountain) in the piazza marks the spot where Savonarola was executed (see page 29).

In gentle contrast to Arnolfo di Cambio's austere Italian Gothic exterior of the **Palazzo Vecchio** or Palazzo della Signoria, Vasari added ornate stucco and frescoes to the first inner courtyard for a Medici wedding in the 1560s. A delightful Verrocchio bronze cherub tops the porphyry fountain in the centre. Upstairs, the **Salone dei Cinquecento** was built in 1495 for Savonarola's short-lived Republican Council before serving as Duke Cosimo's throne room and, three centuries later, the chamber of Italy's first national parliament. The décor celebrates Florentine power—Vasari frescoes of victories over Siena and Pisa and Michelangelo's *Victory* statue. On the second floor, the **Sala dei Gigli** (Hall of the Lilies) is brilliantly decorated in blues and golds with vivid Ghirlandaio frescoes of Roman and early Christian history. It adjoins the **Chancery** *(cancelleria)* where Niccolò Macchiavelli served as secretary to the Florentine Republic. Any world-weary thoughts inspired by the old cynic's portrait and bust are quickly dispelled by the original of Verrocchio's cherub cuddling a dolphin like a baby doll.

The **Uffizi** museum of Italian and European painting stretches in a long U-shape from the Palazzo Vecchio down to the Arno river and back. Duke Cosimo had Vasari design it in 1560 as a series of government offices (hence its name), a mint for the city's florin, and workshops for the Medici's craftsmen.

That makes a lot of museum, but a great one that it would be sad to renounce through visual fatigue. We won't burden you with guilt by telling you "not to miss" this or to "be sure" to see that, but we will just signal some of what really is worth seeing. See all or only half a dozen, stop for an occasional peek out the window over the Arno and Ponte Vecchio—and rendezvous later at the museum's roof garden café above the Loggia dei Lanzi.

Constant reorganization often makes it hazardous to specify room numbers, but the paintings are exhibited chronologically from the 13th to the 18th century. Here are some of the highlights:

Giotto breathes a warm humanity into his *Madonna Enthroned* (1300) that distinguishes it from the more formal pictures of the subject by Cimabue and Duccio in the same room. See also Giotto's Madonna polyptych. Some 30 years later, the *Annunciation* triptych of **Simone Martini**, with Mary shying away from archangel Gabriel, has the characteristic elegance and poetry of his Siena school.

Paolo Uccello shows a dream-like, almost surrealist obsession with his (unsolved) problems of perspective and merry-go-round horses in his *Battle of San Romano* (1456). It contrasts with the cool dignity of **Piero della Francesca** in his *Federigo da Montefeltro* and wife *Battista* (1465), portrayed against their Urbino landscape.

In his graceful *Allegory of Spring* (1478) and the almost too famous but undyingly delightful *Birth of Venus,* **Botticelli** achieves an enchanting mixture of sensuality and purity. His Flemish contemporary **Hugo van der Goes** is more down to earth in the realism of his *Adoration of the Shepherds,* which influenced Florentine painters like **Ghirlandaio**—compare here his *Adoration of the Magi.*

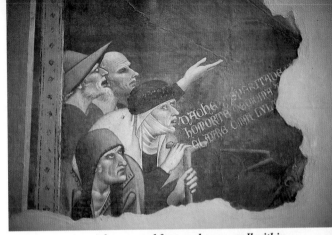

A fragmented fresco adorns a wall within the church of Santa Croce.

In the *Baptism of Christ* (1470) of **Verrocchio**, you can see the earliest identified work of his pupil, **Leonardo da Vinci**—the background landscape and the angel on the left, beautiful enough to reduce his companion angel to wide-eyed jealousy. Leonardo's *Annunciation* of a few years later already shows his characteristic gentle tone and feeling for precise detail, and the *Adoration of the Magi,* even as an underdrawing left unfinished by his departure for Milan (1481), reveals his revolutionary power of psychological observation.

The northern European rooms include a splendid *Portrait of His Father* (1490) by **Albrecht Dürer**; *Adam and Eve* (1528) by **Lucas Cranach**; *Richard Southwell* by **Hans Holbein**; and a moving *Mater Dolorosa* by **Joos van Cleve**.

In the mystic *Holy Allegory* (1490) of **Giovanni Bellini**, we can appreciate the typical Venetian serenity even without understanding its symbols.

"Madonna with Young St. John"
1483–1520 Raphael

The only **Michelangelo** in the Uffizi is the *Holy Family* roundel (1504), his earliest painting, decidedly sculptural in the group's solid plastic qualities. Without Michelangelo's strength and torment or Leonardo's complexity, the third of Italy's three Renaissance giants, **Raphael**, brings his own powers of clarity and restraint to the *Madonna of the Goldfinch* and a revealing *Self-Portrait*.

Titian has a superbly sensual *Venus of Urbino*, less Greek goddess than the prince's mistress she probably was, and an equally disturbing *Flora* (1515). Some are also upset by the eroticism of **Parmigianino** in his strange but undeniably graceful *Madonna with the Long Neck* (1534)—just look at those elongated fingers, too—a masterpiece of the sophisticated and subsequently decadent Mannerism that followed the High Renaissance.

There is an intriguing ambiguity to the half-naked peasant youth posing as a *Bacchus* for **Caravaggio**, but nothing complicated about the robust sexiness of the **Rubens** *Bacchanale*. And compare Caravaggio's mastery of chiaroscuro (the play of light and dark) in the service of realism in his violent *Abraham and Isaac* (1590) with the more contemplative style of **Rembrandt** in his *Old Rabbi* (1658) and other portraits.

For a change from all this fine art, try the **Science History Museum** (*Museo di Storia della Scienza*, Piazza dei Giudici, 1), where you'll find Galileo's telescopes and his (pickled) middle finger and an Edison phonograph.

Designed in the late 13th century by Arnolfo di Cambio but with a neo-Gothic façade added in 1863, the church of **Santa Croce** (east of the Uffizi) has an important series of Giotto **frescoes**. The pathos shines through the heavily restored paintings of St. Francis in the Bardi Chapel, to the right of the apse, and two St. Johns in the Peruzzi Chapel next door. In a chapel in the left transept, the wooden **Crucifixion** by Donatello (1425) is in affecting naturalistic contrast to the Renaissance idealism of the time.

The church is also revered by Florentines as the last resting place of many great Italians. Galileo, Machiavelli, Ghiberti, and composer Rossini are all buried there. **Michelangelo's tomb** (right aisle, second bay) was designed by Vasari, with symbolic statues of Painting, Sculpture, and Architecture mourning beneath a bust of the artist (89 when he died). Michelangelo wanted the tomb surmounted by the *Pietà,* now in the cathedral museum (see page 79), but the Florentines nearly didn't even get his body: they had to smuggle it out of Rome in a bale of sacking. For Dante, they have to be content with a cenotaph, as Ravenna, his burial place, refuses to part with his remains.

At the back of the cloister of Santa Croce's Franciscan monastery adjoining the church, Brunelleschi's **Pazzi Chapel** is a little gem of Renaissance elegance. Its spaciousness is enhanced by geometric patterns of dark stone against whitewashed walls. And Brunelleschi prefers Luca della Robbia's subdued glazed ceramic roundels to Donatello's too competitive wall medallions in the Old Sacristy of San Lorenzo. The most cherished treasure in the Santa Croce **Museum** is Cimabue's 13th-century *Crucifixion,* rescued and painstakingly restored after the town's 1966 flood.

The ominous 13th-century fortress of the **Bargello** (Via del Proconsolo, 4) was Florence's first town hall and very unpleasant prison under the jurisdiction of the Police Chief, or *Bargello,* be-

NOT TO BE MISSED

Geometric designs embellish Brunelleschi's Pazzi Chapel.

fore becoming the National Museum of Sculpture. The old armoury is now the **Michelangelo Hall,** greeting you with a most unhappy bust of the master by Daniele da Volterra. Michelangelo's works here include a marble bust of *Brutus,* a *Virgin and Child* marble roundel, and an early *Drunken Bacchus* (1497)—compare Sansovino's more decorous *Bacchus* of 20 years later. Among the Cellini **bronzes** is an imposing bust of his master, *Duke Cosimo*. The **General Council Hall** is dominated by the works of Donatello: his vigorous *St. George,* intended for the Orsanmichele (see page 83); two statues of David, doubting in marble, naked and restless in bronze; and the stone *Marzocco* lion, the town's symbol, from the Palazzo Vecchio. You can also see the two bronze panels submitted for the Baptistery doors competition by Brunelleschi, the loser, and Ghiberti, the winner (see page 80). On the second floor is a Verrocchio *David,* for which his 19-year-old pupil Leonardo da Vinci is believed to have been the model.

From Mercato Nuovo to Santa Maria Novella

Start out from the centre, on the Via Calimala, the heart of medieval Florence on the street of the drapers' guild taken over today by the colourful **Mercato Nuovo** (the Straw Market). Here, around a 16th-century loggia enclosing the bronze statue of a wild boar known as the *Porcellino,* you can buy a straw hat against the Tuscan sun and a basket to carry off the cheap and not so cheap jewellery, leather goods, and embroidery.

West on the Via Porta Rossa is the 14th-century **Palazzo Davanzati**; its stern, fortress-like exterior still provides rings at ground level for tethering horses and on upper stories to hold torches and lanterns for festive occasions. Inside, on the first floor, is a museum of Florentine domestic life from the 14th to 16th centuries, with furniture, utensils, and ceramics, at their most attractive in the Sala dei Pappagalli (Parrots' Hall) with its *trompe l'œil* tapestries frescoed on the walls.

The church of **Santa Trinità** has a late-16th-century Baroque façade with a Gothic interior. Ghirlandaio decorated the Sassetti Chapel (far right of the high altar) with frescoes of St. Francis, and the *Adoration of the Shepherds* on the altar is considered his masterpiece.

Florence's most elegant shops continue the Via de' Tornabuoni's centuries-old tradition of aristocratic luxury. On the 15th-century **Palazzo Strozzi**, look out for the intricate wrought-iron lanterns by the much sought-after and expensive craftsman Niccolò Grosso, known as *Caparra (*Mr. Down Payment), who coined the philosophy later attributed to Hollywood: "If you want something for nothing, you get what you paid for."

The 13th-century Dominican church of **Santa Maria Novella** is the finest of Florence's monastic churches. Leon Battista Alberti added the graceful white and green marble façade in the 15th century.

The church is rich in artistic treasures, but its most prized, indeed one of the city's greatest paintings, is the **Masaccio Trinity** (left aisle, third bay). Above a pair of stoic kneeling donors, Mary and John stand on either side of the crucified Jesus upheld by his Father, while the dove of the Holy Spirit hovers between them, the whole forming an inspiring triangle under the coffered ceiling of a Renaissance chapel. Painted in weird, rather gruesome counterpoint below is a skeleton (perhaps of one of the donors) and the inscription in Italian: "I was once that which you are and what I am, you will also be."

The Ghirlandaio **frescoes** of the lives of the Madonna and St. John, for the chancel behind the altar, kept the master's whole workshop busy from 1485 to 1490, and a 13-year-old apprentice named Michelangelo Buonarroti picked up some tips for his work a few years later on the Vatican's Sistine Chapel.

The Filippo Strozzi Chapel (right of the altar) is decorated with Filippino Lippi's **frescoes** of saints Philip and John, rich in colour and anecdotal detail: notice in the monumental *Exorcism of Demons in the Temple of Mars* three bystanders holding their nose at the smell.

In the Gondi Chapel (left of the high altar), the Brunelleschi **Crucifixion,** one of his few sculptures (1410), brings to the human body a characteristic idealized harmony, compared with Donatello's more personal piece in Santa Croce (see page 89). Of another age, at once austere and serene, is the Giotto **Crucifixion** (1290) in the Sacristy (left transept).

Through an entrance left of the church, escape the bustle of the piazza in the Dominicans' 14th-century **cloister** (*Chiostro Verde*), with Paolo Uccello's frescoes of the *Flood* now in the refectory.

North of Santa Maria Novella, spare a glance for the simple, clean-lined architecture of the **Stazione Centrale** (main railway station), built in 1935 in Mussolini's heyday but somehow defying the prevailing monumental bombast of the Fascist regime that you can see in Milan's monstrosity.

Heading back down to the river, have a restful drink in the plush neo-Renaissance bar of the Excelsior Hotel (Piazza Ognissanti), even—or particularly—if you're not staying there. Then cross the square to the **Ognissanti** (All Saints Church), 13th century but with a Baroque façade of 1637. In Ghirlandaio's *Madonna of Mercy* (right aisle, 2nd bay), portrayed immediately to the right of Mary is the Florentine banker-navigator Amerigo Vespucci, who gave his name to the continent of America. Botticelli is buried in a chapel (right transept), his *St. Augustine* adorning the church, while in the **refectory** in the adjoining cloister, you'll find Ghirlandaio's *Last Supper*.

South of the Arno

There's nothing very romantic about the muddy green waters of the Arno river, with its broad *lungarni* embankments built in the 19th century to protect from flooding, but it does have two splendid bridges.

The **Ponte Santa Trinità**, destroyed in 1944, has been rebuilt with the original 16th-century masonry scooped from the bottom of the river, including statues of the *Four Seasons*. Bartolomeo Ammanati's three lovely elliptical arches follow drawings by Michelangelo.

The **Ponte Vecchio,** intact since 1345, was Florence's first and for centuries only bridge. The boutiques with their back rooms overhanging the river were built from the 16th to 19th centuries. Vasari provided a covered corridor for Duke Cosimo to keep out of the rain when crossing from his Pitti Palace to the Uffizi. The duke didn't like the smell of the bridge's original butcher shops and had them replaced by the goldsmiths and jewellers, whose descendants offer you their high-quality wares today. Their most famous ancestor, Benvenuto Cellini, has his (1900) bronze bust in the middle of the bridge.

In Renaissance times, the quarter south of the Arno was an aristocratic preserve where the Medici held court. Today, their palace is a museum and the gardens of their private festivities are a public park.

Cross the Ponte Vecchio to the sprawling **Pitti Palace**, its dauntingly heavy and graceless façade belying the ornate and colourful interior. Duke Cosimo's wife, Eleonora of Toledo, acquired the palace from the Pitti merchant family in 1549 as the Medici's official residence, which passed briefly in the 19th century to the king of a united Italy.

Its museums take you into the rich world of the Medici, much as they left it. The **Pitti Gallery** *(Galleria Palatina)* is quite simply, quite opulently, the family art collection. The paintings are displayed just as the dukes themselves hung them, two-, three-, and four-high, by personal preference rather than in historical sequence. The richly decorated halls are named after the themes of their 17th-century frescoes — Venus, Hercules, Prometheus, etc. As in any collection of family pictures, there's a preponderance of portraits, though here the aunts and uncles tend to be princesses and cardinals.

And the Medici's taste and means did permit a considerable number of masterpieces.

Titian displays his masterly use of colour and light in The Concert (Hall 5, Venus), a haunting portrait of T*he Englishman* and bare-breasted *Magdalen* (Hall 6, Apollo).

Early proponent of "make love, not war," Rubens shows Venus restraining Mars in his vivid *Consequences of War* and portrays himself on the far left of his *Four Philosophers* (Hall 7, Mars).

Raphael is well represented by a stately *Veiled Woman* (Hall 8, Jupiter), a classic *Madonna of the Chair* and *Maddalena Doni* (Hall 9, Saturn), deliberately imitating the pose of Leonardo da Vinci's *Mona Lisa*, and *Pregnant Women* (Hall 10, Iliad).

Caravaggio contributes a typically disturbing canvas, an ugly *Sleeping Cupid* with distinct intimations of death (Hall 32, Education of Jupiter).

Up on the next floor, the **Modern Art Gallery** is devoted to 19th- and 20th-century Italian art. Most interesting are the *Macchiaioli* school of Tuscan pre-Impressionists, who met at Florence's Caffè

Michelangelo in the 1860s seeking a new freedom from academic art that paralleled the political liberation of the Risorgimento. Giorgio de Chirico and Eduardo de Pisis are among the more important 20th-century painters exhibited.

Left of the main Pitti entrance, the **Silverware Museum** *(Museo degli Argenti)* has 16 profusely ornamented rooms of family treasures — gold, silver, jewels, beautiful 16th- and 17th-century amber and ivory, crystal and porcelain, and Baroque furniture. The **Carriage Museum** *(Museo delle Carrozze),* in a wing on the far right of the palace, and the **Royal Apartments** *(Appartamenti Monumentali),* upstairs, right of the main entrance, show an opulent, truly palatial life that the Pitti's dour exterior never let you suspect.

Time for a rest in the shade of the cypresses, pines, and holm oaks of the palace's **Boboli Gardens**. To the modern eye, they form a Re-

The Ponte Vecchio, intact since 1385, was Florence's first and, for centuries, only bridge.

naissance and Baroque theme park dotted with loggias, cool fountains, grottoes with artificial stalactites, and myriad statues of gods, nymphs, and grotesques (the word derives from the Boboli grottoes).

Directly behind the palace, the Amphitheatre, shaped like a Roman circus, was the scene of the Medici's most extravagant fêtes and masked balls. In the middle of the nearby Pond of Neptune (*Vasca del Nettuno*), the burly sea god wields his trident in petrified parody of one of the Boboli's gardeners.

After the Pitti's riches, the unadorned white façade of the Augustinian church of **Santo Spirito** is a sobering antidote. Brunelleschi's design was never completed but the interior preserves the spatial clarity of his Corinthian-capitalled colonnades. In the right transept is a strikingly theatrical *Madonna Enthroned* by Filippino Lippi.

Across the church's tree-shaded piazza—popular for its pleasant market—is the **Cenacolo di Santo Spirito**, formerly the monas-

---

War and Flood

In the 20th century, the Arno river has meant nothing but trouble. To slow the Allied advance in August, 1944, the Germans blew up all Florence's bridges except the Ponte Vecchio. And in case their enemy planned to drive vehicles across this ancient footbridge, they blocked approaches by destroying buildings within a radius of 200 metres.

On November 4, 1966, the river burst its banks and flooded the city, destroying and damaging over 1,000 paintings and 500 sculptures as well as countless precious books and manuscripts in its libraries. In places like the Bargello's Michelangelo Hall (see page 90), you can see wall marks recording the flood level—3 metres (10 feet) and more. But this was the golden Age of Aquarius and from all over the world, the sixties' art-loving brothers and sisters of the flower children poured into the city to help with the rescue operation, spearheaded by Florence's own proud citizenry.

tery's refectory, with some 14th-century frescoes of the *Last Supper* and *Crucifixion* by Andrea Orcagna.

The church of **Santa Maria del Carmine** is an essential stop on any artistic pilgrimage to Florence. The church itself is an unprepossessing reconstruction after a devastating fire of 1771, but the Brancacci Chapel with the great **Masaccio frescoes** survived intact. The painter died at 27 after only five years of known creative activity (1423–1428), working with his mild-mannered friend Masolino on scenes from Genesis and the life of St. Peter. Compare Masolino's sweet and harmonious Adam and Eve in his *Original Sin* (chapel entrance, upper right) with Masaccio's agonizing figures in the *Expulsion from the Garden of Eden* opposite to appreciate one of the early Renaissance's most dramatic statements. Florence's greatest artists, Michelangelo at their head, came to sketch Masaccio's trail-blazing use of light and visual depth as instruments of emotional impact, particularly striking in the broad sweep of his *St. Peter Paying the Tribute Money*. The chapel frescoes were completed in the 1480s by Filippino Lippi, who painted the side walls' lower panels.

Drive up the beautiful winding Viale dei Colli for a last panoramic view of the city dominated by the cupola of the Duomo from the vast **Piazzale Michelangelo** (with yet another copy of his David). While you're there, visit the charming Romanesque church of **San Miniato** up the hill behind the square. Antonio Rossellino's monumental 15th-century marble **tomb** of the Cardinal of Portugal, in a chapel off the left aisle, is notable for two beautiful genuflecting angels on the sarcophagus which greatly influenced Michelangelo.

Tuscany *(Toscana)*

The original territory of the ancient civilization of the Etruscans has always been independent-minded, even aloof, in its attitude to Rome and the other regions. For the serious Italophile, its beauty and riches deserve weeks, months, even years of attention, but no first visit

Ancient Roman baths are among the extensive Roman ruins that remain in Fiesole.

would be complete without at least one week here. After an indispensable side-trip from Florence to Fiesole, our itineraries go west to Pisa and Lucca before turning south through the hills to Siena.

Fiesole

Just 8 km (5 miles) northeast of Florence (30) minutes on the number 7 bus from the Duomo, the road winds up a wooded hillside, revealing at each bend ever-changing views of Fiesole's gardens and villas before you and the monuments of the great city below.

Stop on the way at **San Domenico di Fiesole** for its 15th-century church and two important works by Fra Angelico, a *Madonna and Saints* in the first chapel on the left and a *Crucifixion* in the monastery refectory. Just off to the west is the pretty church of Badia Fiesolana, once the town's 10th-century Romanesque cathedral, redesigned by Brunelleschi in the 1450s.

Only some wall fragments remain of the former Etruscan stronghold in Fiesole itself, but there are extensive Roman ruins, including a well-preserved **theatre**, still in use, which seats 2,500 spectators.

Car drivers can negotiate the winding old side-road **Via Vecchia Fiesolana** for glimpses of handsome villas half-hidden among the cypresses and olive trees. The town centre, Piazza Mino da Fiesole, with its austere cathedral, is the starting-point for some exhilarating hill walks, the best being the steep lane leading west to the **San Francesco** convent.

Pisa

The town, like the tipsy stubbornness of its Leaning Tower, is one of the world's blessed wonders. In its heyday from the 11th to the 13th centuries, it created a commercial empire down the Tyrrhenian coast and in Corsica, Sardinia, Sicily, Syria, Palestine, and Egypt. Its riches built that gleaming white marble complex of religious edifices known as the **Campo dei Miracoli** (Field of Miracles), left unscathed by the invasions and wars of succeeding centuries.

Conquering a flat, ungrateful landscape with serene, other-worldly harmony, this assembly of buildings in the **Piazza del Duomo** celebrates the whole cycle of life, from baptistery, cathedral, and campanile to the monumental cemetery of the Campo Santo.

The **Duomo** was built from 1063 to 1118 to honour Pisa's victory over the Saracens in Sicily. With Oriental and Byzantine decorative elements reflecting the Pisan Republic's overseas interests, its four-tiered arcaded façade over three porches is a masterpiece of grace and delicacy. Architect Buscheto didn't hesitate to write in Latin (in the far left arch) "This marble church has no equal." Inside, there was no reason either for Giovanni Pisano to show false modesty about his superbly sculpted 14th-century **marble pulpit** (left aisle).

Thanks to its unstable subsoil, the **Leaning Tower** *(campanile)* is out of alignment by about 5 metres (16 feet). Give or take a micromillimetre or two depending on annual subsidence, that means the 8-storeyed belfry stands 55.65 metres (182.6 feet) high on its north side and 54.8 (179.8 feet) on the south. Scientists are forever seeking new solutions for propping it up, but at its present rate of slippage, you still have another 200 years to see it standing more or less upright.

The lovely circular **baptistery** is topped by a traditional statue of John the Baptist. Inside, left of the baptismal font and altar, is Pisa's greatest work of sculpture, a hexagonal **marble pulpit** by Nicola Pisano, father of the Giovanni who designed the cathedral pulpit. The 1260 carving of biblical themes has clear links to French Gothic sculpture, while drawing on models from Roman and Etruscan sarcophagi—a Herculean Daniel and a Mary inspired by heads of Juno and Phaedra.

In the 13th-century cloistered cemetery of the **Camposanto** (Holy Ground), note the Gothic tabernacle enclosing a *Madonna and Saints.* Within the cloister, in the north gallery, is a striking **fresco** of the *Triumph of Death* (1360) showing how a humble person and an aristocrat face the same destiny.

Away from the Campo dei Miracoli, in a Benedictine monastery down by the Arno, the **San Matteo Museum** houses sculpture from the baptistery and cathedral as well as a gentle Simone Martini *Madonna and Child* and Masaccio's *St. Paul* (part of a polyptych split up among London, Naples, Berlin, and Liechtenstein).

Lucca

The "sights" of this town take scarcely a day, but the seductive tranquillity within its old ramparts is such that people end up staying for weeks. Peace of mind has always been a priority here. In the stormy 15th and 16th centuries, Lucca's prosperous silk merchants preserved the peace by intercepting enemy armies and paying them to bypass the town. It has been particularly rich in musicians, most notably Boccherini and Puccini, and hosts a series of music festivals throughout the summer.

Begin with a stroll around the nicely preserved **ramparts**, along the Passeggiata delle Mura, for a good overall view.

The fine 14th-century cathedral, **Duomo San Martino**, has a Pisan-style arcaded façade with a *Descent from the Cross* carved by Nicola Pisano over the north door. Inside, to the right of the entrance, is a 12th-century equestrian sculpture of *St. Martin and the Beggar,* with a distinctly ancient Roman flavour. In the left transept, see the graceful 15th-century **tomb** of Ilaria del Carretto by Sienese sculptor Jacopo della Quercia.

Northwest of the cathedral, you'll find an even more beautiful adaptation of the Pisan Romanesque style in the church of **San Michele in**

Foro, less encumbered on its site of the old Roman Forum. The arcaded façade varies the patterns of its columns—sculpted, striped, scrolled, chevroned—in pink, green, black, or white marble. With binoculars, you can spot up on the third tier of arches (third from the right), the heads of Risorgimento heroes Garibaldi and Cavour.

To capture something of the town's medieval character, explore the **Via Guinigi**, with its handsome 14th-century palaces, and the towered houses of **Via Fillungo**, leading to the

The Leaning Tower of Pisa is still slipping, due to unstable subsoil.

Roman amphitheatre, now the Piazza del Mercato. Nearby, the façade of the church of **San Frediano** has a 13th-century mosaic of the *Ascension*. In the interior (fourth chapel on left aisle), look for Jacopo della Quercia's marble altar.

Chianti

The best introduction to the Tuscan hill country is a tour of the famous **vineyards** that grace its southern-oriented slopes. The grapes that qualify as *Chianti Classico*, distinguished by a coveted black rooster label, grow in the region between Florence and Siena, most of them along the Via Chiantigiana, which is route 222. The liveliest, most colourful time is during the autumn grape harvest, *la vendemmia*, but tasting—and buying—goes on at the vineyard all year round.

Start out at San Casciano in Val di Pesa, 17 km (11 miles) south of Florence, with a bonus for art-lovers of a Simone Martini *Crucifixion* and other Sienese works in the church of La Misericordia.

Vineyards interspersed with olive groves grace the landscape around Chianti.

Southeast across to route 222, you find the characteristic landscape of vineyards interspersed with equally renowned olive groves as you approach Greve, a major wine centre on the river of the same name. (Americans pay homage at a monument to local boy Giovanni da Verrazzano, navigator-explorer of New York Bay.) The wine route continues through Castellina with its 15th-century castle and ancient town gate. Then on to **Radda**, where you should peep in at the Piccolo Museo del Chianti, and to Gaiole in Chianti, one of the best centres for tasting and a place to linger.

San Gimignano

The haunting silhouette of this medieval Manhattan, a skyline bristling with rectangular towers, and its lovingly preserved historic centre make it the most magical of Tuscany's hill towns. (One of the most photogenic views is from the north, on the road from Certaldo, home and last resting place of Boccaccio.) There were 72 towers—erected as symbols of its merchants' power and prestige—until the town's Florentine conquerors ordered them dismantled in the 14th century. Just 14 remain.

The most important are clustered around three adjoining **squares**: the triangular Piazza della Cisterna, the old banking centre named after the city's 13th-century travertine well, surrounded by elegant palaces; Piazza del Duomo, grouping church and town hall as the centre of civic and religious power; and the Piazza delle Erbe market place with twin Salvucci towers.

The 13th-century town hall, **Palazzo del Popolo**, houses the civic museums. The **Pinacoteca** includes an emotionally intense *Crucifixion* by Coppo di Marcovaldo and a Taddeo di Bartolo painting of St. Gimignano, in which you can see what the towers of the medieval city looked like. Visit the interior of the 12th-century Romanesque **Collegiata** (collegiate church ranking just lower than a cathedral) for its dramatic Barna da Siena frescoes of New Testament scenes along the right aisle. In sharp contrast, the Ghirlandaio **frescoes** in the Santa Fina Chapel (at the end of the right aisle) are a series of sophisticated social portraits. Against the east wall, flanking the church entrance, are wooden statues of Mary and the Archangel Gabriel by Jacopo della Quercia.

For a fine view of the surrounding country, climb up to the ruins of the **Rocca** citadel.

Volterra

This fortified town perched high on its hill works a sober charm among the buff-stone 13th-century edifices of its **Piazza dei Priori** and adjacent Piazza San Giovanni. The Palazzo dei Priori (1208) is the oldest of Tuscany's typical town halls, with a two-tiered tower, battlements, and mullioned windows. It stands opposite the massive triple-arched **Palazzo Pretorio**, medieval police headquarters. The two squares are separated by the austere 12th-century cathedral and 13th-century octagonal baptistery. The latter's baptismal font has bas-reliefs by Andrea Sansovino.

Away from the centre, you can trace the town's ancient beginnings in the **Etruscan Guarnacci Museum** (Via Don Minzoni, 15). The collection includes sculpted stone, alabaster, and terracotta funeral urns dating back to the sixth century B.C. One gaunt statue, *Ombra della Sera* (Evening Shadow), is an uncanny 2,000-year-old precursor of a modern Giacometti.

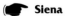 **Siena**

A city of rich russet browns and ochres, Siena is as delightfully feminine as greystone Florence is imposing in its masculinity. Contrasts with its old rival to the north are striking and inevitable. Whereas the nucleus of Florence was built to a strict Roman city plan of straight streets intersecting at right angles, Siena has all the Tuscan hilltown's haphazard organic forms, straggling up and down a forked ridge of not one but three hilltops.

Similarly, while Florentine art developed its formidable intellectual and emotional power, the tone of Sienese painting—Simone Martini, the Lorenzettis, even the Mannerist Sodoma—remained gentle and delicate, bathed in the light and colour of its surrounding countryside. But as its obstinately independent spirit has shown, even after the Florentine conquest of 1555—a spirit epitomized by its lusty Palio tournament—the town is not without vigour.

But go easy on those steep streets, rest awhile in the cool courtyard of a great banker's palazzo, enjoy the spicy cuisine with a good local Chianti. And take time out between two siestas to see some of Tuscany's most exhilarating monuments.

Start at the grand sloping fan-shaped **Piazza del Campo**, site of the old Roman forum and arena of the Palio horse race. The piazza's red-brick herringbone paving is divided by nine marble strips for the nine patrician clans that ruled the city at the end of the 13th century.

Over a late-afternoon coffee on the shady side (next to the tourist office), you can appreciate the painterly impact of the "burnt sienna" glowing in the arcaded Gothic **Palazzo Pubblico** opposite, with its splendid 102-metre- (335-foot-) high **Torre del Mangia** (climb to its first tier at 88 metres [288 feet] for a view of the city). The loggia at the tower's base is a chapel (*Cappella di Piazza*) marking the city's deliverance from the plague of 1348.

The modern town hall offices are on the palazzo's ground floor, but its upstairs chambers, frescoed by the city's foremost artists, have been transformed into a **Museo Civico** (municipal museum). The **Sala del Mappamondo** (named after a lost map of the Sienese world painted by Ambrogio Lorenzetti to trace the city's international banking interests) has two great Simone Martini **frescoes**. To the left is a stately *Enthroned Madonna* (1315) and to the right, *Guidoriccio da Fogliano* (1328, but whose authenticity has recently been disputed), depicting the Sienese captain's ride to a historic victory at Montemassi —in the nicely detailed Tuscan landscape, notice the little Chianti vineyard in the military encampment. In the **Sala della Pace** (Hall of Peace, council chamber of the Nine Patricians), the full force of Siena's civic pride strikes home in the Ambrogio Lorenzetti **frescoes**

The Duomo in Siena is for many the greatest of Italy's Gothic cathedrals.

(1337–1339). One wall is devoted to *Bad Government*, a gloomy portrait of Tyranny, badly damaged, and the other two to Siena's own enlightened *Good Government*, full of fascinating detail of town life—roof-builders, shoe shop, school, outdoor tavern, ladies dancing in the street—and hunters riding out to the surrounding countryside. A second floor loggia is adorned with Jacopo della Quercia's 15th-century carvings for the city fountain Fonte Gaia (of which a poor 19th-century replica stands in the piazza).

Southwest of the Campo, the **Duomo**, built from the 12th to the 14th centuries, is for many the greatest of Italy's Gothic cathedrals. The exterior's majestic polychrome and black- and white-striped marble panelling surrounding Giovanni Pisano's three intricately carved portals presents that quintessential Italian preference for pictorial qualities over *mere* architecture. And that gleaming colour is pure Siena. The interior continues the bands of black and white marble, while **inlaid marble paving** covers the floor with 56 pictures of biblical and allegorical themes done over two centuries by some 40 artists, most notably Beccafumi, di Bartolomeo, and Pinturicchio. Off the left aisle is the early-16th-century **Cardinal Piccolomini Library**, vividly decorated by Pinturicchio's action-packed frescoes of the life of Pope Pius II (the cardinal himself became pope, Pius III, but lasted only ten days). In the left transept is a magnificent octagonal 13th-century **pulpit** carved by Nicola Pisano, with help from son Giovanni and Arnolfo di Cambio. Among the fantastic detail of the new testament scenes, notice the damned being eaten alive in the *Last Judgment*. The 17th-century Baroque Madonna del Voto Chapel (in the right transept) was designed by Bernini, whose statues of St. Jerome and Mary Magdalen flank the entrance.

Riding for the Palio

The Palio horse races held on July 2 and August 16 are part of a traditional pageant dating back to the 15th century and beyond. Colourful Renaissance-costumed pages and men-at-arms put on a procession and show of flag-throwing with emblems—eagle, snail, porcupine, goose, etc.—of the 17 parishes (*contrade*) of the city and surrounding communes. Ten of them compete in the climactic breakneck bareback horse race round the Campo for which a painted silk standard, the Palio, is the prize. (To avoid the sometimes harrowing crush down in the square, you may prefer to reserve a seat in a stand or a place on a balcony.)

In the **Cathedral Museum** *(Museo dell'Opera Metropolitana)*, Giovanni Pisano's original sculptures for the Duomo's façade have strangely distorted poses because they were meant to be seen from below. Look out, too, for Duccio di Buoninsegna's *Enthroned Madonna*, Simone Martini's *Miracles of St. Agostino Novello*, and Pietro Lorenzetti's *Birth of Mary*.

Take a leisurely hour or two for the lovely Sienese paintings in the Palazzo Buonsignori's **Pinacoteca Nazionale**. Besides the works of the 14th-century masters Duccio, Pietro and Ambrogio Lorenzetti, and Simone Martini, see Siena's 16th-century Mannerists, painting at a time when the Renaissance teetered on the brink of effete decadence: Beccafumi's dreamy *Birth of Mary* and a highly decorative *Christ at the Column* by Sodoma.

Montepulciano

On the route to southern Umbria, this is one of Tuscany's most attractive hill towns—with an excellent local wine. Stroll along the Via di Gracciano and Via Ricci to see the town's noble Gothic and Renaissance palazzi.

On the **Piazza Grande**, with a graceful town well decorated with griffins and lions in its centre, the 14th-century **Palazzo Comunale** is a particularly imposing expression of civic dignity. In the austere little **cathedral**, see Taddeo di Bartolo's fine triptych on the high altar. Antonio da Sangallo, architect of many of the town's palazzi, built his masterpiece, the 16th-century church of **Madonna di San Biagio**, southwest of town, at the end of an avenue of cypresses overlooking the Chiana valley.

Monte Argentario

If you're taking the coast road to or from Rome, stop off at the fashionable seaside resorts on this pine-forested peninsula beside the town of Orbetello. The sandy beaches and yachting harbours of **Port'Ercole** and **Porto Santo Stefano** are favourite weekend desti-

Chic Romans head up the coast to Port'Ercole's sheltered harbour playground.

nations for Romans, but they're much quieter during the week. Take a boat excursion out to the pretty island of **Giglio.**

Umbria

The region has a less spectacular reputation than Tuscany (and is blessedly less crowded), but it's highly appreciated both for its great artistic treasures and the dreamy rolling green landscapes that inspired them.

The area was dominated in the past by the papacy, which conquered the Lombard dukes of Spoleto in the Middle Ages, Perugia in the 16th century, and held sway until the unification of Italy. Apart from pilgrims streaming to St. Francis's Assisi and university students heading for Perugia, it has remained a very happy backwater.

On September 26, 1997, two earthquakes rocked the Umbria region, leaving ten people dead and causing extensive damages to local villages. Thousands of people were left homeless, and countless churches and public buildings were forced to close, as aftershocks and additional earth-quakes continued through the early days of October, dozens of buildings suffered structural damage, and many frescoes and other monuments important to the region were severely damaged or destroyed.

Orvieto's rocky perch made it an ideal medieval stronghold.

Orvieto

Half the pleasure of this lovely town high on its rocky precipice is a first glimpse of it from afar (not so very different today from Turner's 1828 painting in London's Tate Gallery). For a good view, approach it from the southwest, on route S71 from Lake Bolsena, or look across from the medieval abbey La Badia (now a hotel), immediately south of town.

Connoisseurs come for the great white wine, art-lovers for the magnificent Gothic **cathedral**. Scores of architects worked on the church from the 13th to the 17th centuries, but its glory remains the gleaming gabled **façade**, with its four slender spired pilasters and its rose-window above the beautifully scrolled porches. At the base of the two northern pilasters, look closely at Lorenzo Maitani's marvellous carved marble **bas-reliefs** of scenes from the Old Testament and the Last Judgment.

Grey and white bands of marble give the interior a spacious simplicity. Off the right transept, the **San Brizio Chapel** is frescoed on the ceiling by Fra Angelico—*Christ in Glory*—and by Luca Signorelli on the walls. To the left, Signorelli portrays himself and Fra Angelico as bystanders in the vivid *Preaching of the Antichrist* (identified here with Savonarola). The nude figures in the *Resurrection of the Dead* on the right wall are less convincing (described by Leonardo da Vinci as "sacks of nuts").

The **Cathedral Museum** in the Palazzo Soliano includes other works by Signorelli, a Simone Martini polyptych, and sculpture by Nino, Andrea, and Giovanni Pisano.

If you want to cool off, explore the monumental **Pozzo di San Patrizio**, a 16th-century well dug 63 metres (206 feet) down into the volcanic rock on the northeast edge of the precipice. Well lit by 72 windows, two spiral staircases of 248 steps take you right down to the water level.

Spoleto

Its greatest tourist attractions are the summer music and theatre festivals, but the town's beautiful natural setting amid densely wooded hills also makes it a base for hikes into the countryside, especially the oak forest on Monteluco.

The sober Romanesque **cathedral** with 17th-century additions is decorated with damaged but still graceful Fra Filippo Lippi **frescoes** in its chancel. In the left transept, son Filippino designed the **tomb** for the licentious painter-monk who seduced Sister Lucrezia—and others—in Florence's Carmine monastery.

Assisi

NOT TO BE MISSED

The enduring popular appeal of St. Francis (1182–1226) has turned his native town into Italy's major pilgrimage destination, second only to Rome. Its basilica, like the peaceful medieval town centre, has been beautifully preserved, and the centuries-old pilgrim trade manages to avoid the commercialism that blights other religious shrines.

Park as close as you can to the lower square *(Piazza Inferiore)* at the west end of town. The basilica of **San Francesco** is in fact two churches, one above the other, built on top of the saint's tomb in the crypt.

The **Lower Church** was begun in 1228, two years after Francis' death, and the frescoes were painted in the 14th century, but a Renaissance porch now precedes the Gothic side entrance. The subdued light of the low vaulted nave evokes the sober piety of the Franciscan tradition. Simone Martini has decorated the **St. Martin Chapel** (first left) with exquisite frescoes, including a most aristocratic Jesus appearing in St. Martin's dream. Stairs in the nave lead down to the crypt and St. Francis's tomb, rediscovered only in 1818, centuries after it had been concealed from Perugian plunderers.

The superb frescoes of the life of Jesus in the **Mary Magdalen Chapel** (third right) and of St. Francis's vows of poverty, chastity, and obedience above the elegant Gothic high altar are attributed to Giotto or his pupils.

In the right transept, the famous Cimabue portrait of **St. Francis**, believed to be a close physical resemblance, shows him to the right of the enthroned Madonna. Over in the left transept, see Pietro Lorenzetti's noble *Descent from the Cross*.

A Saint

Francesco di Bernardone was the spoiled son of a rich family well known for its rumbustious ways. But a sojourn in a Perugia jail at 23, followed by a severe illness, sobered him up. After a vision in the Chapel of San Damiano, he vowed a life of poverty in the service of the Church. He nursed lepers, converted bandits. He travelled to Spain, Morocco, Egypt, and Palestine, but it was his impact on a troubled Italian population that mattered most to a Church beleaguered by heresy. Thousands responded to the simple eloquence of his preaching. They told how the example of his gentle life had tamed wild wolves and taught swallows to sing a sweeter song. In his religious ecstasy on Monte La Verna (near Arezzo), he was marked with Christ's stigmata —a phenomenon the most sceptical scholars have never placed in doubt. He was canonized St. Francis just two years after his death in 1226.

In the **Upper Church**, Cimabue's works in the apse and transepts have turned black, looking like photo negatives because of the oxidized white lead in his paints, yet you can still feel the intensity of the crowd's anguish in his *Crucifixion*.

In the brilliantly illuminated nave, the faithful are exalted by one of the most grandiose series of **frescoes** in Christendom. The *Life of Francis* is movingly celebrated in 28 scenes along the lower tier (starting from the right transept), while 32 frescoes in the upper tier illustrate scenes from the Old and New Testament. Giotto's most fervent supporters say he designed the St. Francis series and himself painted numbers 2 to 11.

Unfortunately, the basilica suffered extensive damage during the earthquakes of September 26, 1997. Several important frescoes were severely damaged or destroyed, notably works by Ciambue featured on a portion of the Upper Church's vaulted ceiling, which plunged to the floor during the quakes.

Penetrate the historic heart of Assisi along the **Via San Francesco**, with its 15th-century Pilgrims' Hostel *(Oratorio dei Pellegrini)* at number 11. Its frescoes are attributed to Perugino. The noble **Piazza del Comune** is the town centre, grouping medieval palazzi around the old Roman forum. A triumph of Christianity over paganism, the Corinthian-columned church of **Santa Maria sopra Minerva** was a Roman temple under Augustus.

The austere little **San Damiano** monastery, where Francis heard the good word, is 3 km (2 miles) south of town, maintaining the purest Franciscan tradition.

Perugia

Dominating the Umbrian countryside from its 494-metre (1,600-foot) hill, the town is emphatically more secular, more profane than its Franciscan neighbour. But the imposing weight of its past is lightened by the lively cosmopolitan studentry of its two (Italian and international) universities. Constantly at war with Assisi in the Middle Ages, Perugia's belligerence is symbolized on the north side of town by the lovingly preserved **Arco Etrusco** (Etruscan—and partly Roman— triumphal arch) that remained part of the medieval ramparts.

And in the town centre, something of the old aggressive civic power is evoked in the formidable **Palazzo dei Priori** (town hall) towering over the Piazza 4 Novembre. But Nicola Pisano's intricately carved 13th-century **Fontana Maggiore** (Great Fountain) does hold its own. Earth tremors badly damaged the buff-stone cathedral opposite.

The third floor of the town hall (entrance around the corner on Corso Vannucci) is given over to the **Galleria Nazionale dell'Umbria**, a splendid collection of Umbrian and Tuscan painting. It includes a Fra Angelico *Triptych* and Piero della Francesca's *Annunciation* and *Madonna with Angels*. But Umbria's pride and joy is the work of Perugino (1445–1523). Look out for his *Adoration of the Magi* and a *Madonna della Consolazione* as sweet and serene as the Umbrian landscape of which you'll catch a glimpse through the museum windows. Pinturicchio, master of narrative fresco, is represented by his *Miracles of the Saints*.

Next door on the busy pedestrian street of Corso Vannucci (Perugino was Pietro Vannucci's nickname) is the **Collegio del Cambio**, 15th-century hall and chapel of the bankers' guild. The vestibule is decorated with 17th-century Baroque walnut panelling. In the **Audience Hall** (*Sala dell'Udienza*) is a delightful series of Perugino frescoes. The left wall is allegorical, devoted to the bankers' widely acknowledged virtues, *Prudence, Justice, Fortitude*, and *Temperance*, while religious themes invoke their piety on the other walls. (*Fortitude* and one of the Sibyls are attributed to Perugino's 17-year-old pupil, Raphael.)

For a feeling of the old medieval town, dodge the chickens scampering across the brick paving of the tiny tunnel-vaulted **Via Volte della Pace**, incongruously linking the modern shopping street of Via Alesse to a parking lot behind the cathedral.

At the south end of the Corso Vannucci beyond the Piazza Italia, the **Carducci Gardens** provide a restful view of the Umbrian countryside.

Gubbio

Some 40 km (25 miles) north of Perugia, this venerable fortress-town is not easy to get to, and once you're there it's hard on you if you don't like climbing steep cobbled streets. But for anyone who cherishes the tranquillity of a totally unspoiled medieval atmosphere, Gubbio is a delight. The **Piazza della Signoria** paved in brick and stone is a fine vantage point for viewing the rest of the city. Its 14th-century battlemented **Palazzo dei Consoli** is one of the grandest civic edifices in all Italy, and from the tall arcade that anchors it to the hillside you have a magnificent panorama of the surrounding country. Then climb (even higher!) to the cathedral and the Renaissance courtyard of the Palazzo Ducale.

THE NORTHEAST

Throughout Italy's history, its northeast regions have linked the country to an exotic outside world of Byzantium and the Orient through Venice, and to the Alpine countries beyond the Dolomites, while the plains of Emilia-Romagna from Ravenna to Parma provide an anchor to the heartland of the Po valley.

The result is a rich variety of distinctive cities and colourful hinterland. The afterglow of Venice's empire is undimmed. Elegant Palladian villas grace its Veneto mainland from Padua to Vicenza. The glories of Verona extend from its grand Roman arena to the palaces of the medieval and Renaissance princes whose intrigues inspired Shakespeare. In Emilia-Romagna, the pride and creativity of the great city-states is still very much in evidence in the monuments and museums of Bologna, Ferrara, and Parma. Stretch your muscles in the Dolomites, with its first-class winter sports and summer hiking, or soak up sun and sea in the Adriatic resorts around Rimini.

Gondolas pole along the Grand Canal to the Rialto Bridge.

Venice (Venezia)

"See Venice & Die"

HAPPY

These palaces, canals, and lagoons claim a place apart in our collective imagination. As our 20th century ends, Venice remains a dreamworld, its myth more powerful than harsh reality. Even when it threatens to disintegrate into nightmare at times of winter flood or overcrowded summer, visitors can take refuge on a boardwalk across the waters or in a quiet corner away from the mob, and continue their dream. One of the city's many blessings is that there still are so many quiet and beautiful corners. Another, so obvious, but impossible to over-emphasize, is the *absence of cars*, the simple joy of wandering around a town relieved of our by now built-in urban traffic stress, of standing on a little humpback bridge far from the Grand Canal and hearing only the water lapping against the moss-covered walls or the occasional swish of a gondola. You may never want to break the spell and go back to the real world.

Go in May or October, if you can—the crowds at Easter and from June to September can be truly horrendous. Venice at Christmas has become fashionable and the February Carnival very commercial. But whenever you go, don't try to do it in a day. Without the time to explore those hidden corners, you risk hating it for the rest of your life. Give yourself a minimum of three days, time to get lost—ultimately, but perhaps regretfully, you'll get back to the main landmarks signposted with bright yellow arrows. The town has more than enough sights to see, but you can taste much of its pleasures before you even set foot inside the museums, churches, and monuments. The only "must" is Venice itself, your own Venice.

 ## Grand Canal

From the railway station or the car park of Piazzale Roma, you begin with a *vaporetto* waterbus along the Canal Grande, the most stunning main street in the world. Use this wonderful first contact with the city as your introductory tour.

Going, Going Gondola

The proud fleet of 10,000 gondolas of a century ago has dwindled to a few hundred, while the prices have gone in the opposite direction. Apart from commuters taking cross-canal ferry gondolas, Venetians leave the sleek and slender black craft to the tourists. Still handing on the business from father to son, the gondoliers in their straw hats and sailor's jumpers or striped T-shirts are as cheerful and witty as, say, any other taxi-driver, but they don't sing as often or as well as they used to. Exorbitant yes, but how will you explain to grandchildren, after the last gondolas have disappeared, that you visited Venice and never went in one?

Vaporetto number 1 takes you to the historic centre of town, Piazza San Marco, but there is another way to go: the faster number 2 takes a shortcut across a loop in the inverted S-shaped canal, missing out three-quarters of the fabulous sights. Airport motor launches cross directly to San Marco from the Lido — just drop your bags off at the hotel and take the Grand Canal in the opposite direction, round-trip. (Save your gondola ride for when you're settled in.)

Along the Grand Canal's 3.8 km (more than 2 miles), varying in width from 30 to 70 metres (100 to 230 feet), are the old trading offices and warehouses of its commercial heyday. Known locally as *ca'* (short for *casa*) as well as *palazzo*, the marble, brick, and white limestone palaces range over 600 years from Venetian-Byzantine to Baroque and Neo classical, but most of them are 14th- and 15th-century Flamboyant Gothic, Venice's "trademark" in architectural styles. Their sea-resistant limestone foundations stand on massive pinewood stilts driven 8 metres (26 feet) into the lagoon bed.

Left Bank

The superb Renaissance **Palazzo Vendramin-Calergi**, where Richard Wagner died in 1883, is today the winter casino. The gilt has gone from the façade of the 15th-century **Ca' d'Oro** (Golden House), but it's still the town's most beautiful Gothic palace. Italy's most impressive post office, **Fondaco dei Tedeschi** was once the trading-centre of Czechs, Hungarians, and Austrians as well as the Germans of its name. Just beyond, the shop-lined **Rialto Bridge** arches the canal at its narrowest point. The 18th-century **Palazzo Grassi** was recently restored for modern art exhibitions. The prefecture puts its bureaucrats in the fine Renaissance **Palazzo Corner** (or *Ca' Grande*), while gondoliers claim Othello's Desdemona lived in the lovely late-Gothic **Palazzo Contarini-Fasan**.

Right Bank

The 700-year-old **Fondaco dei Turchi** was a warehouse in the 17th century for the merchants of Constantinople, now the Natural History Museum. It stands next to the plain brick 15th-century **Megio** wheat granary, decorated only by battlements and the city seal of St. Mark's lion. The imposing 17th-century Baroque **Ca' Pesaro** houses the Modern Art Museum. Come back early in the morning to the **Pescheria** (fish market), 20th-century neo-Gothic, but nicely done. The university has a department in the handsome 15th-century Gothic **Ca' Foscari**. The **Ca' Rezzonico** is itself a fine specimen of the 18th-century Venetian art for which it is now a museum. Beyond

Reflections on the Water

The water explains almost everything. When the Lombards swept east across the Po valley, the Venetians found their salvation literally in the sea—perched on an archipelago of isles and shoals. Ruled by an energetic oligarchy under an elected Doge, or duke, the Serenissima, or Most Serene Republic of St. Mark, turned its back on the hostile mainland and made a fabulous fortune with an empire stretching across the eastern Mediterranean and beyond to the silk and spice routes of Asia allegedly opened up by Marco Polo. Italy had no vital importance for Venice until overseas trade declined and new sources of wealth had to be sought in agriculture on the mainland.

Protected by the lagoons, Venice needed no ramparts; its palaces could be light and decorative rather than the solid fortress-like residences of Florence. Fronting canals instead of streets, the façades are designed to take their colour from the water's reflection as well as from the sunlight. While Florentine art impresses us with its mastery of form and line, the most striking qualities of Venetian painting, with the added influence of Byzantium and the Orient, remain that colour and light.

Piazza San Marco — "the living room of the world," according to Napoleon.

the wooden Accademia Bridge, the perspective is completed by the magnificent Baroque church of **Santa Maria della Salute**.

Around San Marco

Building-space on the water being what it is, Venice has only one real piazza, but in comparison, any other would have died of shame anyway. Gloriously open to skies and sea, **Piazza San Marco**—to locals, just "the Piazza"—embodies the whole Venetian adventure. Its airy arcades reach out to the 900-year-old basilica and turn a corner past the soaring campanile to the Piazzetta and landing stage of St. Mark's basin *(bacino)*, gateway to the Adriatic. The odysseys of victorious commanders began and ended here.

Here, too, the republic fell in 1797, at the hands of Napoleon. While he was removing the four bronze horses from the basilica along with other art treasures to ship back to Paris, he was said to remark that the Piazza San Marco was "the living room of the world." He closed off the Piazza's west end with an Ala Napoleonica (Napoleonic Wing), through which you enter the Museo Correr, devoted to paintings and documents of Venetian history.

The north and south arms of the square, the 16th-century **Procuratie Vecchie** and **Procuratie Nuove**, were the residences of the republic's most senior officials. They are now lined with fashionable boutiques, jewellery shops, and, most important for breakfast *cappuccino* and afternoon tea, two elegant 18th-century cafés. During the Austrian occupation, the enemy frequented Quadri on the north side, while Italian patriots met only at Florian, opposite. To this day, the latter has the favour of Venetians, but also of foreigners who want to avoid foreigners, which complicates things for Venetians. Out in the square, orchestras play "Palm Court" music. Pigeons chase seed-vendors chasing tourists chasing their children chasing pigeons.

Invasion of the Body Snatchers

It's 828 or thereabouts. A couple of merchants—Venice is full of them—hear that the Doge needs a prestigious holy relic, to bolster his position vis à vis the pope. "How about the evangelist Mark?" they ask. "We can get you the whole body."

They go to Alexandria, where Mark had been bishop, and sneak the body out of the mausoleum, after carefully refilling the evangelist's shroud with the remains of Claudian, a minor saint lying nearby. Clever, but not clever enough to fool the Egyptians, who search their ship. "Hallo, hallo, what's in that basket?" they ask. "See for yourselves," say the merchants, uncovering some slabs of meat. "Kanzir, Kanzir! (pork, pork)," cry the Muslim soldiers and flee in horror, leaving Mark's bones safely concealed beneath.

The glittering façade of the **Basilica di San Marco** forms an exotic backdrop, illuminating Venice's role at the crossroads of Eastern and Western culture. What began in 830 as the Doges' chapel for
the remains of the evangelist Mark, the city's patron saint, was rebuilt in the 11th century as a grandiose Byzantine-Oriental basilica.
Greek mosaicists were brought in to decorate the arches and domes.
Five Romanesque portals correspond to the five Islamic-style domes
covering the church's Greek-cross ground plan. Spired Gothic taber-
nacles enhance the teeming richness.

The **San Alipio portal**, first on the left, is the only one decorated
with an original 13th-century mosaic, depicting the *Transfer of St.
Mark's Body*. The mosaic also shows the basilica with the famous
bronze horses brought from Constantinople after the Crusade of 1204.
The ones over the triple-arched main entrance are copies. (Since their
restoration, the originals are kept in the basilica museum.)

Just inside the church entrance, to the right, is the tomb of Doge Vitale Falier, for whom Mark's remains were brought to Venice. In the six
small cupolas of the narthex (vestibule), 13th-century mosaics portray
Old Testament scenes of Abel's murder, Noah, Abraham, and Moses.

The glow in the interior from the **mosaics**, gently illuminated by
high windows, and the soft brown patina of the once-white marble
fully earn the name of "church of gold." The original mosaics on the
five domes and the great barrel vaults separating them date from the
11th to the 15th centuries. Among the best are the 12th-century *Pentecost* dome in the nave and the central dome's 13th-century *Ascension*. Others have been heavily restored or replaced, not with true
mosaics, but with reproductions in coloured stone of drawings by
such artists as Bellini, Mantegna, and Tintoretto.

The **high altar** stands over St. Mark's tomb. Scholars can't decide
whether the altar's carved alabaster-columned canopy is sixth-century
Byzantine or 13th-century Venetian. They agree it's fine work. Beyond it is the **Pala d'Oro**, a great golden altarpiece dating back 1,000
years and bejewelled in its present form in the 14th century. Guides

will tell you that there were once 2,486 precious stones, including 1,300 pearls, 400 garnets, 300 sapphires, 300 emeralds, and 15 rubies. Give or take the few pilfered by Napoleon, it is still precious enough that crowds have to be kept down by charging an entrance fee.

On your way out, stairs right of the main entrance lead to the **museum**, in which you can see the original four **bronze horses**, probably imperial Roman. From the loggia, you get a fine view over the Piazza San Marco, while galleries provide a privileged close-up of the basilica's mosaic ceilings.

North of the basilica, the 15th-century **Torre dell'Orologio** is one of those busy little clock-towers, all gilt and polychrome enamel, that activate statues, in this case two green bronze Moors, to clang out the hour, joined below, in Ascension week in May, by the three Magi and a trumpeting angel revolving around a gilded Madonna. You can watch the Moors from the roof terrace.

The beloved **Campanile** towers 99 metres (324 feet) over the city, for 10 centuries its belfry, lighthouse, weather vane, and gun turret. Emperor Frederick III rode his horse up its spiral ramp. Criminals were suspended from it in wooden cages. In 1902, it cracked, crumbled and collapsed slowly into the Piazza. Ten years later, on its 1,000th anniversary, it was rebuilt a few tons lighter but much the same as before: *"com'era, dov'era"* ("as it was, where it was"). Its collapse hurt no one, but did crush Jacopo Sansovino's beautiful 16th-century **Loggetta**, equally lovingly restored as the entrance to the campanile's elevator for a view high over the Adriatic and all the way north, on clear days, to the Dolomites.

Flanking the **Piazzetta** that leads to the Bacino di San Marco, opposite the Doges' Palace, Sansovino's exquisite white limestone **Libreria Sansoviniana** is the city's most perfectly realized Renaissance structure, fulfilling all the classical ideals of harmonious proportions. The Doric-columned arcade, inspired by the Roman Colosseum, supports an Ionic gallery carrying the eye up to the beautiful roof balustrade with its obelisks and statues of Greek divinities. Its **Marciana Library** contains some 750,000 volumes and manuscripts, including the poetry of Petrarch in his own hand, and Marco Polo's testament.

The two tall **columns** facing out over St. Mark's basin were brought from Constantinople in the 12th century. They are topped by statues of St. Mark's winged lion and the city's first patron saint, Theodore, with his dragon.

The **Doges' Palace** *(Palazzo Ducale)* was for 900 years the focus of Venice's power and pomp, evoked in the imposing elegance of its pink marble and white limestone façades with their airy arcades, loggias, and balconies fronting the Piazzetta and the basin. Erected over an older Byzantine-style castle, the present 14th- to 15th-century Flamboyant Gothic building has three fine sculptural groups at its corners, the *Drunkenness of Noah* by the Paglia Bridge, *Adam and Eve* at the Piazzetta, and the *Judgment of Solomon* by the basilica.

The **Porta della Carta** (Gate of the Paper, where the doge posted his decrees) makes a magnificent entrance. The Gothic sculpture shows the doge kneeling before St. Mark's lion, flanked by *Prudence* above *Temperance* in niches on the left and *Fortitude* above *Charity* on the right. (That book in the lion's paw that you see all

---

It's a Doge's Life

The doges saw their authority wax and wane between that of absolute monarch and pathetic figurehead. Subject to the changing powers of the republic's oligarchic council, many were murdered, executed for treason, or ritually blinded—traditional punishment for a disgraced ruler. Though elected by the council, many created virtual dynasties. When the revered Giustiniani family were reduced by battle and plague in the 12th century to one last male, a monk, he was hauled out of his monastery on the Lido and persuaded to sire nine boys and three girls to continue the line before being allowed to return to his vows of chastity.

over Venice is inscribed: *Pax tibi, Marce evangelista meus,* "Peace unto you, my evangelist Mark.")

In the inner courtyard the **Scala dei Giganti** staircase is so named for Sansovino's giant statues of Neptune and Mars. Visitors take the golden **Scala d'Oro** past the Doge's opulent private apartments to the spectacularly decorated council chambers on the third floor. Here, as in most of the city's palaces and churches, the walls are decorated with painted panels and canvases rather than frescoes, too easily damaged by the Venetian climate.

Look out for Veronese's *Rape of Europa* and Tintoretto's *Bacchus and Ariadne* and *Vulcan's Forge* in the **Anticollegio**; a masterly allegorical series by Veronese glorifying Venice in the **Sala del Collegio**, where foreign ambassadors were received; and weapons and suits of armour in the **Armoury** *(Sala d'Armi)*.

Highlight of the palace tour, back down on the second floor, is the huge **Sala del Maggior Consiglio** (Great Council Hall), where ordinary citizens presented their complaints in person in the Republic's most democratic days before the oligarchy reserved it for their secret deliberations. The last doge presented his abdication to Napoleon here. Of the 76 doges portrayed here, one is blackened out, Marino Faliero, beheaded for treason in 1355. Tintoretto's *Paradise* adorns the entrance wall. Said to be the world's largest oil painting, 22 by 7 metres (72 by 23 feet), it was done, with the help of son Domenico, when the artist was 70. Look, too, for the brilliant colours of Veronese's oval ceiling painting of *Venice Crowned by Victory,* forerunner of the Baroque *tours de force* in perspective.

For those hoping to go from the sublime to the sinister, the palace **prisons**, neat and tidy today along their narrow corridor, become all too romantic with their 17th-century Baroque **Bridge of Sighs** *(Ponte dei Sospiri)*. It's much too *pretty* to serve as such a celebrated passage to doom which supposedly moved its users to sigh on their way to the torture chambers (now off-limits).

Stretch your legs along the **Riva degli Schiavoni** (Quay of the Slavs), named after the Dalmatian merchants who unloaded their goods here. The ghosts of Dickens, Wagner, and Proust wander around the venerable Danieli Hotel.

Probably nowhere is so much spectacular painting on view in such a tiny space as in the **Scuola di San Giorgio degli Schiavoni**. This captivating building was the guildhall of the *schiavoni* who commissioned Vittore Carpaccio to decorate their hall. His nine pictures, completed between 1502 and 1508, cover the walls of the ground-floor chapel. Note also the wonderfully ornate wooden ceiling.

Just four minutes by *vaporetto* from the Schiavoni, on its own little island, is the church of **San Giorgio Maggiore**; its campanile offers the most photogenic view of the city and its lagoon. The 16th-century church is a rare ecclesiastical building by Andrea Palladio, the man whose classic designs have so dominated aristocratic residential architecture throughout Europe and North America. His customary Corinthian-columned elegance prevails here, extended from the façade to an airy interior. Two superb Tintoretto paintings decorate the chancel, *Gathering of the Manna* and an otherworldly *Last Supper*, in which Jesus administers communion while servants bustle to clear up the dishes.

Around the Accademia

With that egocentrism that Venice's admirers find so charming, and justified, the rambling **Gallerie dell'Accademia** is devoted almost exclusively to Venetian painting, from the 14th century of its emerging glory to the 18th century of its gentle decadence. We propose here only some of the collection's most representative highlights:

Room 1: The 14th-century *Coronation of the Madonna* of **Paolo Veneziano**, first of the city's great masters, already glows with characteristic Venetian colour and texture.

Room 2: **Giovanni Bellini**, youngest and most gifted member of the painter family, brings gentle humanity to his *Enthroned Madonna with Job and St. Sebastian* (1485).

Room 4: **Andrea Mantegna** makes his *St. George* a very cool dragon-killer, a most appropriate patron saint for England.

Room 5: **Giorgione's** *Tempest* (1505) is one of the museum's most cherished, most mysterious treasures, a girl calmly nursing her child in a landscape prickling with the electricity of the approaching storm.

Room 7: **Lorenzo Lotto**, troubled loner among Venice's 16th-century artists, portrays a *Gentleman in his Study* with subtle, sombre psychology.

Room 10: Most important of Renaissance rooms. **Titian's** *Pietà*, a vibrant last work completed by pupil Palma il Giovane, was originally intended for his tomb in the Frari church (see page 128); **Veronese's** *Feast in the House of Levi* was meant to be the Last Supper, until the Holy Inquisition complained about its "buffoons, drunkards, dwarfs, Germans, and similar vulgarities"; **Tintoretto** gives full play to his dark sense of drama in the *Miracle of St. Mark*.

Room 17: **Canaletto's** hugely popular 18th-century *vedute* (views) of Venice were aristocratic precursors of modern postcards; in such works as *Island of San Giorgio Maggiore*, **Francesco Guardi** sought more poetry and melancholy, and died a pauper.

Room 20: **Gentile Bellini** breathes little life into the grand pageant of his *Procession on San Marco* (1496), but it remains a fascinating "photograph" of Renaissance Venice.

Room 21: **Vittore Carpaccio** depicts in nine canvases the bizarre *Story of St. Ursula*, a British princess, said to have led 11,000 virgins on a pilgrimage to Rome, all of whom were raped and slaughtered on their way back.

East along the Grand Canal, a breath of the 20th century awaits you at the **Peggy Guggenheim Collection** of modern art in the Palazzo Venier dei Leoni. Home of the American heiress until her death in 1979, this unfinished 18th-century palace provides a delightful setting for Picasso, Marcel Duchamp, Magritte, Kandinsky, and Klee, but above all for Jackson Pollock, Mark Rothko, and Robert Motherwell. In the overgrown garden are sculptures by Giacometti, Henry Moore, and the collector's husband, Max Ernst. She herself is buried here.

Almost as familiar a silhouette as the San Marco campanile, the lovely octagonal domed church of **Santa Maria della Salute**—just *Salute* to its friends—is the masterpiece of Baldassare Longhena, built to mark the city's deliverance from a plague in 1630. For a Baroque edifice, the interior is remarkably sober, even chaste. Tintoretto's *Marriage at Cana* is on the wall opposite the entrance, while three of Titian's

The silhouette of Santa Maria della Salute epitomizes Venice.

most vivid canvases decorate the **chancel**: *Cain and Abel, Abraham Sacrificing Isaac,* and *David and Goliath*, their drama heightened by the perspective *di sotto in su* (looking up from below).

The **Zattere**, along the Giudecca canal, are quays for merchant and industrial shipping serving the Adriatic coast and eastern Mediterranean, a pleasant, uncrowded promenade. Behind the Stazione Marittima, where the big cruiseliners dock, seek out the church of **San Sebastiano**, a veritable monument to the genius of Veronese, whose home was nearby and who is buried in its left aisle. See his magnificent ceiling paintings of the *Story of Esther*, especially the great oval *Triumph of Mordecai*, and the *Apotheosis of the Madonna in the Choir*.

Over on the Grand Canal, the **Ca' Rezzonico** is a grand Baroque palace completed in the 18th century and now a museum dedicated to those sunset years of the Venetian Republic. When the last of the Rezzonico family disappeared, Elizabeth Barrett and Robert Browning bought the palazzo, and the poet died in a first-floor apartment in 1889. The extravagant ballroom and soaring allegorical frescoes like Giambattista Tiepolo's *Merit between Virtue and Nobility* in the "Throne Room" (actually for Rezzonico weddings) and others, more wistful, by Guardi all catch the tone of a declining Venice enraptured by its own legend.

All over the city, you'll find *scuole* that are not schools but old confraternities similar, minus their religious affiliation, to the Freemasons, Rotarians, Elks, or Lions. North of Ca' Rezzonico, the **Scuola Grande di San Rocco** is Venice's richest confraternity, in a fine 16th-century chapter house next to its own church. Happily, Tintoretto was a member and created for the house some 50 paintings over a period of 23 years, a series comparable in grandeur to Giotto's frescoes in Padua or Masaccio's for the Brancacci chapel in Florence. In the Sala Grande, see the high drama of *Moses Striking Water from the Rock* and a fascinating *Temptation of Christ*, with Satan portrayed as a beautiful youth. Titian is something of an interloper here with a remarkable easel painting of the *Annunciation*. Tintoretto's masterpiece in chiaroscuro effects is the grandiose *Crucifixion* in the Sala dell'Albergo. You'll find a self-portrait just right of the room's entrance.

The nearby brick and white-marble Gothic Church of the **Frari** (full name Santa Maria Gloriosa dei Frari) is above all celebrated for the high altar adorned with Titian's jubilant *Assumption of the Madonna*. The master's only painting on such a massive scale is a triumph of primary reds, blues, and yellows that irresistibly draw you up to the altar. Drag yourself away to see his other work here, the *Madonna di Ca' Pesaro* (left aisle), in which St. Peter presents the Pesaro family to Mary. Venetian composer Monteverdi's tomb is in a chapel left of the altar, but Titian's own monumental tomb (in the right aisle) is a cold and ponderous 19th-century monstrosity. Donatello has sculpted a fine polychrome wood *John the Baptist* for his compatriots' **Florentine Chapel**, right of the altar.

Back on the Grand Canal again: Longhena's exuberant Baroque **Ca' Pesaro** is now the town's Modern Art Gallery, devoted principally to purchases from the Venice Biennale exhibitions. Italian artists—Futurists Giovanni Fattori and Telemaco Signorini and the Ferrara trio of Filippo de Pisis, Carlo Carrà, and Giorgio de Chirico—are better represented than other Europeans, of whom Matisse, Klee, and Ernst are the most notable.

Around the Rialto

The ancient commercial heart of the city, named after the ninth-century settlement on *Rivo Alto* (high bank), the **Rialto** spread over both sides of the Grand Canal. Here the Oriental spices and silks were unloaded. The merchants went to the banks and the sailors to the brothels. Today, the action is in the food markets and boutiques. On the west bank, the **Pescheria** (fish market) bustles early in the morning, but the **Erberia** (fruit and vegetables) is worth a return visit in late afternoon when the barges are unloading their fresh produce at the Fabbriche Vecchie warehouses. Nobody knows for sure, but nobody dares dispute the locals' claim for the little 11th-century church of **San Giacomo di Rialto**—San Giacometto to them—as the town's oldest (decipher the Byzantine interior under its Baroque incrustations).

Coming from San Marco, follow the **Mercerie** on the east bank, an ever-busy shopping street, past the 16th-century church of **San Salvatore** (Titian fans pop inside for his *Transfiguration* over the silver reredos on the high altar and his *Annunciation*, right aisle).

The 16th-century **Rialto Bridge** is no architectural gem—Antonio da Ponte wangled the contract over the likes of Michelangelo, Palladio, and Sansovino—but it's still one of the liveliest spots in town. Until 1854, it was the Grand Canal's only bridge. Along the double row of shops with three lanes of pedestrian traffic, you'll find jewellery, clothing and shoes, a few treasures, but a lot of junk, too.

Northeast of the bridge, past the Fondaco dei Tedeschi post office, seek out the little 15th-century church of **Santa Maria dei Miracoli**. Its refined façade of delicate inlaid coloured marble and intricately carved friezes has won it the name of "golden jewel box" *(scrigno d'oro)*, its designer Pietro Lombardo more sculptor than architect.

It's worth mapping out carefully your visit to the **Campo Santi Giovanni e Paolo**. Follow the Calle Larga Giacinto Gallina to the humpbacked Ponte del Cavallo bridge for the all-important first view of the magnificent **equestrian statue** of Bartolomeo Colleoni dominating the square. With his last and greatest piece of sculpture brilliantly evoking all the fierce resolution of a *condottiere* riding into battle, Andrea Verrocchio need not regret abandoning painting to his pupil Leonardo da Vinci. (Verrocchio's clay model was cast in bronze shortly after his death by Alessandro Leopardi.) Colleoni willed his huge fortune to Venice on the understanding his monument would be on Piazza San Marco, but once dead, he had to settle for this spot, in front of the *Scuola* of San Marco, a very Venetian solution. The 13th-century Gothic church of **Santi Giovanni e Paolo**, compressed by Venetians into San Zanipolo, was the doges' funeral church. Some 25 are buried here, many in masterpieces of monumental tombs.

Returning to the Grand Canal: you'll find in the glorious **Ca' d'Oro** the quintessential decorative tradition of Venetian architecture, more successful in its compact form here than in the beautiful but sprawling Doges' Palace. Completed in 1440, its Flamboyant Gothic design has a flair and grace that bewitch you into imagining the long gone gilt of its façade. Take another, more leisurely, boatride for the view from the canal. The treasures of the Ca' d'Oro's

The Rialto Bridge—no architectural treasure, but still one of the liveliest spots in Venice.

Galleria Franchetti of Renaissance art include Andrea Mantegna's *St. Sebastian* and fragments of the Titian and Giorgione frescoes that once adorned the Fondaco dei Tedeschi.

Off the Beaten Track

Among the corners of town far from the madding crowd, the old Jewish **Ghetto** (northeast of the railway station) is particularly peaceful and reveals a fascinating page of Venetian history. It was a local iron foundry, *ghetto* in Venetian dialect, which lent its name to this and scores of other enclaves for the forced isolation of Jewish communities throughout Europe. In 1516, some 900 Jews (rising to a peak of nearly 5,000 by the mid-17th century) were confined to what was then an island beyond the Cannareggio canal.

In the cramped quarters, they had to build the six- and eight-storey tenements you see today, twice as high as those permitted elsewhere. Some 20 Jewish families still live in the Ghetto.

On the island of the **Giudecca**, you'll find another of Palladio's great Venetian churches, the **Redentore**. The grace of its overall form is best viewed from across the canal, because, like St. Peter's in Rome, the dome disappears at closer quarters behind its elongated nave. The Giudecca takes it name either from the Jews *(Giudei)* who lived here in the 12th century or from the *Giudicati*, nobles banished here by ducal judgment. It's now a quiet refuge for fishermen, artists —and tourists seeking to escape the mob. The strange neo-Gothic fortress at the west end of the island is in fact an abandoned 19th-century grain mill, the **Mulino Stucky**.

Out in the lagoon, Venetians have been manufacturing glass on the island of **Murano** since 1292, when the hazardous furnaces were moved away from the city centre. Today, its factories and shops are an undeniable tourist trap, but the **museum** *(Museo Vetrario)* tracing the glass industry back to Roman times is worth a look. And many enjoy watching burly fellows blowing molten globules into cute little green giraffes. The island's quiet spot is the 12th-century Venetian-Byzantine church of **Santa Maria e San Donato**, with a good mosaic in the apse.

The island of **Burano** is a simple fishing village, true haven of tranquility, old ladies making lace on the doorsteps of their brightly coloured houses, a few artists on the quay, no hustlers.

Hemingway's favourite old hangout, the romantically overgrown island of **Torcello**, beyond Burano, is one of the lagoon's oldest inhabited spots, very prosperous until emptied by malaria. The mosquitoes have gone, but its superb **cathedral** remains. Founded in the seventh century and reconstructed in 1008, it's probably the finest of the Venetian-Byzantine churches. In the apse there's a moving mosaic of the Madonna above a frieze of the 12 Apostles. Notice, too, the fine Corinthian capitals on the slender Greek marble columns.

With its fine sandy beaches and smart hotels, the **Lido** is as restful as any fashionable seaside resort, but after a couple of days in

Venice, its cars come as something of a shock. Nostalgics take tea in the Grand Hôtel des Bains to recall the decadent 1900s evoked there by Thomas Mann's novella (and Luchino Visconti's movie) *Death in Venice*.

Veneto

The Venetian mainland reflects some of the *Serenissima's* artistic glories, but the cities that came under its domination in the 15th century retain their individuality.

An *autostrada* links Venice to Padua, Vicenza, and Verona for those in a hurry, but others should take the charming back roads.

The Brenta Canal

When Venetian aristocrats gave up the high seas for a more leisurely life on the land, they built Palladian Renaissance villas and extravagantly frescoed Baroque country houses on the banks of the Brenta Canal between Venice and Padua. A romantic way to visit some of the best is on the *burchiello*, a modern version of the rowing barge that took the gentry, Casanova, and Lord Byron to their trysts and parties in the country. (Get details from the city tourist office on the eight-hour trip which goes in either direction on alternate days, optional return by bus, from March to October.)

> Every worker has the legal right to 20 paid vacation days during the summer and one week during the winter.

Otherwise, follow the canal along the pretty country road (route S 11) to Padua. First stop, off a side road to Fusina, is Palladio's **La Malcontenta** (1571), to which a too-flighty Venetian countess was sent to pine, malcontentedly, in exquisite isolation on the canal. The villa, with its classical portico to catch the summer breezes, was the architect's "visiting card" for scores of commissions, copied worldwide, especially on the cotton plantations of America's Deep South,

An Italian Adriatic painting in Padua's Museo Civico.

where elegant porch-living became an article of faith.

At nearby Oriago, the Palladian style can be seen in **Villa Gradenigo** and, at Mira, in the 18th-century **Villa Widmann**. The influence is clear even in the most spectacular of the Brenta villas, at Stra, the opulent **Villa Pisani** or Villa Nazionale. Built for the Pisani doges in 1756, with 200 rooms, Tiepolo frescoes in the ballroom, and vast park with pond, labyrinth, and stables, it was bought by Napoleon in 1807 and subsequently hosted Tsars, Habsburg emperors, and, for their first meeting in 1934, Hitler and Mussolini.

Padua *(Padova)*

This proud university town—Galileo taught physics here from 1592 to 1610—was a major centre of the Risorgimento reunification movement. Something of the old spirit remains at the handsome Neoclassical **Caffè Pedrocchi**, the activists' meeting place on a little square off bustling Piazza Cavour.

North along the Corso Garibaldi is the 14th-century **Scrovegni Chapel**, also known, because of its site among ruins of a Roman amphitheatre, as the Arena Chapel. As a penance for his father's usury, the patrician Enrico Scrovegni built the simple little hall in 1303 specifically for the great **Giotto frescoes**, beautifully preserved and indisputedly his. In 38 pictures arranged in three rows under a starry heavenly-blue vault, Giotto tells the story of Mary and Jesus. Among the most moving, look for the *Kiss of Judas*, the *Crucifixion,* and the *Lamentation*. A monumental *Last Judgment* covers the entrance wall.

The entrance to Piazza del Santo south of the city centre is guarded by Donatello's grand **statue of Gattamelata**, the 15th-century condottiere Erasmo da Narni, perfect ideal of a Renaissance hero, whose "honeyed cat" nickname still mystifies historians. Behind him looms the 13th- and 14th-century **Basilica of Sant'Antonio**, known as Il Santo, named after the Portuguese-born Franciscan monk who died in Padua. The Romanesque façade makes a striking contrast with the eight Byzantine cupolas and two minaret-like towers around a central Gothic cone-shaped dome. In the lofty Gothic interior, Donatello's sculptures at the **high altar** include a stoical *Crucifixion* and large bronze reliefs narrating St. Antony's miracles, notably the *Mule Adoring the Eucharist* and the healing of the *Irascible Son*, who cut off his foot in remorse at kicking his mother. The Scuola di Sant'Antonio, right of the church, has some Titian frescoes of the saint.

Vicenza

This is Andrea Palladio's home town, and he has made of it a place in many ways more truly serene than the often more excitable Venice. At the centre, **Piazza dei Signori** is graced by his **basilica** (1549), not a church, but the old Roman concept of a gathering place for the lawcourts of the Gothic Palazzo della Ragione that it encases with a colonnade and loggia. If you wonder what to think of it, Palladio's modest opinion was that it "ranked among the most noble and most beautiful edifices since ancient times, not only for its grandeur and ornaments, but also its materials" (hard white limestone). Inside is a museum of his designs and models.

The main commercial street is, inevitably, **Corso Palladio**, lined with the master's elegant mansions at numbers 42 and 165, and others by disciples. The 15th-century **Palazzo da Schio** (number 147) is also known as Ca'd'Oro, after the famous Venetian Gothic palace. You'll find Palladio's best town palace where the Corso widens out into the Piazza Matteotti to give him more freedom for the wonderfully airy **Palazzo Chiericati**. Its Museo Civico houses works by Tintoretto, Veronese, Hans Memling, and Van Dyck.

Set in a little garden, the audacious **Teatro Olimpico** is Palladio's last work (completed by Vincenzo Scamozzi in 1584). Facing an amphitheatre auditorium is a fixed décor of classical Roman statuary and columns with what look like three long streets leading away from the stage. It's quite a shock when you go through the archways and find the streets go back only a few feet, a simple illusion of perspective.

Take route N 247 to Monte Berico and Palladio's most celebrated building, the hilltop **Villa Rotonda**. Designed as a belvedere for Cardinal Capra in 1551, it's an exquisite piece of applied geometry, a domed rotunda set in a square surrounded on all four sides by simple Ionic-columned porticoes, offering different views of town and countryside with the changing light of day. Film-director Joseph Losey used the villa for his *Don Giovanni*, in which valet Leporello unrolls down the long staircase the list of his master's mistresses—1,003, *mill'e tre*.

Verona

A favourite of Roman emperors and the "barbarian" rulers that followed, the city likes to be known as *la Degna*, the Dignified, but it also has a very lively atmosphere, stimulated by its Adige river flowing swiftly down from the Dolomites. And perhaps by a memory of its fierce medieval history. The family feuds that inspired Shakespeare's *Romeo and Juliet* ended only with the 14th-century ascendancy of the tough Scalageri dynasty, in turn conquered by Venice in 1405.

The hub of city life is the vast Piazza Brà, with the town hall on its south side and the great **Roman Arena** dating back to A.D. 100. Only four of its outer arches survived an 1183 earthquake undamaged, but the inner arcade of 74 arches is intact. It seats 22,000. People in the top rows during the summer opera festival get a terrific view of the surrounding city.

Along the north side of the piazza, the Liston, a people-watcher's delight lined with smart cafés and restaurants, is the street for the Veronese bourgeoisie's evening stroll *(passeggiata)*. It leads to the boutiques, galleries, and antiques shops of the equally fashionable Via Mazzini.

Turn right at the end down Via Cappello for the 13th-century tavern that the local tourist industry understandably insists was **Juliet's House** *(Casa di Giulietta Cappelletti)*, complete with balcony.

The **Piazza delle Erbe** along the ancient elongated Roman forum makes the prettiest of

Padua's market is held outside the Palazzo della Ragione.

market-places. Its medieval houses and old umbrella-covered stalls surround a 14th-century fountain and a line of columns, one of which bears the lion of St. Mark, in former allegiance to Venice.

West of Piazza Brà, the massive brick 14th-century **Castelvecchio** fortress on the Adige river now houses an art museum. Its collections are principally of the Venetian school, notably Mantegna's *Holy Family*, a Giovanni Bellini *Madonna*, and Lorenzo Lotto's

Portrait of a Man, attributed by some to Titian.

The austerely handsome 12th-century church of **San Zeno Maggiore**, with superb bronze doors and an imposing free-standing brick campanile, is a rare jewel of Italian Romanesque architecture. (The 14th-century battlemented tower to the left is the remnant of an old abbey.) The dignity to which the town aspires is there in the simple interior, illuminated by the magnificent Mantegna **triptych** on the high altar.

Dolomites

The landscape of Italy's eastern Alps is a mixture of rich green Alpine meadows with jagged white limestone and rose-coloured granite peaks. Summer hiking in the largely German-speaking region of Alto Adige

The Dolomites offer a striking contrast of granite, limestone, and vegetation.

(Austrian South Tyrol till 1918) is a delight. Well-marked paths lead to farmhouses and rustic mountain-restaurants where you can try the local bacon *(Speck)* or spinach dumplings *(Spinatknödl)* as a change from spaghetti —saves you carrying a picnic.

On winding mountain roads it's advisable to sound your horn.

Bolzano *(Bozen)*

South Tyrol's historic capital makes a good base for hikes. It has a 14th-century Gothic **church** with a characteristically Austrian polychrome tiled roof. Inside is a 16th-century sculpted sandstone pulpit and marble altar. Get your hiking equipment on the old arcaded shopping street, Via dei Portici *(Laubengasse).* Then head northeast of town to the **Renon** *(Ritten)* plateau for views of the Dolomite peaks, reached by cableway and rack railway.

Cortina d'Ampezzo

The queen of Italian winter-sports resorts has elegant hotels, smart boutiques, and a bouncing nightlife. In a sunny sheltered basin high in the Boite valley of the eastern Dolomites, it provides excellent skiing facilities as well as skating and bobsledding. It, too, is a favourite with summer hikers. Take the cable car to **Tofana di Mezzo** for an awesome view clear down to the Venetian lagoon. Equally spectacular are the panoramas from the **Belvedere di Pocol** and **Tondi di Faloria.**

Emilia-Romagna

The two regions were united at the time of the Risorgimento, with Emilia following the Apennines from Bologna to Piacenza while Romagna covers the eastern area of Ravenna and the Adriatic resorts around Rimini down to Cattolica.

Rimini

The Adriatic coast, of which Rimini is the chief resort, has wide sandy beaches, at some points stretching 300 metres (1,000 feet) from the water's edge back to the dunes. Its lively hotels, beach clubs, and myriad discos make Rimini a favourite playground for the sun-soakers, while the fishing port remains peaceful.

Inland, on the other side of the railway, is the old city that was Ariminium to the Romans. The 27 B.C. **triumphal arch** *(Arco d'Augusto),* anachronistically ornamented with medieval battlements, stands at the junction of the imperial highways from Rome: Via Flaminia and Via Emilia (which gave the region its name). The

Ponte di Tiberio bridge built over the Marecchia river in A.D. 21 is still in use. The unfinished 15th-century **Tempio Malatestiano** is an important Renaissance design of Leon Battista Alberti, incorporating elements of the Arco d'Augusto in the façade. More pagan temple than church, it served as a mausoleum for the cultivated but cruel tyrant, Sigismondo Malatesta, and his mistress (later wife), Isotta degli Atti.

To the south of Rimini are the resorts of **Riccione**, very popular, and the quieter **Cattolica**, while **Cesenatico**, to the north, has a colourful fishing port.

☞ Ravenna

For those who find it difficult to appreciate mosaics as we usually see them, in fading indecipherable fragments, the beautifully preserved mosaic decoration of Ravenna's churches, up to 1,500 years old, come as an exciting revelation. They stand at the summit of the art as originally practised by the Greeks and Romans.

Now some 10 km (6 miles) from the sea, the ancient capital of the Western Roman Empire was once a flourishing port on the Adriatic. Emperor Honorius made it his capital in 402, followed by his sister Galla Placidia. Ruled in the early sixth century by Theodoric, king of the Ostrogoths, it was recaptured for Emperor Justinian, and Byzantine culture left its mark for another two centuries.

You'll see something of the town's Venetian-dominated era on the graceful **Piazza del Popolo**, bordered by the 17th-century Palazzo Comunale—Venetian insignia on the piazza's two columns have been replaced by local saints Apollinaris and Vitalis. Next to the church of San Francesco, in a building of 1780, is the **tomb of Dante**, who died here, in exile, in 1321, with a fellow poet's epitaph: "Here I lie buried, Dante, exile from my birthplace, son of Florence, that loveless mother."

A mosaic at Sant'Apollinare depicts the theme of sacrifice.

The oldest of the Byzantine monuments, in the northern corner of the city centre, is the fifth-century **Mausoleum of Galla Placidia**. Three sarcophagi stand in the cross-shaped chapel, but no one knows if her remains are in one of them. The deep blue, gold, and crimson mosaics on the vaults and arches depict *St. Laurence*, the *Apostles,* and the *Good Shepherd Feeding His Sheep* (over the entrance).

In the same grounds is the magnificent three-storey brick church of **San Vitale**, consecrated in 547. Its narthex is set at an angle to the main entrance (through a Renaissance porch). The octagonal construction provides the interior with seven *exedrae,* or recesses, the eighth being the choir and apse. Try to come on a bright morning when the sun provides natural illumination for the mosaics. The Old Testament scenes, such as *Abraham Sacrificing Isaac*, are more lively than the rigidly formal Emperor Justinian and Empress Theodora, with their court retinue, and Christ between two angels, St. Vitalis, and, far right, Bishop Ecclesius holding a model of the church. The cloisters house a National Museum of Roman, early Christian, and Byzantine Sculpture.

DANTI·ALIGHERIO
TVSCI
HONORARIVM·TVMVLVM
A·MAIORIBVS·TER·FRVSTRA·DECRETVM
ANNO·M·DCCC·XXIX·
FELICITER·EXCITARVNT·

The Santa Croce church in Florence contains this funeral monument to Dante.

You can see the art of mosaics still being practised in workshops along the nearby Via Giuliano Argentario.

Next to the cathedral, the fifth-century **Battistero Neoniano** (Baptistery of Bishop Neon) has a fine mosaic procession of the Apostles. It was originally a Roman bath.

East of the city centre, the early sixth-century church of **Sant'Apollinare Nuovo** was built by the Christianized Ostrogoth king Theodoric. In the nave, classic Byzantine mosaics show, on the left, Ravenna's fortified port of Classe, from which a procession of 22 virgins follows the three Magi with gifts for Jesus on his mother's lap; on the right, from Theodoric's palace, 26 martyrs carry jewelled crowns.

Five km (3 miles) south of the town, protected only by a couple of cypresses from an incongruous wilderness of highways and bleak urban development, stands the lovely church of **Sant'Apollinare in Classe** (549), and, next to it, a splendid cylindrical 11th-century Romanesque campanile. In the apse of the Greek-columned interior is a delightful mosaic of St. Apollinaris, Ravenna's first martyr and bishop, surrounded by sheep, with Moses and Elijah in the clouds above him.

Bologna

The capital of Emilia-Romagna is a thriving town with a certain patrician atmosphere to its elegantly arcaded historic centre. It is the home of Europe's oldest university, established in the 11th century on the foundation of a renowned law school dating back even earlier, to the end of the Roman empire. Bologna also boasts of the diploma its Philharmonic Academy gave Mozart in 1770—though he might have done quite well without it. The town's revered place in Italian gastronomy compares to that of Lyon in France.

On the west flank of the handsome Piazza Maggiore, the massive medieval **Palazzo Comunale** with its Renaissance porch is a striking expression of Bologna's civic power. The 14th-century basilica of **San Petronio** ranks among the most imposing of Italy's Gothic churches. It has a fine **central portal** with reliefs of Old Testament scenes on its pilasters sculpted with great dignity and power by Jacopo della Quercia. Adam's pose in the *Creation* scene (top left) inspired the Michelangelo figure reaching out to God on the Sistine Chapel ceiling. The soaring vaults of the sober interior have the monumentality of French or German Gothic.

In the adjoining square, the 16th-century **Neptune Fountain** is one of the town's most popular symbols, for which Giambologna sculpted the bronze sea god surrounded by nymphs and cherubs.

A medieval atmosphere clings to the old houses in the tiny streets behind the Metropolitana cathedral to the north. At the end of the busy Via Rizzoli, the two **leaning towers** are all that remain of a whole forest of medieval status-symbols—like those of San Gimignano in Tuscany (see pages 102–103). The 12th-century Torre degli Asinelli, 98 metres (320 feet), is the taller, with 498 steps to its rooftop view.

You'll find the city's characteristic arcaded **palazzi** along the Via Zamboni leading past the university to the **Pinacoteca Nazionale.** The Pinacoteca's fine collection is devoted in large part to the Bologna school, most notably the Baroque paintings of the Carracci family, of whom Annibale was the most gifted—see his *Annunciation* and *Madonna in Glory*. Look out for Raphael's important *Ecstasy of St. Cecilia* and Parmigianino's *Madonna di Santa Margherita*.

South of the city centre, the founder of the Dominican order is buried in the church of **San Domenico**, 13th-century but with many 18th-century Baroque modifications. The monk's marble **tomb** (*Arca di San Domenico*, 6th chapel, right aisle) was designed by Nicola Pisano with additional works by Nicolò dell'Arca and the 20-year-old Michelangelo. He did the saints Petronius and Proculus, and the angel on the right—the first and last time he ever put wings on an angel.

Ferrara

A mere half-hour's drive from Bologna on the *autostrada* takes you to this stronghold of the high-living d'Este dukes, archetypal scheming, murderous, lovable Renaissance villains. In their formidable **Castello Estense**, a 14th-century moated fortress,

For some, cheese and ham rival art and architecture as Italy's main attractions.

guides tell delightfully dubious stories of what went on in the dungeons.

You get a sense of the dukes' grandeur among the Renaissance palazzi of the **Corso Ercole I d'Este**, part of a 15th-century urban expansion, *Addizione Erculea*, that was one of the most ambitious pieces of town planning of its age. The d'Estes' **Palazzo dei Diamanti** (12,000 pieces of diamond-shaped marble on its walls) houses the Pinacoteca Nazionale, with works of the Ferrara masters Cosmè Tura, Ercole de' Roberti, Garofalo, and Dosso Dossi.

The triple-gabled 13th-century **Cathedral** still has its loggia of shops attached to the south wall. The cathedral museum exhibits two major works by Cosmè Tura, *St. George* and the *Annunciation,* and sculptures by Jacopo della Quercia, *Madonna of the Pomegranate* and *St. Maurelius.*

Parma

The home of two famous painters, Correggio and Parmigianino, has much more to offer than just that great cheese and ham. The **Piazza del Duomo** forms a wonderfully harmonious space for the graceful octagonal baptistery and the austere nobility of the 12th-century Romanesque **cathedral** and its 13th-century campanile. Inside, on the ceiling of the central octagonal dome, are the grandiose Correggio **frescoes** of the *Assumption of the Virgin* (1530). In this, his masterpiece, Correggio has achieved, in the truest sense, exalting emotion without the sentimentality of Mannerist imitators.

The lovely 13th-century pink Verona marble **baptistery** has superbly sculpted doors by Benedetto Antelami, who also carved most of the 12 statues of the months in the interior.

Behind the cathedral, the 16th-century Renaissance church of **San Giovanni Evangelista** also has in its dome a fine Correggio fresco of the *Vision of St. John on Patmos.* Look out, too, for the Parmigianino frescoes in the first, second, and fourth chapels on the left aisle. In the 16th-century Renaissance church of **Madonna della Steccata** (Via Garibaldi), Parmigianino painted the frescoes of the *Foolish and Wise Virgins* on the arch above the high altar.

In the charming **Camera di San Paolo** (Via Melloni), you'll find the Benedictine convent's private dining room for the highly unconventional abbess, Giovanna da Piacenza. She commissioned Correggio to decorate it in 1519 (his first work) with mischievous putti

angels and a very pagan view of Chastity as symbolized by the goddess Diana.

The **Galleria Nazionale** (on Piazzale Marconi) exhibits more excellent works of Correggio and Parmigianino, and a sketch of a
young girl, *Testa di Fanciulla*, by Leonardo da Vinci.

THE NORTHWEST

Lombardy, Piedmont, and the Ligurian coast together make up the
country's most prosperous region. Industry and commerce have
made the fortune of its three great cities—Milan, Turin, and Genoa.
If the latter has drawn on the riches of the seas, Milan and Turin, in
close contact with France and Germany across the Alps, have had
the added underpinning of a flourishing agriculture in their Po valley
hinterland. The early lords of this constant economic expansion also
called on the greatest artists both from Italy and beyond, from Jan
Van Eyck to Leonardo da Vinci.

The region has won world recognition in the vanguard of the arts,
of modern design in clothes and furniture, and of the automobile and
communications industries.

For relaxation, the Italian Riviera east and west of Genoa alter-
nates a rugged coastline with fine sandy beaches. Hugging the
slopes of Mont Blanc (Monte Bianco), Courmayeur is Italy's oldest
ski resort. North and east of Milan are the romantic lakes Como,
Maggiore, and Garda.

Milan

Quite happy to leave the politics of national government to Rome,
Milan is clearly the country's economic
and cultural capital. Despite its prestigious museums and magnificent cathedral, tourists do not think of Milan as an
obvious holiday destination (though some
do make the pilgrimage just for Leonardo

> **Underground fare
> in Milan is the
> same irrespective
> of the distance
> you travel.**

Candle lighting for a moment of prayer in Milan Cathedral.

da Vinci's *Last Supper*). But anyone interested in contemporary Italian life will want to hang out a few days in its cafés and restaurants, elegant shopping avenues, and side-street art galleries. If the main railway station is a monstrous reminder of Mussolini, the Pirelli skyscraper opposite is a more graceful symbol of the new era. With its vivacious residents, fashion-conscious and self-assured to the point of pushy, this is *the* modern city of Italy.

Around the Duomo

Nowhere does a cathedral more dominate a major city centre. Almost non-stop throughout the day, but especially at that magic moment of the *passeggiata*, the **Piazza del Duomo** is one of the liveliest squares in all Europe. People gather around the cafés, kiosks, and shopping arcades, the young discussing music and clothes, their fathers arguing politics and business, and everybody talking football.

And all in the shadow of the **Duomo**, most grandiose of Italy's Flamboyant Gothic cathedrals. Teams of Italian, French, Flemish, and German architects and sculptors contributed to this astonishing

*It took a good five hundred years to complete
the Duomo's Gothic façade.*

cathedral, begun in 1386. For the best view of that awesomely rich façade, finished in 1813, and bristling silhouette of marble pinnacles and statues, stand in the courtyard of the Palazzo Reale south of the cathedral. (It houses the Cathedral Museum, which displays fine examples of Gothic sculpture from the façade.) The cathedral's interior is a vast and noble space, showing its North European influence in the soaring columns and a decoration of **stained-glass windows**, from the 15th century to the present day.

Give yourself plenty of time for a spectacular walk out on the **roof**. The elevator entrance (clearly signposted outside the cathedral) is in the right transept. Wander high above the city turmoil under the flying buttresses and around the statues (2,245 in all) and pinnacles (135), up to the roof-ridge for an unbeatable view of the city. To go down, take the staircase (158 steps) for some fascinating close-ups of the cathedral's construction.

West of the Piazza del Duomo, tucked away between the busy Via Orefici and Via Mercanti, is the last vestige of the medieval city, **Piazza Mercanti**. The 13th-century seat of communal government on its south side, Palazzo della Ragione, has a fine Romanesque equestrian relief of a *podestà* (chief magistrate). It stands opposite the elegant porticoed Palazzo dei Giureconsulti (1564).

Leading north from the Piazza del Duomo, the huge cross-shaped shopping arcade of the **Galleria Vittorio Emanuele** is a splendid monument in steel and glass to the expansive commercial spirit of the 19th century. Today, cafés, restaurants, bookshops, and boutiques bathe in its unabashed neo-Renaissance décor.

In the winter, the Galleria provides a sheltered, albeit draughty, passage from the Duomo to another holy of holies, the 18th-century **La Scala** theatre, high temple of opera. Even if you can't be there for an opera (opening with a gala to end all galas every sacrosanct December 7), attend a concert there or at least visit the little museum (left of the theatre), if only for a chance to see the sumptuous Neoclassical auditorium with its six tiers of balconies and galleries.

Milan's most prestigious thoroughfare is **Via Monte Napoleone**, an august parade of Neo classical palazzi and luxury shops. Narrow side streets such as Via Borgospesso, Via Sant'Andrea, and Via Bagutta take you into a more tranquil 18th-century world, now graced by art galleries, antiques shops, and the town's smarter *trattorie*.

Around Castello Sforzesco

The massive brick fortress, the **Castello Sforzesco**, northwest of the city centre, was rebuilt in its present form in the 15th century by Duke Francesco Sforza. The bulk of the solid square structure stands around a vast courtyard, Piazza d'Armiles. Beyond, in the handsome old residential quarters of the Corte Ducale, is the entrance to the Castello Sforzesco **art museums**, devoted to sculpture, painting

(Pinacoteca), ceramics, furniture, and archaeology. In collections that include important works by Giovanni Bellini, Mantegna, Titian, Correggio, and Tintoretto, pride of place—and a room to itself—goes to Michelangelo's last work, the unfinished Rondanini *Pietà* (1564). Working on it until six days before his death, the sculptor chiselled a pathetic Mary struggling to hold up the dead Jesus, strange throwback to medieval sculpture for his last tussle with recalcitrant stone.

Behind the castle is a delightful English-style **park** for a rest away from the city and even a dream of tropical lands among the exotic fish of the municipal aquarium in one corner.

Even without Leonardo da Vinci's masterpiece in the adjoining refectory, the church of **Santa Maria delle Grazie** (Via Caradosso, southwest of the Castello) would be worth a visit as a jewel of Renaissance architecture. Adding to an earlier Gothic design, Donato Bramante—Pope Julius II's chief architect in Rome—fashioned in 1492 a magnificent red brick and white stone chancel *(tribuna)*. The graceful lines of the rectangular choir and 16-sided cupola are best viewed from the little cloister that he built on the north side. Inside the church, stand in the choir to appreciate the majesty of the dome.

Leonardo da Vinci's **Last Supper** *(Cenacolo)* has been lovingly resuscitated in the little Dominican refectory to the left of the church. Despite centuries of deterioration and clumsy restoration since it was completed in 1497, there is enormous psychological impact in Leonardo's depiction of the trauma for each of the disciples when Jesus declares: "One of you will betray me." As a result of the painstaking centimetre-by-centimetre recovery of the fragmentary but still powerful traces of the "real Leonardo," we can now see, for example, that Philip (third to the right) has an expression of acute grief rather than the simpering pathos left by "restorers" who presumed to improve on the original.

For another aspect of Leonardo da Vinci's talents, visit the **Science Museum** *(Museo della Scienza e della Tecnica)* in the nearby

Via San Vittore. Among the rooms devoted to the history of science and technology, one gallery is reserved for Leonardo's inventions, displayed as models constructed from his notebooks. You'll see his aircraft, a machine for making screws, hydraulic timber-cutter, revolving bridge, various machine-tools, and a system of map-making by aerial views long before any aircraft, even his, was operational.

At the eastern end of Via San Vittore, beyond a noble atrium courtyard, the church of Sant' Ambrogio is the city's most revered sanctuary, built from the ninth to the 12th centuries. It stands on a foundation that dates back to the time of St. Ambrose (340–397), first bishop of Milan and one of the Church's four founding fathers (with Peter, Paul, and Jerome). Its sober five-bayed façade is char-

---

Autopsy of a Masterpiece

The great culprit in the disintegration of the *Last Supper* was not so much Milan's infamous humidity or modern pollution as Leonardo himself—or at least the understandable demands of his genius.

For this summit of his life's work, Leonardo did not want to suffer the restrictions of fresco—painting onto damp plaster. A fresco was painted section by section without modifying once dry, thus denying him the chance to add that overall shadowy *sfumato* effect that gave his paintings their psychological depth and subtlety. Nor would the sustained effort demanded by a fresco's damp plaster permit him, as was his habit, to leave the painting when inspiration deserted him, to go and work on something else.

So Leonardo preferred a tempera with oil and varnish on an ideally dry surface, in fact a disastrous choice for the damp climate. Deterioration was already noted in 1517, when Leonardo was still alive. By the time fellow artist Giorgio Vasari saw it a generation later, there was "nothing visible but a muddle of blots." It's a miracle that 400 more years of dust and smog have left anything at all.

acteristic Lombard Romanesque, flanked by a ninth-century campanile and taller 12th-century tower topped by a modern loggia. In the interior, left of the centre nave, notice an 11th-century pulpit standing on a Christian sarcophagus of the Roman era. Under the canopy carved with Romanesque-Byzantine reliefs is the high altar, richly encased in elaborate, bejewelled, and enamelled plates of gold and silver.

The Brera and Other Museums

The handsome 17th-century palace of the Jesuits is now the **Pinacoteca di Brera**, one of the country's foremost art museums. In its fine arcaded courtyard, notice a bronze statue of Napoleon, remarkable rare example of the emperor with no clothes. (It was he who turned the Brera into a national gallery with confiscations from the Church and recalcitrant nobles.)

Among the highlights: two paintings by Giovanni Bellini of the *Madonna and Child* and a highly personal *Pietà*; Veronese's *Jesus in the Garden*; Tintoretto's dramatic *Discovery of St. Mark's Body*; and an impressive *Christ at the Column* by Donato Bramante.

Mantegna has a touching *Madonna*, but his masterpiece here is the *Dead Christ*, achieving a gripping emotional effect with its foreshortened perspective. Piero della Francesca's celebrated *Montefeltro altarpiece* (1474) is his last work.

The gentle beauty of Correggio's *Nativity and Adoration of the Magi* and Raphael's stately *Betrothal of the Virgin* contrast with the earthier inspiration of Caravaggio's *Supper at Emmaus*.

The non-Italian artists include El Greco, Rubens, Van Dyck, and Rembrandt. In the modern collection, look out for Modigliani, Boccioni, de Chirico, Carrà, and de Pisis.

The **Biblioteca Ambrosiana** (Piazza Pio XI) was the 17th-century palace and library of Cardinal Federigo Borromeo. Its principal treasure is Leonardo da Vinci's luminous *Portrait of a Musician* (1485), unfinished but at the same time the best preserved of the master's few surviving works. You can see his pervasive influence on Milanese artists in the decorative paintings of Bernardino Luini and a fine *Portrait of a Young Woman* by Ambrogio de Predis. Nothing sweet about Caravaggio's *Bowl of Fruit*—the worm is in the apple and the leaves are withering. Travellers on their way to or from Rome will be especially interested in Raphael's cartoons (preparatory drawings) for his *School of Athens* fresco in the Vatican.

The **Poldi-Pezzoli Museum** (Via Manzoni 12) is a small, formerly private collection. Its prize pieces include Piero della Francesca's *San Nicola da Tolentino*, Mantegna's *Madonna and Child*, a Botticelli *Madonna*, and Antonio Pollaiuolo's lovely *Portrait of a Young Woman*.

Lombardy

This central part of the Po valley is only a fraction of the Italian lands conquered by the Lombards when they crossed the Alps from eastern Europe in the early Middle Ages. But it has proved the most fruitful, all too tempting to the acquisitive appetites of France, Spain, and rival Italian duchies and city-states such as Venice, which pushed its Republic as far west as Bergamo. Natural fertility was enhanced by Europe's most advanced systems of irrigation, still operating in the medieval canals that you'll see on your way south to Pavia. Lombardy's rice, wheat, and maize are the main basis of the nation's *risotto, pasta,* and *polenta.*

On a more sentimental note, the three major lakes at the foot of the Lombardy Alps—Garda, Como, and Maggiore—are perfect settings for mending broken hearts, breaking mended hearts, and all romantic conditions in between.

Pavia

The Lombards' first capital, before Milan, is now a sleepy redbrick university town. Its principal attraction, the spectacular Charterhouse or **Certosa di Pavia,** is in fact some 10 km (6 miles) north of the city,

Santa Maria Maggiore in Bergamo.

a 30-minute drive from Milan. Built by Gian Galeazzo Visconti, Duke of Milan, for his family mausoleum, the monastery's 15th-century church is a high point in the transition from Flamboyant Gothic to Renaissance. Even without the originally designed crowning gable, the sculpted marble façade makes an impact, with its statues of prophets, saints, and apostles above the medallion reliefs of Roman emperors.

The Gothic interior is lightened by the brightly coloured paving and groin-vaulting. Among the chapels which were given Baroque finishings in the late 16th century, notice an exquisite Perugino altarpiece of *God the Father*. Right of the triumphant Baroque high altar is a beautifully carved 15th-century lavabo (ritual basin) and a charming *Madonna and Child* by Bernardino Luini. In the right transept is the Visconti tomb, and a door leading to the lovely small cloister of russet terracotta, with a fine view of the church's galleried octagonal tower. Since 1947, Cistercians have taken over from the Carthusian monks but continue the manufacture of herbal liqueurs.

Bergamo

Rising out of the plain of the Po valley on its own steep little hill, 47 km (29 miles) east of Milan, the delightful town of Bergamo makes a welcome break in the monotony of the *autostrada*. The city has a proud soldiering history, giving the Venetian Republic a famous *condottiere,* Bartolomeo Colleoni (see page 130), and the largest contingent in Garibaldi's 1,000 Red Shirts. The Città Bassa (lower city) at the foot of the hill is the modern town of shops, hotels, and restaurants—serving a savoury *risotto* they insist is superior to Milan's. **Piazza Matteotti** is the hub of the town's lively café scene, along the Sentierone arcades. Opposite is the Teatro Donizetti and a monument showing the Bergamo-born opera composer accompanied by the naked lady he is said always to have needed for inspiration.

Venetian ramparts still protect the historic **Città Alta** (Upper City) on the hill. The gracious **Piazza Vecchia** is surrounded by Renaissance public edifices, notably the **Palazzo della Ragione** with a medieval Torre del Comune—take the lift to the rooftop view over the Po valley to the Alps. The town's most venerable edifice is the 12th-century Romanesque church of **Santa Maria Maggiore**. Notice the finely carved monumental north porch and slender campanile. The Baroque interior has impressive 16th-century tapestries and inlaid wooden choir stalls and beautiful intarsia work at the altar rail. Adjacent to the church is the Renaissance **Colleoni Chapel**, an ostentatious mausoleum in red, white, and green marble.

A short walk from the Città Alta's Porta Sant'Agostino, the **Galleria dell'Accademia Carrara** has an important Mantegna *Madonna and Child* and interesting works by Bellini, Lotto, Raphael, and Titian.

Lake Garda

On the lake's west shore, the people of Salò, where Gaspare Bertolotti is regarded as originator of the violin, suggest his design was inspired by the contours of the lake. But Italy's largest lake is shaped more like a banjo, 52 km (32 miles) from the ruggedly romantic cliffs of the neck down to its broad "sound box," 18 km (11 miles) across, surrounded by rolling green hills. Graced with vineyards (notably Bardolino), lemon trees, olives, and cedars, the lake enjoys mild winters and mellow summers.

At the south end, boat cruises start out from Peschiera, Sirmione, and Desenzano, particularly recommended for dramatic

Harvest time is a joy in Lake Garda's vineyards.

views of the east shore's mountains and the beautiful **Punta di San Vigilio**, with its little church and 16th-century Villa Guarienti. Begin your road tour out on the narrow **Sirmione** promontory. This fishing village and renowned spa resort affords a splendid view of the lake from the tower of the 13th-century castle, **Rocca Scaligera**. The drive itself, along the winding **Gardesana Occidentale** cut through the cliffs of the west shore, is spectacular.

The resort town of **Gardone Riviera** is much appreciated for its parks and botanical gardens and as a base for hikes back into the hills. Above the resort, in Gardone di Sopra, is a 20th-century "folly," **Il Vittoriale**, the bizarre and disturbing residence of Gabriele D'Annunzio, poet, adventurer, fascist. Melancholy gardens of dark laurel and cypresses lead up to a mausoleum of the writer's sarcophagus flanked by those of his disciples.

It overlooks the prow of a World War I warship, the *Puglia*, hauled up the hillside as the crowning piece of his relics, for which the villa is a museum: two cars in which he drove to his war exploits and the aircraft from which he dropped propaganda leaflets over Vienna (see page 37).

 Lake Como

Embraced by green wooded escarpments, the lake favoured by some of England's most romantic 19th-century poets, Wordsworth, Shelley, and Byron, retains a certain wistful atmosphere for the leisure hours of the Milanese. As at Garda, a mild climate nurtures luxuriant vegetation in the villa gardens and parks.

The lake divides into two arms on either side of the tranquil resort town of **Bellagio,** which juts out on a hilly promontory. Up on the heights above the town, the elegant 18th-century **Villa Serbelloni** stands in the middle of a beautiful park of rose trees, camelias, magnolias, and pomegranates. (Not to be confused with the Villa Serbelloni luxury hotel down near the lakefront.) You can take a bracing swim at the lido at the southern end of town. Lake cruises—and car-ferries—leave from the Lungolario Marconi.

The lake's southwest arm is the most attractive for your excursions. From Lezzeno, take a boat cruise to see the colourful grottoes, and look out for the waterfall at Nesso. **Como** itself is a factory town, but has a handsome Gothic-Renaissance cathedral crowned by a superb Baroque dome added in 1744 by Turin's great architect, Filippo Juvarra. It stands next to the arcaded Broletto, 13th-century seat of municipal government.

The western shores of the lake are lined with gracious villas nestling in perfumed gardens. At **Cernobbio**, the 16th-century Villa d'Este is now a hotel where you can at least take tea as an excuse to stroll among the cypresses and magnolias. Between the genteel resort towns of Tremezzo and Cadenabbia, you'll find one of the lake's most beautiful residences (open to the public), the 18th-century **Villa Carlotta**. There's a marvellous view of the lake from its terraced gardens, famous for the display of camelias, rhododendrons, and azaleas in late April and May.

Lake Maggiore

The northern, more blustery end of the lake lies in Switzerland, but the rest shares the other lakes' mellow climate. The resort towns offer excellent opportunities for relaxation and sports on longer stays, but for short visits you'll get a better idea of the lake on a boat cruise (3–4 hours, with a meal on board, from Stresa, Baveno, or Pallanza) than by road.

Close to the western shore, the **Borromean Islands** *(Isole Borromee)* are celebrated for their Baroque palazzi and magnificent gardens. They are still the property of the Borromeo family that provided Milan with its greatest cardinals. The 17th-century palazzo on **Isola Bella** is decorated with admirable paintings by Annibale Carracci, Tiepolo, Zuccarelli, and Giordano. The terraced gardens constitute one of the finest ensembles of the Italian formal style. View the lake from the uppermost of the ten terraces, by the unicorn statue that is the Borromeo family emblem. **Isola dei Pescatori** is a delightfully peaceful fishing village with tiny narrow streets, while **Isola Madre**, farther out in the lake, is the largest of the islands and almost deserted, except for its palazzo and botanical garden inhabited by peacocks and pheasants among the palms and rhododendrons.

A maiden watches over the Isola Bella's garden-terraces of Lake Maggiore.

Stresa is the principal resort. The lakeside promenade, Lungolago, is famous for its flowers and bewitching view of the islands. Take the cable-car to the peak of the **Mottarone** at 1,491 metres (4,892 feet) for its exhilarating view of the Lombardy lakes, the Alps, and the Po valley. A toll road will also take you there via the Giardino Alpinia (Alpine Garden), which displays over 2,000 varieties of mountain plants.

Piedmont *(Piemonte)*

As its name suggests, this region of the upper basin of the Po river lies in the foothills of the Alps.

From the fall of the Roman Empire to the 19th century, it stood outside the mainstream of Italian history. Its royal House of Savoy walked a diplomatic tightrope between the rivalries of France, Switzerland, Spain, and the German emperors until the fall of Napoleon. The new nationalism led Piedmont into the Italian orbit at the head of the Risorgimento unification movement, and the House of Savoy provided the first king of united Italy.

Close links to France have left their mark. A French patois is still spoken in hill villages and you'll notice bilingual street signs in the Aosta Valley (geographically part of Piedmont, but administratively separate). The country's most venerable ski resort, on the Italian side of Mont Blanc, is known as Courmayeur, not Cortemaggiore. The classical palaces and squares of Turin, Piedmont's royal capital, are in many ways closer in spirit to France than the rest of Italy. But whatever Gallic ambience this may have created has been thoroughly "Italianized" by the steady influx of workers from the south for the steel, chemical, automobile, and communications industries.

Turin *(Torino)*

Best known for its industry, most notably the giant Fiat automobile works, the proud Piedmontese capital is far from being a dull or dismal factory town. It has retained the checkerboard layout of its origins as a Roman *castrum*. Its rise to prominence in the 17th and 18th centuries was accompanied by Italy's first coherent urban planning; classical and Baroque palaces and monuments give its main streets and squares a great dignity and panache.

The tone is set by the formal elegance of the **Piazza Castello**, dominated by Filippo Juvarra's richly articulated Baroque façade for the

Palazzo Madama. The original medieval castle received its new name when transformed in the 17th century into the royal residence of Vittorio Amedeo I's widow, Maria Cristina. It now houses the **Civic Museum** *(Museo Civico di Arte Antica)* beside a splendid ceremonial staircase, also designed by Juvarra. The paintings include Jan Van Eyck's 14th-century miniatures for the *Book of Hours of the Duc de Berry,* Pontormo's *St. Michael,* and a particularly handsome *Portrait of a Young Man* by Sicilian master Antonello da Messina. On upper floors are the royal collections of furniture, ceramics, and carved ivories.

Across the square is the former royal chapel, the 17th-century church of **San Lorenzo**, designed by Turin's other great Baroque architect, Fra Guarino Guarini. Philosopher and mathematician as well as priest, he has created a marvellously intricate interior surrounding the octagonal space with 16 red marble columns. Arches rise to hold the central lanterned cupola formed by an 8-pointed star.

At the **Armoury** *(Armeria Reale)*, take a look at the interesting collection of Asian and European weapons and armour dating back to Roman and Etruscan times. Then relax a while behind the Palazzo Reale in its **Royal Gardens**, designed by Louis XIV's Versailles landscape-architect, André Le Nôtre.

The late 15th-century **cathedral** cherishes one of Italy's most celebrated relics, the shroud said to have enveloped Jesus on his descent from the cross, taking the imprint of his face and body. Kept in the **Chapel of the Holy Shroud** *(Cappella della Santa Sindone)*, it was brought to Turin in the 17th century after a journey 200 years earlier from Jerusalem to France via Cyprus. Measuring 4.1 by 1.4 metres (13 by 5 feet), the sheet is kept in an iron-boxed silver casket placed in a marble urn on the altar. Modern scientific tests have proved it is a medieval forgery, but crowds still visit its black marble chapel, a masterpiece of Guarini's High Baroque, with its cone-shaped dome formed by a web of intersecting arches that rise to a 12-pointed star. From outside, the chapel's spire looks like a three-tiered pagoda.

The pride of Turin, as in so many Italian cities, is not in one monument but in a glorious square, the **Piazza San Carlo**, one of the most beautiful in Europe. The 17th-century palazzi make an exquisite setting for your late afternoon *passeggiata* along the arcades of shops and cafés, culminating in the graceful symmetry of two Baroque churches, Juvarra's Santa Cristina and its twin, San Carlo. Stretching north and south of the square is the town's most elegant shopping street and main axis, Via Roma.

Northeast of the piazza, in the Palazzo dell'Accademia delle Scienze, is the **Egyptian Museum** *(Museo Egizio),* second in importance only to Cairo's. Its treasures include statues of the Pharaohs of the period around 1500 B.C., of Tutankhamen, and of the god Amen Ra, as well as a mummified crocodile, and artefacts of everyday life, combs, clothes, kitchen utensils, even food.

On the second floor is the **Galleria Sabauda** (Savoy Gallery), with an important collection of Italian and European art. The Italian works include a Fra Angelico *Madonna and Angels,* Veronese's *Supper at Simon's House*, and Pollaiuolo's *Tobias and the Archangel.* Among the European paintings are Jan Van Eyck's *St. Francis Receiving the Stigmata* and works by Roger Van Der Weyden, Van Dyck, Rembrandt, Hans Memling, and François Clouet.

One of the city's more bizarre monuments is the **Mole Antonelliana,** with its swordfish-like 167-metre- (547-foot-) high granite spire, named after its engineer designer Alessandro Antonelli. Planned originally in 1863 as a synagogue, it's now a beloved city symbol used for exhibitions and elevator trips to its panoramic terrace.

The designing talents of Fiat, Alfa Romeo, Bugatti, and Ferrari (but also Benz, Peugeot, and Ford) are celebrated out at the **Museo dell'Automobile** (Corso Unità d'Italia, 40), south of the city centre beside the Po river.

Take the pretty excursion up on a hill across the river to Sassi, 10 km (6 miles) east of Turin, to see Juvarra's Baroque masterpiece, the splendid domed **Basilica di Superga** and the hilltop view of the Alps and the Po valley. Kings of the House of Savoy are buried in the basilica's crypt.

Courmayeur

The 4,810-metre (15,781-foot) peak of Mont Blanc (Monte Bianco) may be in France, but the Italian side of the mountain gets the better weather. The Aosta Valley's Courmayeur is as pleasant a base for hiking—and more strenuous mountain-climbing—in summer as it is for skiing in winter. Adepts recommend the mineral waters for whatever ails you—and a shot of *grappa* for whatever doesn't. This is Italy's oldest ski resort and an Alpine Museum traces its history in the Casa delle Guide *(Maison des Guides)*.

One of the most spectacular excursions in the whole country is the 90-minute **cable-car ride** from La Palud, north of Courmayeur, to the Colle del Gigante, 3,354 metres (11,004 feet) and Aiguille du Midi, 3,842 metres (12,606 feet). This gives you a wonderful view across to the peak of Mont Blanc and the whole roof of the western Alps. (The Aiguille cable-car station is across the French border, so take your passport.)

Italian Riviera

The Ligurian coast that holidaymakers have dubbed the Italian Riviera has an ancient history of piracy and commerce, not always easily distinguishable. The great port city of Genoa made the Mediterranean more or less safe for respectable traders, and the rest of the coast settled down to some quiet fishing, sailing, and harmless traffic in postcards and suntan lotion.

The picturesque, more rugged coast east of Genoa is known as the Riviera di Levante (Riviera of the Rising Sun), while the coast west to the French border at Ventimiglia is the Riviera di Ponente (Riviera of the Setting Sun), better known for the sandy beaches of its family resorts.

Genoa (*Genova*)

Hemmed in between the Apennine mountains and the sea, Genoa has tended, like historic rival Venice on the east coast, to turn its back on Italy to seek its fortune on the high seas. This may account for a cool reserve, almost aloofness, that some read even into the architecture of the tall houses in the straight and narrow streets behind the port.

With 28 km (17 miles) of docks, Italy's biggest port remains the key to the city's identity. Start your city tour with a motor-launch **harbour cruise** from the Calata degli Zingari quay between the passenger and cargo terminals.

This glorious statue celebrates the triumphs of Christopher Columbus.

Then, at the end of the main shopping street of Via XX Settembre west of the Piazza De Ferrari that constitutes the city's bustling modern centre, enter the historic quarters. **Piazza San Matteo** was the medieval home of the august Doria family, navigators and merchants who helped build the city's great commercial empire. Their arcade houses, with grey and white striped façades (numbers 15–17) were built from the 13th to 15th century. The Romanesque-Gothic church of **San Matteo** has the same grey and white façade. In the crypt, you'll find the tomb of Andrea Doria, great 16th-century admiral who took Genoa into the Spanish camp against the French and became the city's virtual dictator.

The Renaissance and Baroque palaces of the **Via Garibaldi** are a unique testimony to the town's historic prosperity, many of them now banks or museums. The **Palazzo Bianco** (number 11) makes a handsome setting for its collection of Genoese painters: Cambiaso, Strozzi, and Magnasco, as well as works by Pontormo and Palma il Vecchio, and the Flemish school: Rubens, Gérard David, and Van Dyck. The 17th-century Baroque **Palazzo Rosso** (number 18), taking its name from the red façade, displays works by Veronese, Titian, Dürer, Rubens, and Van Dyck.

Perhaps because his home town is ashamed of not financing his crazy trip to America, Genoa still has no decent monument to Christopher Columbus. The closest reference you'll find is on a ramp leading to the **Porta Soprana** medieval turreted gate on Piazza Dante, an obscure plaque indicating the house of the discoverer's father.

Riviera Resorts

 Along the mostly rugged Riviera di Levante east of Genoa, by far the prettiest spot is **Portofino**, more fishing and sailing harbour than resort, though it does have some fine hotels back in the hills. From the colourfully painted houses clustered around the harbour, set out on a cliff walk past the church of San Giorgio to the **lighthouse** *(faro)* at the end of the promontory for a superb view along the coast. The cliffs are clothed in a profusion of exotic vegetation, with occasional glimpses of imposing villas framed by cypresses, palm trees, and cascades of bougainvillaea. Boat excursions will take you to other beautifully secluded fishing villages, such as **San Fruttuoso** and **Camogli**. By road, you can visit the charming little town of **San Rocco** and take a 40-minute walk over to Punta Chiappa, looking out over the whole Riviera.

Santa Margherita Ligure is a jolly resort town with lively cafés, discos, and *trattorie*. The family resort of **Sestri Levante** has fine sandy beaches. Most popular of all, down the coast beyond the naval city of La Spezia, are the beaches of **Viareggio**, favourite resort of the Tuscans and famous for its pine groves, mostly of the umbrella variety.

A picturesque bridge in the Ligurian village of Dolceácqua, about 10 miles west of San Remo.

Cool off with an excursion inland to **Carrara**, where the marble quarries provided the raw material of Italy's greatest achievements, the monuments of the Roman Empire and the Renaissance. The town is still full of sculptors, and Piazza Alberica is the scene of a summer sculpture competition—14 days to produce a masterpiece. Visit the still active **quarries** of Fantiscritti and Colonnata. The marble that Michelangelo chose for his *Moses* and *Pietà* is now hewn, at $3,000 a cubic metre, for replicas at Caesar's Palace, Las Vegas, and tombstones in the Los Angeles Forest Lawn cemetery.

The Riviera di Ponente west of Genoa is an almost continuous chain of family resorts. **San Remo** is the best known, with its casino and elegant promenade along the Corso Imperatrice. For time away from the beach, explore the narrow winding medieval streets of the **La Pigna** quarter, leading up to the 17th-century sanctuary of Madonna della Costa.

Evening is the time for a drink on Portofino's harbour.

Nearby **Bordighera** is particularly proud of the palm trees along the Lungomare Argentina promenade. Since the 16th century, the town has had the exclusive privilege of providing Rome with its palm fronds for the Sunday before Easter. **Alassio** completes this coast's trio of major resorts, justifiably proud of its gardens nurtured by a particularly mild winter. Take an excursion east to the quiet medieval town of **Albenga**, with its Romanesque-Gothic houses around the 11th- to 14th-century cathedral and early Christian (fifth-century) baptistery.

THE SOUTH

One of the great joys of the south is the extent to which it is still virgin land for the majority of Italy's visitors. It has its perennial favourites: the islands of Capri and Ischia in the Bay of Naples, the ruins of Pompeii, and the resorts of the Amalfi coast. Otherwise, southern Italy is overlooked by tourists almost as much as it has been by the national government since the 1871 reunification. Less prosperous than the north, it cannot offer the same wealth of modern hotel facilities. Monuments and museums have suffered from earthquakes, the last catastrophic one in 1980, and civic neglect. But things are improving fast and the compensations for the more venturesome visitor are considerable. The chief pleasure of the south, or *Mezzogiorno*, is the people, who tend to be warm-hearted, outgoing, and gregarious.

Naples *(Napoli)*

The very idea of this teeming, undisciplined town may intimidate the faint-hearted, but for those as enterprising and cheerful as the Neapolitans themselves, the rewards are rich. Indeed, two of its museums are among the most important in Europe, but they and the monuments play second fiddle to the street life. In the outdoor theatre that is Italy, Naples is unabashed melodrama: around the port, the popular quarters of Spaccanapoli, even the more bourgeois neighbourhoods of Vomero and Posillipo. Spend hours in the restaurants. Whether the Chinese or the Italians invented noodles, Naples is where real *spaghetti* began and where the Spanish brought Italy's first tomato.

The cautious tell you not to drive in Naples, where one-way signs are meaningless and red and green lights purely decorative, and they are right.

The face of Naples has been made and remade by its many earthquakes, permitting—imposing—transitions from Gothic to Renaissance and Baroque. Remember that today many of the city's churches, palaces, and museums may still be closed for ongoing reconstruction and restoration after the devastating earthquake of 1980.

The Port and Spaccanapoli

Traffic roars down the broad Corso Umberto I to the pivotal **Piazza Municipio** to serve the docks or spin off into the commercial district behind Santa Lucia, the teeming historic centre of Spaccanapoli, or the residential districts of Vomero and Posillipo.

Towering over the long rectangular square on its south side is the massive dry-moated **Castel Nuovo**. Originally the 13th-century fortress of Naples' French ruler Charles d'Anjou, it was rebuilt in the 15th century as a palace for the Spanish kings of Aragon. Entrance to what is now administrative offices and a communal library is between two towers on the west side, away from the harbour, through a fine two-storey Renaissance **triumphal arch** crowned by a statue of St. Michael. Francesco Laurana's sculpted reliefs celebrate the ceremonial entry of King Alfonso in 1443.

Celebrated in song, the old popular harbour district of **Santa Lucia** is now lined with elegant hotels and restaurants contrasting with the formidable medieval **Castel dell'Ovo** out on the promontory. The sunset walk gives you a great view of the bay and Mount Vesuvius. At the Mergellina (western) end of the harbour, the fishermen bring their morning catch into Porto Sannazaro.

South of the Piazza Municipio, the Via San Carlo curves round to the 19th-century steel-and-glass shopping arcade of **Galleria Umberto I**, opposite the great Neo classical temple of Neapolitan *bel canto,* the **Teatro San Carlo** opera house, built in 1737. The solemnly monumental hemicycle of the **Piazza del Plebiscito** was laid out by Napoleon's marshal Joachim Murat when, as King of Naples, he occupied the Spaniards' **Palazzo Reale** on the east side of the piazza. The rooms are still decorated and furnished with the Baroque pomp of the 17th and 18th centuries.

Leading north from the palace, the Neapolitans' favourite shopping street of **Via Toledo** is named after Viceroy Dom Pedro Alvarez de Toledo. It separates the town hall *(Municipio)* and broad commercial streets going down to the harbour from a checkerboard of narrow alleys to the west, a Spanish neighbourhood of the 16th century that is now a mass of tall crowded tenements.

Via Toledo takes you into the city's historic heart, **Spaccanapoli** (around a Roman road that "splits Naples" into upper and lower districts). In an area stretching from the permanently traffic-jammed Piazza Dante, between Via San Biagio dei Librai and Via Tribunali and over to the Porta Capuana, the popular image of old Naples survives. A permanent festival of laundry hangs across the narrow streets. Gossip, business, and vendettas fly between balconies, while ropes haul up baskets of vegetables, letters, and pet cats.

For a sense of the neighbourhood's old splendour, start on **Piazza Gesù Nuovo**, with its characteristically extravagant Baroque Immacolata column *(guglia)* in the centre. Behind an embossed façade, the same architectural exuberance continues inside the Jesuit church. But the jewel here, on the south corner of the square, is the 14th-century church of

The island of Ischia in the Bay of Naples is a perennial favourite in the South of Italy.

Santa Chiara, built for the wife of Robert d'Anjou and retrieved from its 18th-century Baroque additions and 20th-century fire-bombing. The original rose window and elegant porch survive and the French Gothic interior is beautifully restored. In the choir are the **sculpted tombs** of Marie de Valois (on the right) and Robert d'Anjou (behind the high altar). Through an entrance between the church and campanile, visit the lovely 14th-century **cloister** *(Chiostro delle Clarisse)*, converted in 1742 into a country garden —a delightful haven of tranquillity.

Take the Via Tribunali to the Franciscan church of **San Lorenzo Maggiore**, with its Baroque façade incorporating the 14th-century marble porch, which was added after the earthquake of 1731. Inside, the sober French Gothic chancel, exceptional in Naples for its ambulatory around the nine chapels, contrasts with the Baroque chapel left of the choir.

The **cathedral's** three handsome 15th-century portals are somewhat overpowered by the ugly 19th-century neo-Gothic façade. Inside, left of the Baroque nave, go down to Naples' earliest known Christian sanctuary, the fourth-century Basilica of **Santa Restituta**, in which the original Roman columns survived the 1688 earthquake. At the end of the right nave is the fifth-century domed baptistery with remnants of some fine mosaics in the dome.

The eastern end of Spaccanapoli is dominated by the Hohenstaufen emperors' medieval **Castel Capuano** (law courts since the 16th century) and a Renaissance city gate, **Porta Capuana,** flanked by massive towers from the Spanish ramparts. Between the gate and the fortress, a boisterous market offers a veritable open-air "museum" of counterfeit luxury brands of luggage, wristwatches, polo shirts, and tennis shoes.

Street scene in Naples, a city known for its unabashed melodrama.

The Museums

The roguish image of the city's present might make it easy to forget the city's glorious past. Luckily, two truly magnificent museums preserve the region's treasures from the ravages of earthquake and theft. Inquire at the tourist office (main railway station or Via Partenope 10a in Santa Lucia) about ever-changing details of opening times.

Originally a 16th-century cavalry barracks, the **Archaeological Museum** *(Museo Archeologico Nazionale)* is in no way a dry bundle of old bones and stones, but sheer pleasure for anyone even remotely interested in southern Italy's Greek, Etruscan, and Roman past. All visits to Pompeii and Herculaneum should begin or end here. The collections display, beautifully, not only the paintings and mosaics buried there nearly 2,000 years ago by Mount Vesuvius, but a host of other sculptures from the region's villas and temples. (As some pieces are exhibited on a rotation basis, you may want to identify those on display with the museum guide cataloguing them by number.)

The ground floor is devoted to **sculpture,** including many Roman copies of classics from Greece's Golden Age in the fifth century B.C. which are our only access to these lost masterpieces. The most famous of these is the *Doryphorus* (Spear-carrier) of Polycletus, second in fame among Greek sculptors only to Phidias. The Emperors' Gallery includes busts and statues of Julius Caesar, Augustus, Claudius, and Caracalla.

The **Pompeii mosaics** and **Herculaneum bronzes** are on the mezzanine floor. The lively secular and pagan mosaics from Pompeii's patrician villas make a striking contrast with the rigid formality of church mosaics that we see elsewhere in Italy. They include *Clients Consulting a Sorceress* and *Strolling Musicians,* vivid little friezes of an octopus, a cat catching a quail, and the huge exciting mural of *Alexander* driving Darius of Persia from the battlefield at Issus in 333 B.C. The **paintings** here are the best preserved of any from Roman antiquity—frescoes in brilliant blues, greens, and the inimitable Pompeii reds. The most celebrated is the sophisticated portrait of *Paquius Proculus and his Wife,* but look out, too, for the elegant *Hercules* and *Telephus* and four delicate portraits of women, including *Artimedes* and the *Flower Gatherer.*

The **Capodimonte Museum** (currently undergoing extensive restoration) is housed, as its name suggests, in an 18th-century hill-top palace. The garden offers a welcome rest before and after a visit to the rich collections of Italian and European painting.

Highlights include: Giovanni Bellini's gentle *Transfiguration of Christ* standing serenely between Moses and Elijah; Mantegna's *Portrait of a Boy*; and Michelangelo's drawing of *Three Soldiers* for his Vatican fresco of *St. Peter's Crucifixion*. The Titian room contains half a dozen of his great works, among them a brilliant *Pope Paul II with his Farnese Nephews*, the artist's daughter *Lavinia Vecellio* and *Philip II of Spain*. The stark realism you'll see in Caravaggio's *Flagellation* and the *Seven Works of Mercy* launched a whole Neapolitan school of "Caravaggeschi" displayed here. Most notable among the museum's non-Italian painters are El Greco, Breughel (*Blind Leading the Blind* and the *Misanthrope*), Cranach, Holbein, Dürer, and a Van Dyck *Crucifixion*.

Vomero and Posillipo

Much of Naples' middle class looks out over the city from the hill-top Vomero neighbourhood in geometrically laid out, treeshaded streets respectably named after artists and musicians of the Renaissance and Baroque periods: Michelangelo, Giordano, Scarlatti, and Cimarosa. On the southeast edge of the Vomero hill just below the massive Castel Sant'Elmo, the elegant Baroque Charterhouse **Certosa di San Martino** offers a soothing haven of tranquillity in its cloisters and monastery gardens. The 16th-century church is rich in Neapolitan Baroque paintings, notably by Caracciolo, Stanzione, and Giordano. The monastery's museum traces the kingdom of Naples' long history in costumes, sculpture, paintings, and prints. Both children and adults adore the monumental Christmas crib of 1818, a Neapolitan speciality presenting the characters of the Nativity accompanied by peasants and artisans.

A fresco in the Villa of Mysteries, Pompeii's most cherished artistic treasure.

The 19th-century **Villa Floridiana** houses a fine museum of ceramics from all over Europe and Asia. From its delightful gardens, you have a superb view of the Bay of Naples.

The genteel **Posillipo** neighbourhood enjoys a privileged position on a promontory at the western edge of town. Drive around its gardens and villas, some of them romantically dilapidated but still graceful, such as the 17th-century Palazzo di Donn'Anna on the bay front.

Campagnia

The green and fertile region round Naples, between the Tyrrhenian coast and the western slopes of the Apennines, was originally colonized by the Etruscans and Greeks. The volcanic soil has produced a profusion of tomatoes, olives, walnuts, grapes, oranges, lemons, and figs.

The succession of authoritarian rulers from the Middle Ages to the 18th century—Norman and Angevin French, German emperors, and the Spanish—kept in place a feudal system that has left the region to this day socially backward compared with the north. Village festivals and processions bear witness to the heavy rural attachment to religion and even pagan superstition harking back to Roman times. Holidaymakers favour the islands in the Bay of Naples and the resorts of the Amalfi coast. All are in easy reach of the remains of Pompeii and Herculaneum, the Vesuvius volcano and, farther down the coast, the Greek temples of Paestum.

Capri

Ferries or hydrofoils leave from Naples, Sorrento, and Positano. Look out for the dolphins accompanying the ship across the Bay of Naples. With its fragrant subtropical vegetation, mountainous terrain, and dramatic craggy coast, this still-beautiful island manages to cater to the boisterous fun of the package tours while providing quiet hideaways for the idle rich. Winters here are marvellously mild and deserted, but even in summer you can seek out the island's many enchanted corners away from the mob.

To drive your own car on the island, you need a special permit (not usually available at the height of the holiday season). At the main harbour of Marina Grande, take a minibus or the funicular railway up to the main town of **Capri**. (Or rent a canopied limousine or taxi for the day, not cheap, but negotiable.) Souvenir shops and pizzerias cluster around the pretty 17th-century domed church of Santo Stefano. Escape down the little paved road south of town to the peace of the shady Romanesque and Renaissance cloisters of the **Certosa di San Giacomo**.

Dominating the western half of the island, the quieter resort town of **Anacapri** derives a sleepy charm from its white villas along narrow flowery lanes. A short walk from the Piazza della

Vittoria takes you to Swedish doctor-writer Axel Munthe's famous **Villa San Michele**. The house is an intriguing mixture of Baroque furniture and Roman antiquities, but the main attraction is the charming garden with its trellised arches and terraces looking out over the bay. Back at the piazza, take the chairlift for a soaring view of the whole island on your way up to the terraced gardens and chestnut trees of **Monte Solaro**, 589 metres (1,933 feet).

The island's most popular excursion—prettiest by boat from Marina Grande, but also possible by road northwest of Anacapri—is to the celebrated cave, the **Blue Grotto** (*Grotta Azzurra*), most effective at noon. The sun shining through the water turns the light inside the cave a brilliant blue, and objects on the whitesand seabed gleam like silver. Duck your head as the rowboat takes you through the one-metre- (3-foot-) high cave entrance. The cave, 54 metres (177 feet) long, 15 metres (49 feet) high, and 30 metres (98 feet) wide, is believed from the man-made niches to have been a *nymphaeum*, a kind of watery boudoir for the Emperor Tiberius, who retired to Capri in the first century A.D.

Of the dozen villas that Tiberius built on Capri, the best preserved are the ruins of **Villa Jovis**, sprawling across an eastern promontory opposite the mainland. The spectacular view from the 297-metre- (974-foot-) high Salto di Tiberio precipice is said to be the last pleasure enjoyed by the emperor's enemies before they were hurled over the edge.

Ischia

Lying at the western end of the Bay of Naples—reached by ferry or hydrofoil from Naples and Pozzuoli—the island has won the overwhelming favour of German tourists in the summer, thanks to thermal springs, fine sandy beaches, and good facilities for watersports. Casamicciola Terme and Lacco Ameno are among the smarter spa resorts.

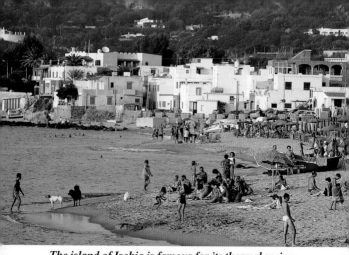

The island of Ischia is famous for its thermal springs and fine sandy beaches.

One of the best beaches, pockmarked with volcanic steam spouts, is the Lido dei Maronti on the south coast near the pretty little fishing village of Sant'Angelo. The island interior has a rich vegetation of vines, olive trees, and exotic plants. Nature lovers can hike up the extinct volcano of Mount Epomeo, 788 metres (2,585 feet), starting from Fontana.

Pompeii

More than in any of the empire's colossal arenas, soaring aqueducts, or triumphal arches, you'll find the reality of Roman life in the bakeries, wine shops, groceries, and brothels of Pompeii. The town that Vesuvius blotted out along with Herculaneum (see pages 180-181) on August 24, A.D. 79, is still being meticulously excavated from its ashes. It was rediscovered in 1594 by an architect cutting a new channel for the Sarno river, but excavation did not begin till 1748.

The road from the main gate (Porta Marina) passes on the right of the basilica law courts and stock exchange to reach the **Forum**, the town's main public meeting place directly facing Mount Vesuvius. Imagine a square looking originally something like Venice's Piazza San Marco, with two-storey porticoes running along three sides and the six-columned **Temple to Jupiter** flanked by ceremonial arches at the north end. (After earlier earthquake damage, the temple was used as the *Capitolium* and city treasury.) You can still see plinths from the square's statues of local and national celebrities and the white base of the orator's platform. In the northeast corner is the market *(macellum)*.

On the **Via dell'Abbondanza** running east from the Forum, those are ancient, not modern graffiti you find scratched and daubed in red on the walls of the houses and shops. Election slogans, insults, obscene drawings—our subway kids continue a venerable tradition.

The ruins of Pompeii are still being excavated some four hundred years after the city was rediscovered.

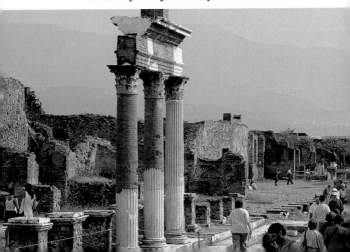

Prominent phallus signs often indicate a house of joy, with an arrow pointing upstairs to where the action was, but sometimes they're just a shopkeeper's good luck sign. Notice the oil and wine jars in the shops, the bakers' ovens and flour-grinding mills shaped like giant cotton-reels (excavators found a donkey lying by one he'd been turning when Vesuvius erupted).

At the Stabian Baths *(Thermae Stabianae),* you can see the separate men's and women's facilities, changing room, with clothes-locker niches, and three baths: cold, lukewarm, and hot *(frigidarium, tepidarium, and calidarium).* The **Teatro Grande** seated 5,000 spectators. Behind the stage was the gladiators' barracks, where 63 skeletons were found. Their weapons, along with Pompeii's more fragile works of art, are exhibited at Naples' Archaeological Museum (see page 171), which provides an invaluable adjunct to your visit here.

At the far end of the Via dell'Abbondanza, visit two of the town's best villas: the **House of Loreius Tiburtinus,** for its beautiful peristyle garden of fountains, water channels, and cascades, one of them with paintings of **Narcissus** and **Pyramus and Thisbe**; and the **House of Julia Felix,** big enough to have been perhaps a luxury hotel, with its own bathhouse and a handsome portico of slender mar-

---

House and Garden

Unlike the predominantly aristocratic Herculaneum, Pompeii's population of 25,000 was a mixture of patricians, nouveau riche merchants, small shopkeepers, artisans, and slaves. They made their money from commerce in wool and wine.

The typical patrician house had two storeys, with servants and lodgers living upstairs. The family's living and sleeping quarters surround a first courtyard or atrium. Opposite the entrance is a main living room (*tablinum*) backing onto the dining room (*triclinium*). This looks onto another courtyard or Greek-style porticoed garden (*peristylium*).

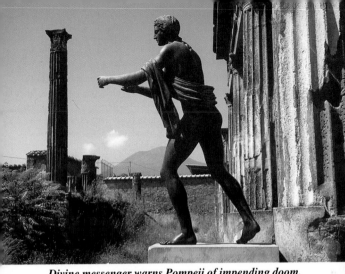

Divine messenger warns Pompeii of impending doom.

ble columns around the peristyle. At the great **Amphitheatre** just to the south, you get a fine view back over the town from its upper tiers.

A short walk outside the main site to the north, the **Villa of Mysteries** *(Villa dei Misteri)* is Pompeii's most cherished artistic treasure. The "mysteries" are those depicted in **frescoes** of a woman's initiation into the Dionysiac cult. Archaeologists suggest that the scenes of dancing satyrs, flagellation, and a woman kneeling before a sacred phallus indicate rites that the town preferred to keep at a decorous distance, in this splendid suburban villa.

Vesuvius *(Vesuvio)*

The old Roman name of Europe's most famous volcano means "Unextinguished" and there's no reason to change it. In the 1980s, it was 1,281 metres (4,203 feet) high, having added 79 metres (259 feet) with the big eruption of 1944 and subsequent smaller ones.

Barring risks from "unscheduled activity," you can peek inside the steaming crater. From the Ercolano *autostrada* exit, take the winding mountain-road's right fork for a short chairlift ride to the summit. Exploiting the fertile volcanic soil, some vineyards still produce the esteemed *Lacryma Christi* white wine. The **Eremo Observatory** halfway up the mountain has been studying eruptions since 1845 and has an impressive display of relief plans, seismographs, and geological specimens spewed out of the volcano.

Herculaneum *(Ercolano)*

Herculaneum is smaller and perhaps less spectacular than Pompeii, but its very compactness and better preservation give a more immediate sense of the shape and ambience of a whole Roman town. While Pompeii was incinerated by volcanic cinders, the mud swamping Herculaneum covered the houses in a protective crust that kept upper stories and even some of the woodwork intact. The gardens have been lovingly replanted.

Rediscovered by well-diggers in the 18th century, the town is still being excavated, a delicate business as much of it is covered by modern buildings.

The entrance off the Corso Ercolano takes you around the site for a striking view across the town of terraced villas from which wealthy Roman landowners looked out to sea towards Ischia on the horizon. The streets (Cardine III, IV, and V) have curbed pavements, lined with two-storey houses with balconies and overhanging roofs for shade.

At the southern end of Cardine V, the spacious **House of the Stags** *(Casa dei Cervi)* is named after its two marble sculptures of stags attacked by hounds. In one of the rooms off the garden is a statue of a shockingly drunken Hercules. In the middle of Cardine IV, the **House of Charred Furniture** *(Casa del Mobilio Carbonizzato)* has

The town of Herculaneum is still being excavated, after being rediscovered by 18th-century well-diggers.

Peek among the bougainvillaea at a church on the Amalfi Coast.

a marvellously preserved latticed divan bed and small table. Next door, the **House of Neptune** has lost its upstairs façade but the ground floor wine shop with its narrow-necked amphoras on the shelves looks open for business. The inner courtyard has a lovely green and blue mosaic of Neptune with his wife Amphitrite.

The grandest of the villas, the **House of the Bicentenary** (excavated 200 years after the first "dig" in 1738) stands on the avenue Decumanus Maximus on the northeast edge of town. It has splendid marble paving and, etched in the wall of one of the smaller rooms, a controversial cross regarded by some as evidence of a Christian chapel, though others insist the emblem was not adopted until the conversion of Constantine three centuries later.

Sorrento and the Amalfi Coast

The coast curving along the southern arm of the Bay of Naples round the Sorrento Peninsula to Salerno is one of the most romantic in Italy. The sinuous coast road tames even the most audacious Italian driver overlooking the sheer drop of rugged cliffs and ravines. In olden days, only brigands and pirates ventured out here, their ruined redoubts still dotting the hillsides. Now, wild roses and camelias tempt lovers out onto jutting crags high above terraces of orange and lemon groves, vineyards, walnut, and almond trees.

Surrounded on three sides by ravines above the sea, the pretty tree-shaded resort of **Sorrento** makes a perfect base for excursions along the coast. Its craftsmen are famous for their inlaid walnut woodwork. Compare their modern wares with their forefathers' Baroque furniture exhibited at the **Museo Correale**, in an 18th-century palazzo at the east end of town.

Positano spills down its hillside in a spectacular cascade of gleaming white houses dotted with gardens of oranges and lemons. Take the **cliff walk** from the town's main beach, the broad Spiaggia Grande, to the long and narrower Spiaggia Fornillo. In the little church of Santa Maria Assunta, with the region's characteristic majolica-tiled dome, see the 13th-century Byzantine-style altar painting.

Most charming and lively of the coast's resorts, **Amalfi** was once a powerful rival to the maritime republics of Pisa and Genoa, with trading posts in the 10th and 11th centuries in Palestine, Egypt, Cyprus, Byzantium, and Tunis. Its two destinies come together in the **Piazza del Duomo**, where open-air cafés and ice-cream parlours look up a long staircase to the Arab-Norman **campanile** and polychrome mosaic façade of the Romanesque **cathedral**. It was built in the ninth century, with the façade added in the 13th, when the remains of St. Andrew were brought to its crypt from Constantinople. The interlacing Arab-Norman arches of the 13th-century cloister, **Chiostro del Paradiso**, make a handsome setting for the summer recitals of chamber music. Amalfi has excellent facilities for sailing and other watersports. Take a trip to nearby Conca dei Marini to visit the stalactites and stalagmites of the **Grotta di Smeraldo**, where the waters are as brilliantly emerald green as those of Capri's Grotta Azzurra are blue.

Set back on a high ridge behind Amalfi is the peaceful village of **Ravello**, once a hideout for Romans fleeing the Huns and Visigoths. Today it's a delightful resort of modest but elegant hotels and villas, notably **Villa Cimbrone**, where the fragrant gardens command a

The goddesses of Paestum have gone, but not their devotees.

marvellous view of the Gulf of Salerno. The exotic flowers and palm trees of the **Villa Rufolo**, with its mysterious polychrome arcaded cloister, gave Richard Wagner inspiration for his last opera, *Parsifal*.

Paestum

Italy has no more magnificent testimony of its Greek colonies than this complex of wonderfully preserved Doric temples, a 40-minute drive south from Salerno, dating back to the fifth and sixth centuries B.C. Standing alone in fields leading to the sea, their buff-stone columns take on a wonderful golden glow at sunset. Four temples loom over the forum and residential quarters of Poseidonia (as it was known before the Roman era). After the town was abandoned to malaria and Arab invaders in the ninth century, the monuments disappeared under wild vegetation until their rediscovery 900 years later. The most spectacular, directly opposite the entrance to the site, is the fifth-century **Temple of Neptune**. The roof has gone, but with its entablature and 36 columns still standing, it is, with Athens' Theseion, the best preserved of all

Greek temples. To the south, the more dilapidated **Temple of Hera** (also known, mistakenly, as the Basilica) is a hundred years older. The northernmost **Temple of Ceres** was used as a church in the early Middle Ages, as attested by three Christian tombs.

Puglia

Known to many under its Roman name of Apulia, the region stretches from the "spur" of the Gargano peninsula to the heel of Italy's boot, endowed with a wild and unspoiled beauty over the gently undulating stony plateaus grazed by sheep and goats. Massive fortresses and fortress-like churches testify to the passage of the Normans and then the German emperors in the Middle Ages. In among the groves of olive, almond, and fig trees, the stones have been gathered up from time immemorial to build the smaller, but equally sturdy, corbelled *trulli*.

Gargano Peninsula

The peninsula's seaside resorts have good beaches among the pine groves, first-class camping and water-sports facilities, and are a base for excursions and hikes into an attractive hinterland of rolling hills. Before starting out on the coastal circuit from Manfredonia, visit the 12th-century church of **Santa Maria di Siponto** (southwest of town), built over a fifth-century crypt.

Pugnochiuso is among the best of the beach resorts, along with Vieste, where Emperor Frederick II left a castle from which to view the Adriatic, and the pretty fishing village of **Peschici** climbing up its rocky promontory.

Go inland through Vico to join the wild deer for picnics in the **Umbra Forest**. Perched on the Gargano heights south of the forest, **Monte Sant'Angelo** was a major medieval pilgrimage town, celebrated for its fifth-century sanctuary of **St. Michael** in a mountain cave which the archangel revealed to the Bishop of Siponto in a dream. The sanctuary inspired the building of the great French island-monastery of Mont-Saint-Michel after Bishop Aubert travelled to Gargano to collect a piece of St. Michael's red cloak. From a Gothic portico in the middle of town, beside the massive 13th-century **Campanile**, a staircase of 90 steps takes you down to the sanctuary's 11th-century bronze doors. Notice to the left of the altar the beautifully carved stone episcopal throne.

From the north-coast resort of Rodi Garganico, you can take a 90-minute boat trip out to the pine-tree-covered **Tremiti Islands**.

Alberobello

This agricultural town is the centre of Puglia's famous *trulli*, the whitewashed houses with ruddy or grey dry-stone roofs, cone-shaped, dotting the landscape like giant spinning tops turned upside down. The cone is formed by small limestone slabs set in a spiral without mortar to bind them. Though the region's oldest surviving *trulli* date back only to the 16th century, the construction technique is prehistoric, brought here perhaps from Greece or the Middle East.

In Alberobello, two neighbourhoods of *trulli* houses, shops, and churches, **Rioni Monti** and **Aia Piccola**, are protected as a *zona monumentale*. Shopkeepers are happy to let you climb up to their roof terraces for a striking view across a whole forest of *trulli* domes. Out in the country in and around **Locorotondo** and **Selva di Fasano**, you'll find *trulli* farms, barns, grain silos, even filling stations.

Northwest of Alberobello, a *strada panoramica* along a ridge overlooking the Adriatic coast leads to **Castellana Grotte**, a group of spectacular caves 60 metres (190 feet) underground. Take a guided tour of the translucent stalactites reaching down to fuse with stalagmites in glowing columns of red, green, and pink.

Sicily *(Sicilia)*

The Mediterranean's largest island is in many ways a country to itself and deserves a separate holiday to do it proper justice. Here, for anyone who has a few days to spare for a first impression, we'll just provide

*The drystone trulli houses of Alberobello use
prehistoric building techniques.*

some highlights representative of its many facets: the capital Palermo,
the ancient Greek settlements, and the coastal resort of Taormina.

Palermo

This bustling capital deserves the necessary effort to get at its
colourful past. Cleverly integrating designs of Arab and Byzantine
predecessors, the Norman palaces and churches join the crumbling
grandeur of Spanish Baroque façades in momentary triumph over
the chaos of the modern port city.

The intersection of Via Vittorio Emanuele and Via Maqueda is the
town's historic centre, **Quattro Canti** (Four Corners), in a characteristic setting of Baroque churches (San Giuseppe and Santa Caterina)
and the monumental **Pretoria Fountain.** Behind the town hall, **Piazza Bellini** evokes Palermo's cosmopolitan history. The 12th-century
church of **San Cataldo** with its three little red domes and Arabic in-
scriptions was originally built as a synagogue. Beside it, the Norman
Gothic **Martorana** church, partly remodelled with a Baroque façade
and porch, has a fine campanile with four storeys of slender mullioned

windows. Inside the porch, 12th-century mosaics show, to the right, Jesus crowning Sicily's Norman king, Roger II, and to the left, his admiral, Georges of Antioch, at the feet of the Madonna. In the nave are **mosaics** of Christ Pantocrator (Omnipotent Lord) with angels.

West along Via Vittorio Emanuele, the **Palace of the Normans** *(Palazzo dei Normanni)* turned the Arabs' ninth-century fortress into a royal residence, appropriate setting for the later brilliance and luxury of Emperor Frederick II's Sicilian court (see page 23). In the royal apartments, see the hunting mosaics in **King Roger's room** *(Stanza normanna)*, but the jewel of the palace, one of Norman architecture's greatest achievements in Italy, is the 12th-century **Palatine Chapel** on the first floor. The noble Romanesque interior has a magnificent painted wooden ceiling with Arabic honeycomb motifs and stalactite pendentives. The **mosaics** of the dome and apse depict Christ Pantocrator with the Evangelists and Jesus blessing Peter and Paul. The combination of figurative and intricate geometric designs was a collaborative effort of Syrian Muslim craftsmen with Byzantine Christians.

The pink-domed church of **San Giovanni degli Eremiti** (Via dei Benedettini) is another intriguing example of 12th-century Arab-Norman design. Its exotic character is enhanced by the twin-columned **cloister** overgrown with tropical plants, orange, lemon, and palm trees.

Housed in a 17th-century monastery, the town's **Archaeological Museum** (Piazza Olivella) displays superb statues and sculpted metope (friezes) from the Greek temples of Selinunte (600–500 B.C.), on Sicily's south coast. The **Palazzo Abatelli Art Gallery** includes in its collection a gripping fresco of the *Triumph of Death* by an anonymous 15th-century artist, Antonello da Messina's exquisite *Annunciation*, and Francesco Laurana's sculpture of *Eleonora of Aragon*.

 Monreale

This hilltop suburb southwest of Palermo boasts Sicily's finest **cathedral** (12th century). Go round to the back of the church to see its wonderful russet and brown stone chancel of interlacing arches,

Gothic rose windows, and Arab windows with pointed arches. In the grandiose interior, the 12th- and 13th-century mosaics of the nave and apse depict Old Testament scenes and Christ Pantocrator with saints, while the aisle mosaics narrate the miracles of Jesus. The more warmly human figures are believed to be the work of Venetian mosaicists, as opposed to the more rigidly formal Byzantine figures of Palermo's Palatine Chapel.

The beautiful cloister offers strangely mixed sensations: spiritual meditation along the arcades of delicate chevron-fluted columns and an almost sensual pleasure among the exotic flowers and trees and Arab fountain of its garden.

Agrigento

If you can make only one pilgrimage to the great Greek sanctuaries of Sicily, let it be to Agrigento's magical **Temple Valley** *(Valle dei Templi)* dating back to the fifth century B.C. The **Temple of Juno** with its sacrificial altar stands in majestic isolation high on a ledge at the eastern end of the Via Sacra. The **Temple of Concordia** is the best preserved, thanks to its subsequent use as a church in the sixth century A.D. But the golden glow of the temples' Doric columns and the idyllic setting amid acadia and almond trees on a precipice overlooking the Mediterranean are enough to start you worshipping a whole pantheon of Greek gods. Nearby is the even older **Temple of Hercules**.

North of Temple Valley, next to the 13th-century Norman church of San Nicola, the **Archaeological Museum** has a fine marble sculpture of *Ephebus* (fifth century B.C.), a gigantic *telamon,* a male figure used to hold up a temple roof's entablature, and some superb Greek wine vessels.

Syracuse *(Siracusa)*

This east-coast Corinthian settlement, founded in 734 B.C., was the most powerful of Greece's overseas colonies and, under Dionysius

(405–367 B.C.), a direct rival to Athens. In its heyday, its population was nearly triple the size of today's 118,000. It was here in the third century B.C. that mathematician Archimedes proved his water displacement theory in the bath and ran naked into the street crying "Eureka!"

Syracuse's original settlement was the port island of Ortigia, joined by causeway to the mainland. Two pillars surviving from the Greek Temple of Apollo stand like a gateway, but the Spanish era has given it a charming 17th-century ambience of Baroque houses with balconies supported by floral carvings and an occasional stone nymph. The graceful crescent-shaped Piazza del Duomo is the perfect place for breakfast surrounded by 17th- and 18th-century palazzi and the cathedral. The church is in fact a Baroque elaboration of the Greeks' Temple of Athena (fifth century B.C.), with its columns incorporated into the masonry of the outside walls. On the island's west side, the Fontana Aretusa is a freshwater spring with black and white ducks swimming in its semi-circular papyrus pond.

The principal excavated site, **Parco Archeologico**, is located on the northwest corner of the modern city. Rebuilt by the Romans to hold 15,000 spectators, the **Greek Theatre** dates back to the fifth century B.C. when Aeschylus himself arrived from his home at Gela to supervise productions of his tragedies. A classical drama festival is held here in May and June. The nearby **Paradise Quarry** *(Latomia del Paradiso)* provided the city's building materials and is now a pleasant garden of oleander and orange trees. Its popular attraction is the cave called **Orecchio di Dionisio** (Dionysius' Ear), carved from the rock.

Taormina

This attractive resort town, already very popular in antiquity as a vacation spot for the Greek bourgeoisie from Syracuse, commands a splendid view of the Mediterranean from its hillside villas and hotels. No Sicilian *passeggiata* is more celebrated than a promenade on the elegant shopping street of **Corso Umberto** and out along the **Via Roma**

*The Greek Theatre in Taormina offers spectacular
views, and not just of the stage.*

past the subtropical vegetation of the terraced gardens. With great
views south along the coast and to the volcano of Mount Etna to the
west, the **Greek Theatre** (third century B.C.) provides a wonderful setting for the summer classical drama—and a slightly surreal one for the
Taormina film festival. Excursions further up the mountain take you to
two medieval fortresses, on foot to **Castello di Taormina** and, by car
along a winding road, to **Castelmola**, for grand views.

Mount Etna

Europe's tallest volcano is still very active, as you'll see from tell-tale
yellow sulphur stains of mini-eruptions as you approach the crater. The
summit stood at 3,343 metres (10,975 feet) above sea level in 1985, but
varies according to the eruptions' destruction or lava deposits. Because
of the erratic nature of the eruptions, approaching the crater is no easy
business. The routes by bus, special Land Rover, and cable car from
Taormina or Catania change from year to year, lava permitting. Inquire
at local tourist offices and travel agencies before setting out. In any
case, the last stretch to the crater itself is on foot, so take sturdy shoes
and warm clothing—it's cool and windy up there, even in summer.
From October to May, the summit is covered in snow.

WHAT TO DO

While you're wandering around the country's myriad palazzi and churches, ancient ruins, and modern museums, you may occasionally wonder what the Italians are doing—and feel a great urge to join them. If the ephemeral idea of *la dolce vita* didn't outlive the early '60s and even then was the preserve of a happy few, today's widening prosperity has resurrected and expanded the Italians' propensity for the sweet life.

Their mania for sport is contagious, elegant shops all too seductive, and the time-honoured theatricality extends from grand opera and flamboyant discos to traditional carnivals and colourful religious processions.

SPORTS

It would be an understatement to describe the Italians as sports crazy, at least as far as spectator sports are concerned. For millions, Sundays are less sacred for mass in the morning than football in the afternoon. In a country with just a century of national unity and the scalding experience of Mussolini's fascism, sport seems almost the only activity which can inspire in Italians any semblance of patriotic fervour.

Witness the crowd's ferocious, unashamedly chauvinistic partisanship at Rome's international open tennis championships or the Davis Cup. On a day when Italy is involved in an international football match, streets all over the country are deserted—until the cars come out honking for a frenetic victory parade or the men shuffle on foot to the Piazza del Duomo for a funereal post-defeat commiseration and recrimination.

You can observe the **football** (soccer) phenomenon, with the *tifosi* (fans) in full cry, in all the major cities, the most celebrated teams studded with top foreign stars being in Turin (Juventus and Torino),

Milan (A.C. and Inter), Florence (Fiorentina), Genoa (Sampdoria), Rome, and Naples.

Cycling races are still popular—especially the round-Italy *Giro d'Italia* in June. You can watch World Cup **skiing** at Cortina d'Ampezzo and Val Gardena. **Bocce**, the bowls game similar to French *boules* or *pétanque*, is played wherever there's a patch of tree-shaded sand gravel and a bar *(osteria)* close enough at hand to serve a glass of wine or *grappa*.

Motor racing fans can watch the Grand Prix of Italy at Monza, near Milan, or Imola, near Bologna.

Heading for a hike in the Alps above Piedmont's Aosta Valley.

On the beaches of the Adriatic coast, the Italian Riviera, Sardinia, and Sicily, **swimming** is a pleasure that needs a few words of warning. Conditions of water pollution vary from year to year, but observe the general rule of thumb of avoiding a dip in the immediate vicinity of major industrialized port cities: Genoa, Naples, and Palermo. Look out for red flags warning about dangerous undercurrents, and for small children check that beaches are patrolled by lifeguards. Remember, for many smart resorts like the Venice Lido or Sardinia's Costa Smeralda, to budget for umbrellas, deck chairs, and mattresses.

For watersports at the resorts, you can usually hire equipment on the spot for **snorkelling** and **wind-surfing** (particularly good on the lakes). The Italians are great experts at **scuba diving** and have skillful instructors. You may well come across archaeological finds—

Amalfi is a great place for swimming, or just sunning.

ancient anchors, wine-jars, even sculpture which *must* be reported to local municipal authorities. It's not difficult to get hitched up to a motorboat for **water-skiing**.

Sailing is great sport around Sardinia and Sicily, but also on the Argentario peninsula (see pages 107-108).

Offshore **fishing** is popular all along the coasts, notably for tunny (tuna) off western Sicily, for swordfish on the east coast, and spear-fishing at Bordighera. For freshwater fishing in the inland lakes and rivers, you should get a permit from the local municipality.

Hiking is the simplest and most exhilarating way of seeing the countryside, up in the Dolomites or the Alps, around the lakes and the Abruzzo National Park. Remember good shoes, light but solid, and some warm clothing. You can hire horses for **riding** at resorts like Sestri Levante, Alassio, San Remo. To explore the back country on horseback, inquire at the A.N.T.E. (National Association of Equestrian Tourism), Largo Messico 13, Rome.

Golf players can usually play on local private courses with proof of their home club membership. Venice has an 18-hole course at the Lido's Alberoni. On the Riviera, try Rapallo, San Remo, or Garlenda (near Alassio). **Tennis** is less widespread than in other major Western European countries, but growing in popularity. Your hotel can help you find a hard or clay court.

Skiing is first-class in the established resorts of Cortina d'Ampezzo and Courmayeur, with a more explosive thrill on Mount Etna.

194

ENTERTAINMENT

From time to time, the Italians move the melodrama of their lives indoors and call it **opera**. Most famous of the high temples of this art is, of course, Milan's La Scala (see page 149), showcasing the works of Verdi, Bellini, Rossini, and Puccini. The taste for the grandiose musical spectacle has spread all across the Western world, but the greatest stars and divas need a triumph at La Scala for true consecration. Its season is from December till mid-May. For good tickets, you should plan well in advance through your travel agency, but your hotel may be able to help with seats from last-minute cancellations.

The other great opera houses are La Fenice in Venice, Florence's Teatro Comunale, and the great Teatro San Carlo of Naples. But Bologna, Parma, Perugia, Rome, and Palermo also have fine regional houses, beginning around December or January and going on till late spring or early summer.

In the summer, **open-air opera** is the great attraction in Rome's ancient Baths of Caracalla and Verona's Roman Arena, when performances of *Aida* and other extravagant productions may bring horses, camels, or even elephants onstage.

Orchestral concerts of symphonic and chamber **music**, for which it is usually easier to get tickets, are held in the opera houses outside and sometimes concurrently with the opera season, but also in Milan's Conservatorio and Rome's Accademia Filarmonica Romana. Florence, Spoleto, Perugia, Ravenna, Rimini, and Stresa all hold important music festivals. In Tuscany, San Gimignano and Lucca stage open-air concerts, while Amalfi's are given in the cathedral cloisters.

Lovers of **Neapolitan folk music** can enjoy a whole week of it in early September at the Piedigrotta festival.

A great open-air festival of **jazz, pop,** and **rock** music is held in the parks and gardens of Rome for the *Estate Romana* (Roman Summer). Alassio's jazz festival is in September. Milan has the best discos and night-clubs, while others are attached to hotels at the seaside resorts.

FESTIVALS

The attachment to regional customs and religious festivals has dwindled in the 20th century, but many keep going for the tourist trade. We offer here a far from exhaustive list of processions and festivities around the country.

January:

Piana degli Albanesi (near *Palermo*). Colourful Byzantine ritual for Epiphany

February or early March:

Venice Carnival, masked balls and processions in magnificent costumes; *Viareggio* Carnival; *Agrigento* Almond Blossom Festival

April:

Rome Pope's Easter Sunday blessing

May:

Assisi Calendimaggio Christian and pagan festival; *Naples* Miracle of San Gennaro (liquefaction of the saint's blood); *Camogli* (Riviera) Fish Festival, communal fish-fry in giant pan; *Gubbio* candle race, crossbow competition; *Orvieto* Pentecost feast of the Palombella (Holy Ghost)

June:

Pisa San Ranieri, jousting and torchlit regatta on Arno river; *Florence* costumed medieval football game

July:

Siena first Palio (July 2, see page 106); *Palermo* Santa Rosalia; *Venice* Redentore regatta; *Rimini* Festival of the Sea; *Rome* Noiantri street-festival in Trastevere (see page 66)

August:

Siena Second Palio (August 16)

September:

Naples Piedigrotta, Neapolitan music and cuisine; *Venice* Historical Regatta

October:

Assisi Feast of St. Francis; *Perugia* Franciscan Mysteries

December:

Rome Christmas food and toy market on Piazza Navona; *Assisi* and *Naples* cribs in streets; *Alberobello* celebrations in *trulli*

Naturally enough, **theatre** requires a good knowledge of Italian. You'll find the best productions in Rome and Milan, the latter famous for Giorgio Strehler's Piccolo Teatro.

One of the most entertaining ways to polish your Italian is at the **cinema**, where all foreign films are dubbed into Italian (though a minor revolution is taking place in a few movie houses playing original versions in Milan and Rome). In summer, Rome's great cinema event is the series of Italian and foreign films projected at the Massenzio Basilica near the Colosseum. International film festivals are held at Venice and Taormina.

In July the Redentore regatta comes to Venice turning the city's canals into a raceway.

SHOPPING

The inspired vanity of the Italians has turned their country into a delightful bazaar of style and elegance for the foreign visitor. Of stupefying junk, too. The luxury goods of Milan, Venice, Rome, and Florence, jewellery, clothes, especially shoes, but also luggage and household goods of impeccable modern design, are second to none in the world. Not inexpensive, but then the bargain here is not in the price, it's in the meticulous workmanship. But the souvenirs also merit a homage to endless invention in the realm of the cheap—and not-so-cheap—and nasty.

A cameo carver displays his wares — and special tools — in Naples.

Some souvenirs are, or course, more tasteful: gourmet delicacies, but save these purchases for the end, to get them home as fresh as possible—cheeses, salami, Parma ham, Milanese sweet *panettone* brioche, Lucca's olive oil, Siena's cakes and famous *panforte*, a spicy fruit-and-nut concoction, and the better Chianti and Orvieto wines that you may not find back home.

And if you've fallen in love with Italian coffee, why not buy a compact version of the *espresso* machine or streamlined coffee pot that does practically the same job on the stove? Italian kitchenware is in general beautifully styled with a great sense of colour and line.

In a country where civilizations have come and gone like commuter trains, there's a considerable traffic in archaeological antiquities. But when anybody at an ancient site in Rome, Pompeii, or Sicily offers you a Roman coin, Greek pot, or statue, you can be fairly sure it's a fake.

For quality goods, Italians prefer shopping in small boutiques with a long tradition, very often a family business guaranteeing generations of good craftsmanship. As a result, you won't find upmarket department stores, but popular, lower-price chain-stores—Coin, Standa, Upim, or Rinascente. But these are useful for your extra T-shirts, suntan lotion, or throwaway beach sandals.

If you want friendly treatment in the more expensive stores, you must dress decently. Even the warmest-hearted Italian can, perhaps understandably, be snooty towards people dressed like slobs. Credit cards work almost everywhere these days, apart from a few Sardinian basket weavers and Apulian potters.

Haggling is a thing of the past. You can get an occasional small *sconto* (discount) for bulk purchases, but the spread of foreign travel has taught shopkeepers in the remotest province the going international price for everything. Except among antiques, art, and second-hand dealers, where negotiation is part of the business, you may get a very cool response if you question the marked price.

Many cities are renowned for products of their traditional crafts: Naples' costumed terracotta figures for its Christmas cribs, Sorrento's inlaid walnut furniture and music boxes, Ravenna's mosaics, Pisa's alabaster, Gubbio's ceramics. For the rest, the widest range of products will be found in the big cities.

Shopping in Rome

The capital's smartest and most expensive boutiques (even if you're not buying, they're worth window-shopping just for the superb displays) are conveniently concentrated in a four-by-four-block area around Via Condotti. Closed to cars, it's bounded by Piazza di Spagna to the east and Via del Corso to the west. Here you'll find the finest leather goods (Gucci, Fendi, Pier Caranti). Women's fashions include the major French designers as well as the natives (Valentino, Armani, Gianni Versace, and Missoni). Almost as expensive are the two children's clothing shops of Tablò. Among the men's clothes meccas are Cucci (with a C) and Battistoni.

In **jewellery**, for sheer exclusivity, there's nothing like the imposing marble façade of Bulgari (Via Condotti), the ultimate monument to Roman luxury.

Two streets dominate the market in **art** and **antiques**, Via Margutta and Via del Babuino.

An *edicola* is an outdoor kiosk that sells newspapers, magazines, and, often, tickets for public transportation.

On the outskirts of this high-class shopping district, you'll find mass-produced sweaters, jeans, and other casual wear, as well as more moderately priced leather goods, on the bustling Via Tritone and Via del Corso.

If you're looking for second-hand *bric-à-brac*, try shops around the Campo de' Fiori and Piazza Navona. The Sunday morning **flea market** at Porta Portese in Trastevere is as much fun for the street musicians as for the chance of picking up bargains. Keep your own valuables safe—pickpockets love this place.

Shopping in Florence

If it has ceded to Milan its place as Italy's fashion capital, the old Renaissance city is still a centre of exquisite, if conservative, elegance. The principal thoroughfares for the smarter **fashion** boutiques, for men and women, are Via de' Tornabuoni and Via de' Calzaiuoli.

Florentine **leather goods** remain unequalled. You can smell out the country's, indeed Europe's, finest craftsmen at work in leather factories around San Lorenzo and Santa Croce. Watch the making of handbags, wallets, gloves, belts, and desk equipment without any obligation to buy. Look out, too, for the leather school tucked away behind Santa Croce's sacristy in what were once Franciscan monk's cells.

The Ponte Vecchio is the most picturesque place to shop for very reasonably priced **gold, silver,** and **jewellery**, designed with centuries of tradition behind them.

Multicoloured glass mosaic jewellery—brooches, pendants, bracelets, and rings—are all over town, handmade in local cottage industries, amazingly cheap and very attractive.

Inlaid wood or *intarsia* is a venerated craft here, perfected in the 16th century with the inlay of semi-precious stones. Using the same techniques, **furniture** is likely to be expensive, but framed pictures of Tuscan landscapes or views of Florence are more moderately priced and, as souvenirs go, tastefully done. The town also specializes in **bookbinding** and stunningly beautiful **stationery**.

Antiques shops are centred mainly around Borgo Ognissanti and San Jacopo, Via della Vigna Nuova, and Via della Spada. Even if you cannot afford the mostly prohibitive prices, they're worth visiting as veritable little museums of Renaissance and Baroque sculpture and furniture. If the creative geniuses are long dead, master craftsmen continue the tradition of superb reproductions, at negotiable prices.

Italian shoes are certainly a step above the rest of the world's footwear.

Shopping in Venice

One of the many great adventures here is separating the treasure-house from the tourist trap, distinguishing priceless gems from pricey junk. By and large, the better but more expensive shops are around the Piazza San Marco. The busy shopping street of Mercerie has good quality boutiques growing progressively moderate in price as they approach the Rialto. For cheaper purchases, head for the Strada Nuova leading behind the Ca' d'Oro to the railway station.

The bargains or at least more authentic and tasteful products are to be found, like the havens of tranquillity, far from these main tourist centres, in artisans' workshops on the Giudecca, in the Dorsoduro behind the Zattere, over by the Ghetto, to be hunted down individually and guarded as precious secrets.

Two institutions stand out among the **jewellery** shops: Missiaglia on Piazza San Marco and Sfriso on Campo San Tomà near the church of the Frari. For a cross-section of Venetian craftsmanship in more moderately priced jewellery, as well as **ceramics** and **glass mosaics**, take a look at Veneziartigiana, just off San Marco in Calle Larga.

The famous **glassware** poses a problem of quality and price. Much of the stuff is unspeakably ugly, but there is also an admirable renewal in both classical and modern design. Just hunt carefully. Necklaces of crystal or coloured beads are popular. Prices in the Murano island factories are marginally better than "downtown." When choosing gifts to be packed, remember: if real giraffes are fragile enough as it is, glass ones will never make it home; go for a rhinoceros.

Visit the island of Burano to see intricate **laceware** being made in the time-honoured manner, on the doorstep. Modern reproductions of traditional patterns can be bought on and around Piazza San Marco, along with beautifully embroidered tablecloths and napkins.

The venerable Legatoria Piazzesi (by Santa Maria Zobenigo) is the last of the great Venetian printing presses, still producing exquisite handmade **paper-goods**, stationery, and bookbindings. And you can give your fancy-dress balls a touch of Renaissance class with the finely crafted papier-mâché **masks** produced for the great Mardi Gras Carnival by workshops also turning out delightful toys, dolls, and funny hats.

The range of **fashion** boutiques around San Marco is small but select, with an emphasis on top-class **shoes** and other **leather goods**.

Shopping in Milan

With the commercial leadership of the country, Milan has also taken over as **fashion** capital. For women's and men's clothes, you'll find all the great Italian designers—Valentino, Versace, Fendi, Krizia, Armani, Missoni, and Ermenegildo Zegna—on and around Via Monte Napoleone. Here, too, are the leading **jewellery** shops.

The Galleria Vittorio Emanuele has plenty of smart, bright, and more moderately priced boutiques for younger tastes. Bargain-hunters in jeans, shoes, and cheaper fashions head for the popular stores along Via Torino and Via Manzoni.

You'll find the **modern art** galleries and **antiques** shops in the neighbourhood of the Brera Gallery and along the side streets of the Via Monte Napoleone—Via Borgospesso, Via della Spiga, and Via Sant'Andrea.

EATING OUT

The spice of life so treasured by Italians is in abundance every meal-time. From the punch of the early morning coffee to a last shot of after-dinner grappa, eating and drinking here is always a heart-warming experience.

Where to Eat

For **breakfast**, head for a *caffè* on the piazza and settle, happily, for the local *prima colazione* of superb coffee, *espresso* black or *cappuccino* with foaming hot milk (sprinkled in the best establishments with powdered chocolate), and toast or a sweet roll.

Ideal for those adopting a healthy "sightseer's diet" of one main meal a day, preferably in the evening, with just a snack for **lunch**, stand-up bars in the city known as *tavola calda* serve sandwiches and hot or cold dishes at the counter. If you want to picnic in the park or

Pizza is a speciality of Naples, where the tomato is king, but of course you can find it anywhere in Italy.

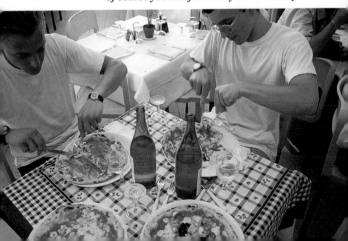

out in the country and don't feel like preparing the food yourself, get your sandwiches made up for you at the *pizzicheria* delicatessen. Ask for *panino ripieno*, a bread roll which they fill with whatever sausage, cheese or salad you choose from the inviting display at the counter.

For **dinner**, even if you don't have to be overly budget-conscious, it's useful to know that the most elaborate restaurant *(ristorante)*, with prices matching the real or apparent opulence of its décor, is almost invariably the worst value. In a family-run *trattoria*, Venetian *locanda,* or, especially in Naples and the south, a *pizzeria* which serves much more than just pizza, the ambience—half the value of an Italian meal—is infinitely more enjoyable and the food has more character.

It's the custom to round off the bill with an extra tip in addition to the service charge.

What to Eat

The classical cuisine of Tuscany and Bologna and the pizza and pasta dishes of Naples are available everywhere, but you can try other regional specialities as you travel around the country. Despite the vast array of sauces for the pasta, the essence of Italian cooking is its simplicity: fish cooked with perhaps just a touch of fennel, other seafood served straight, cold as an hors d'oeurve, Florentine steak charcoal-grilled, vegetables sautéed without elaborate disguise, at most marinated in lemon, olive oil, and pepper.

Any *trattoria* worth its olive oil will set out on a long table near the entrance a truly painterly display of its **antipasti** (hors d'œuvre). The best way to get to know the delicacies is to make up your own assortment *(antipasto misto)*. Both attractive and tasty are the cold *peperoni*, red, yellow, and green peppers grilled, skinned and marinated in olive oil and a little lemon juice. Mushrooms *(funghi)*, baby marrows *(zucchini)*, aubergines eggplant *(melanzane)*, artichokes *(carciofi),* and sliced fennel *(finocchio)* are also served cold, with a dressing *(pinzimonio)*. One of the most refreshing hors d'œuvre is the *mozzarella alla caprese*, slices of soft white buffalo cheese and tomato in a dressing of fresh basil and olive oil.

Try the tunny or tuna fish *(tonno)* with white beans and onions *(fagioli e cipolle)*. Mixed seafood hors d'œuvre *(antipasto di mare)* may include scampi, prawns *(gamberi)*, mussels *(cozze)*, fresh sardines *(sarde)*, but also squid *(calamari)*, and octopus *(polpi)*.

Ham from Parma or San Daniele (near Udine) is served paper thin with melon *(prosciutto con melone)* or, even better, fresh figs *(con fichi)*. Most salami is mass-produced industrial sausage from Milan, but try the local product of Florence, Genoa, Naples, and Bologna and look out for Ferrara's piquant *salame da sugo*.

Popular **soups** are mixed vegetable *(minestrone)*, clear soup *(brodo)*, and *brodo* with an egg beaten into it *(stracciatella)*.

Remember that Italian restaurants traditionally serve **pasta** as an introductory course, not as the main dish. While they won't kill you, even the friendliest restaurant owners will raise a sad eyebrow if you make a whole meal out of a plate of spaghetti.

It is said that there are as many different forms of Italian pasta noodles as there are French cheeses—some 360 at last count, with new forms being created every year. Each sauce—tomato, cheese, cream, meat, or fish—needs its own kind of noodle. In this land of painters and sculptors, the pasta's form is an essential part of the taste.

Besides spaghetti and macaroni, the worldwide popularity of pasta has familiarized us with *tagliatelle* ribbon noodles (known in Rome as *fettucine*), baked *lasagne* with layers of pasta, meat sauce, and béchamel, rolled *cannelloni*, and stuffed *ravioli*. From there, you launch into the lusty poetry of *tortellini* and *cappelletti* (variations on *ravioli*), or curved *linguine*, flat *pappardelle*, quill-shaped *penne*, and corrugated *rigatoni*. Discover the other 350 for yourselves.

And there are almost as many sauces. The most famous, of course, is *bolognese*, known more succinctly in Bologna itself as *ragù*. The best includes not only minced beef, tomato purée, and onions but chopped chicken livers, ham, carrot, celery, white wine and, vital ingredient in Bolognese cooking, nutmeg. Other popular sauces range from the simplest and spiciest *aglio e olio* (just garlic, olive oil, and chilli peppers), *marinara* (tomato), *carbonara* (chopped bacon and eggs), *matriciana* (salt pork and tomato), Genoese *pesto* (basil and garlic ground up in olive oil with pine nuts and parmesan cheese) and *vongole* (clams and tomato), to the succulent *lepre* (hare in red wine) and startling *al nero*, yes, pasta blackened by the ink of the cuttlefish—wonderful. Don't be ashamed to ask whether Parmesan cheese should or should not be added.

There's no shortage of meat in Italy. A waiter at the Savoy Hotel shows off a special cut.

For prince and peasant alike, the Po valley's rice fields have made **risotto** a worthy rival to pasta, particularly in and around Milan and Bergamo. The rice is cooked slowly in white wine, beef marrow, butter, and saffron, and served with Parmesan cheese. Delicious with mushrooms, chicken, or seafood.

For the main dish, veal *(vitello)* has pride of place among the **meats**. Try the pan-fried cutlet *(costoletta)* Milanese-style in breadcrumbs, *scaloppine al limone* (veal fillets with lemon), *vitello tonnato* (veal in tunny fish sauce), *alla fiorentina* (with a spinach sauce). The popular *saltimbocca* (literally "jump in the mouth") is an originally Roman veal-roll with ham, sage, and Marsala, while *osso buco* is stewed veal shinbone. You'll find calf's liver *(fegato)* served in a Marsala sauce, *alla milanese* in breadcrumbs, or *alla veneziana*, thinly sliced, fried with onions in olive oil.

Beef *(manzo)*, pork *(maiale)*, and lamb *(agnello)* are most often served straightforwardly, charcoal-grilled or roasted *(al forno)* but, particularly in the south where the beef may be less tender, the meat is cooked in a tomato and garlic sauce *(alla pizzaiola)*.

The most common **chicken** dishes are grilled *(pollo alla diavola)*, and fillets with ham and cheese *(petti di pollo alla bolognese)* or, like veal, in a tunny fish sauce *(tonnato)*.

All the **fish** that you see displayed as *antipasti* are prepared very simply, grilled, steamed, or fried. You should also look out for *spigola* (sea bass), *triglia* (red mullet), *pesce spada* (swordfish) and *coda di rospo* (angler fish). Be careful when ordering the *fritto misto*. Although this most often means a mixed fry of fish, it may be a mixture of breaded chicken breasts, calf's liver, veal and vegetables.

Aristocrats among the cooked **vegetables** are the big boletus mushrooms *(funghi porcini)*, which sometimes come stuffed *(ripieni)* with bacon, garlic, parsley, and cheese. Try red peppers stewed with tomatoes *(peperonata)* or aubergine *(melanzane)* stuffed with anchovies, olives, and capers. Baby onions *(cipolline)* and zucchini are both served sweet-and-sour *(agrodolce)*.

Of the **cheeses**, the famous Parmesan *(parmigiano)*, is eaten separately, not just grated over soup or pasta. Try, too, the blue *gorgonzola*, *provolone* buffalo cheese, creamy Piedmontese *fontina*, the pungent cow's milk *taleggio*, or ewe's milk *pecorino*. *Ricotta* can be sweetened with sugar and cinnamon.

Dessert means first and foremost *gelati*, the creamiest ice cream in the world. But it's usually better in an ice-cream parlour *(gelateria)* than in the average *trattoria*. Connoisseurs send you to Parma and Bologna for the best, but they lower their voices around Neapolitans. The delicious coffee- or fruit-flavoured *granita* is always refreshing.

Zuppa inglese (literally "English soup") may be an extremely thick soup of fruit and cream and cake and Marsala or just a very disappointing sickly slice of cake. You may prefer the coffee trifle or *tirami sù* ("pull me up"). The *zabaglione* of whipped egg yolks, sugar, and Marsala should be served warm or sent back.

Easier on the stomach is the fruit: grapes (*uva*), peaches (*pesche*), apricots (*albicocche*), and wonderful fresh figs (*fichi*), both black and green.

Regional Specialities

Though most regional delicacies have spread nationwide, a few specialities are still to be found principally in their place of origin.

Rome goes in for hearty meat dishes. If its *saltimbocca* veal-rolls have gone around the world, gourmets insist you mustn't wander too far from the Piazza Navona to get a real *stufatino* (beef stew) or *coda alla vaccinara* (oxtail braised with vegetables). Romans also claim the best roast kid (*capretto*) or spring lamb (*abbacchio*). The capital's Jewish Ghetto originated the spectacular *carciofi alla giudea*, whole artichokes, crisply deep-fried, stem, heart, leaves, and all.

Tuscany produces Italy's best chicken. Try *pollo alla cacciatora*, "hunter's style," with mushrooms, tomatoes, shallots, herbs, and strips of ham. The flavoursome charcoal-grilled T-bone or rib steak (*bistecca alla fiorentina*) is often big enough to cover a whole plate and will serve two people, very, very happily. Hearty stomachs enjoy the *trippe alla fiorentina*, tripe with tomato, marjoram, and parmesan cheese. On the coast, look out for the *cacciucco*, a spicy fish stew of red mullet, squid, and crab in tomatoes, onions, garlic, Chianti, and croûtons. *Baccalà* is a simpler but similarly spicy cod stew.

> Cooking is essentially regional. But the terminology may vary. There are at least half a dozen names for octopus or squid.

The cuisine of **Umbria** has great finesse. The roast pork (*porchetta*) is especially fragrant with fennel and other herbs, and look out for a succulent spit-roasted wild pigeon (*palombacce allo spiedo*). They are proud, too, of the *cacciot-*

_to_ and _raviggiolo_ ewe's cheese. In and around **Perugia**, the supreme pasta dish is spaghetti _ai tartufi neri_ (with black truffles). Especially at Christmas time, the traditional _cappelletti in brodo_ is served, a soup of ravioli stuffed with pork and veal.

Milan has contributed its risotto, breaded veal, _osso buco,_ and sweet _panettone_ brioche to the nation. But it's kept for itself and its more robust visitors

Fruit figures prominently in many of the fine desserts of Italy.

the _casoeula_, pork and sausages stewed in cabbage and other vegetables. Tough industrialists are weaned on _busecca alla milanese_, tripe with white beans. To fend off the autumn rains, the polenta maize flour bread served with so many savoury **Lombardy** dishes becomes, as _polenta pasticciata_, a stout pie of mushrooms and white truffles in a béchamel sauce.

The herbs of **Liguria** make for some superb pasta sauces, most famous of all, the basil of **Genoa's** _pesto_, best with the local _trenette_ (large-size spaghetti). Rosemary is sprinkled on flat rounds of bread, _focaccia_, with olive oil; and wild aromatic greens are pounded together with ricotta cheese to make a delicious stuffing for the ravioli-like _pansoti_, always served with walnut sauce. The harvest of the land is just as important as that of the sea. On trattoria menus, _misto di mare_ is followed by _misto di terra_.

Cooking in **Alto Adige** or South Tyrol is still predominantly Austria-style and in German on the menu. The home-cured ham, _Speck_, is often served in the farmhouse manner, a chunk on a wooden board with a sharp knife for you to cut it yourself in paper-thin slices. Up in the mountains, you'll appreciate the _Knödelsuppe_, a chicken or beef broth with dumplings of flour, bread crumbs, onions, bacon, parsley, and garlic. Austria meets Italy with *Spinat-spätzle*, gnocchi-like spinach noodles with bacon and cream. **Friuli-Venezia Giulia** also continues the cuisine of the Austro-Hungarian empire—goulash and barley soup. And here, the great ham is San Daniele. In **Trieste**, the seafood is excellent and the desserts, they claim, as good as Vienna's, especially the apple *Strudel* and almond *mandorlato*.

In **Venice**, when you see someone smacking a cod against a gondola's mooring post, likely as not it's being "tenderized" for the great *baccalà mantecato* (cream of dried cod), a smoother version of the French *brandade de morue*. The *grancevole*, beautiful red Adriatic spider crabs, are treated more delicately as a centrepiece of Venetian seafood. Risotto is as popular here as in Lombardy, particularly with scampi or mussels, as well as the delightfully named *risi e bisi*, rice and green peas. An original creation of Harry's Bar, rendezvous of the international smart set down by the Grand Canal, beef *carpaccio* is sliced raw and thin as Parma ham and served with an olive oil and mustard sauce. During Carnival time, have the mussel soup (*zuppa di peoci*) to resist the February mists. But **Ravenna** can lay claim to the Adriatic's most bracing fish soup, *brodetto*, full of sea bass, squid, eel, red mullet, and all kinds of shellfish.

Bologna has a position of leadership in Italian gastronomy similar to that of Lyon in France. Its old specialities are now the mainstays of the national cuisine, but some things are just not as good away from home: *tortellini* pasta coils stuffed with minced pork, veal, chicken, and cheese; *costolette alla bolognese* (breaded veal cutlets with ham and cheese); and the monumental *lasagne verde*, baked green pasta with beef *ragù*, béchamel sauce, and the all-important nutmeg. The key to the classic Bologna *mortadella* sausage is the flavouring of white wine and coriander. One of the great rice dishes of **Parma** is the *bomba di riso*, pigeons cooked in a risotto with their livers and giblets, tomato purée, and, of course, parmesan. Parma's *prosciutto* (raw ham) is world famous. Real Parmesan cheese must be labelled *parmigiano-reggiano*.

Turin is famous for its *bollita*, a most aristocratic boiled beef dish, with sausage, chicken, white beans, cabbage, potatoes, and a tomato sauce. Not to be confused with the *fondue* from across the Swiss border, the *fonduta* of **Piedmont** is a

How could you resist stopping for lunch at a tempting trattoria like this?

hot dip of buttery *fontina* cheese, cream, pepper, and white truffles (more delicate than black).

In **Naples**, the tomato has been king since the Spaniards brought it here from America in the 16th century. It's there, deliciously, in the simplest pasta, the thinner *vermicelli* for which *alla napolitana* just means with a tomato sauce. And it dominates the greatest not-so-fast food ever invented, the *pizza*, for which the classic version also includes anchovies *(acciughe)*, mozzarella cheese, and oregano. A handy, purely local version is the *calzone*, pocket-size pizzas filled with ham and mozzarella and folded over in a half-moon. The seafood is excellent, especially the sea bass *(spigola)*, swordfish *(pesce spada)*, squid *(calamari),* and octopus *(polpi)*. Have your morning coffee with a crisp Neapolitan *sfogliatella* croissant filled with sweet ricotta cheese.

The lamb of **Puglia** is a royal dish. Try the *agnello allo squero* spit-roasted on a fire of twigs perfumed with thyme and fine herbs; or *cutturidde*, baked with onion, parsley, tomatoes, and sprinkled with pecorino cheese. *Gnemeridde* are chitterlings of baby lamb roasted or stewed with ham, cheese, and herbs. On the Adriatic coast

Wash down a bite of local cheese with some regional wine.

and the Gulf of Taranto, the seafood is excellent: squid and octopus in Bari, red mullet in Polignano, oysters and mussels in Taranto. Two great fish soups: Gallipoli's sweet-and-sour with shellfish and white fish in a bouillon of tomatoes, onions and vinegar; or Brindisi's spicier version with sea bream, eel, squid, and mussels.

The coastal resorts of **Sardinia** cook up a pungent fish soup *(cassola è pisci)* and roast eel *(anguidda arrustia)*. Inland, kid *(capretto)* and suckling pig *(porceddù)* are roasted on the spit, as is the island's greatest delicacy, wild boar *(cinghiale)*.

There's a great variety of country bread, the best being the charcoal-baked *civriaxiu*. Try it with the local *pecorino* ewe's cheese.

Wines

Italian wine is more than just Chianti, but it wouldn't be a catastrophe if that's all it was. The best Chianti Classico produced in an area of 70,875 hectares (175,000 acres) between Florence and Siena (page 101) and distinguished by the *gallo nero* (black cockerel) label will please most discerning palates. In a Bordeaux-style bottle, it's a wedium-bodied red with a fine bouquet. Whereas most Italian wines can and should be drunk young, the Chianti Classico ages very well.

The best of the other Chianti reds, some in the familiar fat basket-bottles, are *Rufina, Montalbano,* and *Brolio,* distinguished by a cherub on the neck labels. While straw is no guarantee of quality and authenticity, it's a fair rule-of-thumb that if the bottle's basket is plastic, the contents are similarly mass-produced and characterless. Of the other Tuscany wines, the most appreciated reds are the earthy *Montepulciano* and rather dry *Brunello di Montalcino*. The best of the whites are the *Montecarlo* and *Vernaccia di San Gimignano*, both dry.

Orvieto in Umbria produces superb white wines, both dry and semi-dry. East of Rome in the Alban Hills is the refreshingly light *Frascati*. The famous *Est! Est! Est!* comes from Montefiascone on Lake Bolsena.

The very popular wines are centred around Verona and Lake Garda, notably the velvety *Valpolicella*, light and fruity, and the light *Bardolino*. *Soave* is a dry white with a faint almond flavour. The rosé *Chiaretto* comes from south of Lake Garda and another rosé, *Pinot Grigio*, from Treviso.

Piedmont boasts some of Italy's finest reds, particularly the powerful, full-bodied *Barolo*, with a slight raspberry tang. *Barbera* has a lot of bouquet and tends to referment in the bottle, producing a slight "fizz" that horrifies Frenchmen and delights Italians. The *Barbera* that's exported doesn't usually fizz. Watch for the word *frizzante* on the label if you like it sparkling. The *Barbaresco* is the lightest of Piedmont reds. From south of Turin comes the sparkling *Asti spumante*.

The *trulli* country of Puglia turns out some first-class white wines, notably *Locorotondo* and *Martina Franca*. Castel del Monte produces fine red, white, and rosé wines. If you like sweet wines, try Trani's *Moscato*.

Among apéritifs, bitters such as *Campari* and *Punt e Mes* are refreshing with soda and lemon. For after-dinner **drinks**, try the anise-flavoured *sambuca* with a *mosca* (literally a fly) coffee-bean swimming in it, or *grappa* distilled from grapes. Among the best are *grappa moscato* and *grappa di Barolo*.

INDEX

HANDY TRAVEL TIPS

An A–Z Summary of Practical Information

A

ACCOMMODATION (See also CAMPING)

Hotels, called *hotel* or *albergo*, are classified in categories by stars from five (luxury) down to one. Minimum prices in cities, where most hotels are open all year round, are usually charged from November to April; in seaside or lakeside resorts, where many establishments are open only half the year, the low season is May–June and September in the north, a month earlier and later in the south. Breakfast is usually optional, but during high season, many resort hotels require guests to stay a minimum of three nights on half-board terms.

Pensioni. The term *pensione* encompasses everything from simple, family-style boarding houses to comfortable small hotels (breakfast included). These establishments are also rated by stars. A *locanda* is an inexpensive country inn, providing basic accommodation. Full-board *(pensione completa)* or half-board *(mezza pensione)* may be offered.

Motels in Italy are increasing in number and improving in service. Many have a swimming pool or private beach, tennis courts, and more.

Religious institutions. Some monasteries and convents take in guests at very reasonable rates. They provide comfortable rooms as well as meals. For information, write to the tourist board in the region of your choice (for addresses, see page 242).

Self-catering accommodation. Families staying for a week or longer in one locality may find it more convenient and economical, especially in tourist resorts, to hire a furnished apartment *(appartamento ammobiliato)* or villa. Many tour operators offer self-catering packages which include travel to and from Italy. Lists of operators are available from the Italian National Tourist Office (see page 242).

You can also stay on a **farm** in Italy, in a spartan cottage, a modern farmhouse, or a 17th-century castle, and enjoy threshing, grape-harvesting or mushroom-gathering, fishing, horse riding, golf. Contact Agriturist, the National Association for Rural Tourism:

Corso Vittorio Emanuele 101, 00186 Rome; Tel. (06) 685 23 42.

The Italian Alpine Club (CAI) owns several hundred **mountain huts**, and both this organization and the Italian Touring Club (TCI) publish books with detailed information. Write to:

Club Alpino Italiano, Via Ugo Foscolo 3, 20121 Milan; Tel. (02) 86 43 80/80 57 519

Touring Club Italiano, Corso Italia 10, 20122 Milan; Tel. (02) 852 61

Youth and student hostels. Italy's 50-plus youth hostels *(ostello della gioventù)* are open to holders of membership cards issued by the International Youth Hostels Federation. Book well in advance. Cards and information are available from your national youth hostels association and from the Associazione Italiana Alberghi per la Gioventù (AIG), the Italian Youth Hostels Association, at:

Via Cavour 44, 00184 Rome; Tel. (06) 46 23 42, (06) 474 12 56

Do you have any vacancies?	***Avete camere libere?***
I'd like a single/double room.	***Vorrei una camera singola/doppia.***
with bath/shower/private toilet	***con bagno/doccia/gabinetto privato***
What's the rate per night/week?	***Qual è il prezzo per una notte/una settimana?***

AIRPORTS *(aeroporto)*

Rome and Milan are Italy's principal gateway cities, but scheduled international flights also operate to Genoa, Naples, Turin, Venice, and other major centres.

Rome is served by two international airports, Leonardo da Vinci, commonly referred to as Fiumicino, about 30 km (18 miles) southwest of the city centre, and Ciampino, 15 km (10 miles) southeast. Fiumicino is mainly used for scheduled air traffic, while Ciampino mostly serves charter flights. Fiumicino has two terminals, one for domestic and one for international traffic.

Buses leave Fiumicino every 15 minutes from 7 a.m. to 9:30 p.m., every half-hour until midnight and each hour between midnight and 7 a.m. for the city air terminal in Via Giovanni Giolitti 36, just around the corner from Stazione Termini, Rome's main railway station. From Ciampino, there is a (fairly infrequent) bus connection to Anagnina, where you can pick up the underground/subway (Line A) to Stazione Termini.

Italy

Airport information:

  Fiumicino   (06) 6 01 21   Ciampino (06) 46 94

Milan has two airports, Malpensa, 45 km (28 miles) northwest of the city centre, for intercontinental traffic, and Linate, about 10 km (6 miles) to the east, mainly for domestic and European flights. There is a bus service to Milan's central railway station, Stazione Centrale, about every 20 minutes from Linate and a less regular one from Malpensa.

  Alitalia, airline information   54 56

  Taxi fares from airports to the respective city centres are approximately ten times higher than the bus fares.

C

CAMPING

There are more than 2,000 official campsites *(campeggio)* in Italy. Addresses and full details of amenities are given in the directory *Campeggi in Italia,* published annually by the Italian Touring Club (TCI). The directory is on sale in bookstores in Italy. A free list of sites, with location map, published by the Federcampeggio *(Federazione Italiana del Campeggio e del Caravanning),* is available from the Italian National Tourist Office (see page 242) or from Federcampeggio:

Via Vittorio Emanuele 11, P.O. Box 23, 50041 Calenzano (Florence); Tel. (055) 882 391

  The *International Camping Carnet,* a pass that entitles holders to modest discounts and insurance coverage throughout Europe, is required at many campsites in Italy. It can be obtained through your camping or automobile association or through the TCI or Federcampeggio.

  It is inadvisable to camp outside official sites. If you do so, at least choose sites where there are other campers, and always obtain the permission from the owner of the property or ask at the local police station or tourist office.

Is there a campsite near here?	**C'è un campeggio qui vicino?**
Have you room for a tent/caravan (trailer)?	**C'è posto per una tenda/roulotte?**
May we camp here?	**Possiamo campeggiare qui?**

CAR HIRE

The major international car rental companies are listed in the yellow pages of the telephone directory under "Autonoleggio." Local firms generally offer lower rates, but the car may have to be returned to the starting point. Weekend rates and weekly unlimited mileage rates are usually available, and it's worth inquiring about any seasonal deals. There are also some bargains to be had if you book your car together with your plane ticket or hotel package, or order it in advance through your automobile association or a company in your home country.

To hire a car, you must show your driving licence and passport or national identity card. The minimum age is 21 or 25 depending on the company and the car's engine size or even 30 if a particularly expensive car is involved. And you must have held a licence for at least one year. A substantial deposit is usually required unless you hold a credit card recognized by the rental firm. Third-party insurance is included.

I'd like to hire a car.	***Vorrei noleggiare una macchina.***
for one day/a week	***per un giorno/una settimana***
Do you have any special rates?	***Avete tariffe particolari?***
I want full insurance coverage.	***Voglio l'assicurazione completa.***

CLIMATE and CLOTHING

In the Alpine region, winters are long and cold, but often sunny, while summers are short and pleasantly cool. The northern lakes and the Po valley see cold and foggy winters and warm and sunny summers. The rest of the country, even the Ligurian coast, enjoys mild weather in winter. Summers are dry and hot to scorching depending on how far south you go, but sea breezes often compensate for the torrid heat.

The best time for a visit to the Ligurian and northern Adriatic coasts is May/June to September. Before or after this period it can be rather chilly. Many hotels will be closed and the resorts and beaches practically deserted. The best time to visit the cities of Italy is in spring or autumn—between April and June and again in September—when the weather is most pleasant and the streets less crowded.

If you're travelling in northern Italy in winter, you'll need boots and an overcoat, but in the south a lightweight coat will be adequate. During early spring and late autumn, you should bring light- to medium-weight clothing and rainwear for those brief but torrential showers. Summer evenings can be cool, so don't forget to pack a jacket or wrap. All year-round, comfortable walking shoes are indispensable.

Average daily temperatures in degrees Fahrenheit:

		J	F	M	A	M	J	J	A	S	O	N	D
Milan	max.	40	46	56	65	74	80	84	82	75	63	51	43
	min.	32	35	43	49	57	63	67	66	61	52	43	35
Rome	max.	52	55	59	66	74	82	87	86	79	71	61	55
	min.	40	42	45	50	55	63	67	67	62	55	48	44
Naples	max.	53	55	59	65	72	79	84	84	79	71	63	57
	min.	40	41	44	48	54	61	65	65	61	54	48	44

and in degrees Celsius:

		J	F	M	A	M	J	J	A	S	O	N	D
Milan	max.	5	8	13	18	23	27	29	28	24	17	10	6
	min.	0	2	6	10	14	17	26	19	16	11	6	2
Rome	max.	11	13	15	19	23	28	30	26	22	16	13
	min.	5	5	7	10	13	17	20	20	17	13	9	6
Naples	max.	12	13	15	18	22	26	29	29	26	22	17	14
	min.	5	5	6	9	12	16	18	18	16	12	9	6

COMMUNICATIONS

Post offices (*posta or ufficio postale*), identified by the "PT" sign, handle telegrams, mail, and money transfers. They are generally open from 8:15 or 8:30 a.m. to 2 or 2:30 p.m. (main post offices till around 8 p.m.), Monday to Friday, closing at 11:45 a.m. on Saturdays and on the last day of the month.

Postage stamps can also be purchased at tobacconists and at some hotels. Letter boxes are painted red; the slot marked "Per la Città" is for local mail, while the one labelled "Altre Destinazioni" is for all other destinations .

Poste Restante/General Delivery. You can have mail addressed to you in any town c/o Fermo Posta. In municipalities with more than one post office, it will be sent to the main post office (ufficio postale centrale)—address it to the office at Piazza San Silvestro in Rome, to Via Pellicceria in Florence, to Piazza Edison in Milan, to Piazza Matteotti in Naples, to Rialto in Venice. You'll have to show identification to retrieve mail. A small fee is charged for the service.

Telegrams (*telegramma*). All post offices accept domestic and international telegrams. You can also dictate a telegram over the phone (dial 186). Italcable sends messages abroad both by radio and telegraph.

Telephone (*telefono*). The older type of public phone takes tokens (*gettoni*) available at bars, tobacconists, and from automatic dispensers installed in some call boxes (phone booths). Either gettoni or coins may be used in the modern type of public phone, equipped with two separate slots. You can make direct international calls from telephones labelled "Teleselezione": be sure to have a reserve of coins or tokens. It may be more convenient to go to a major post office or main railway station.

Some telephones are card-operated. Phone cards (*scheda telefonica*) are available at SIP (*Società Italiana per l'Esercizio Telefonico*) offices, where you can also make long-distance and international calls; they are usually open from 7 a.m. to around 10 p.m.

Area codes for main cities: Bari 080, Bologna 051, Catania 095, Florence 055, Genoa 010, Messina 090, Milan 02, Naples 081, Palermo 091, Rome 06, Turin 011, Trieste 040, Venice 041, Verona 045. Drop the "0" when dialling Italy from abroad.

To make a direct international call, dial 00 and wait for a change of tone before dialling the country's code, area code, and subscriber's number. To telephone Italy from abroad, dial the international access code, followed by 39.

Charges for international phone calls are reduced by about 30% between 11 p.m. and 8 a.m. on weekdays and all day on Sundays.

Where's the nearest post office?	***Dov'è l'ufficio postale più vicino?***
A stamp for this letter/ postcard, please.	***Un francobollo per questa lettera/cartolina, per favore.***

COMPLAINTS

In hotels, restaurants, and shops, complaints should be made directly to the manager (*direttore*) or proprietor (*proprietario*). The threat of formal declaration to the police should be effective in such cases as overcharging for car repairs (but carrying out the threat could consume days of your visit). Arguments over taxi fares can usually be settled by referring to the notice affixed by law in each taxi, specifying charges in excess of the meter rate.

CRIME and THEFT

Cases of violence against tourists are rare, but petty theft is an endless annoyance, and tourists are always easy targets for robbery.

Check whether your home insurance policy covers theft or loss of personal effects while abroad; if it does not, it is advisable to take out separate insurance.

Italy

Carry as much of your money as possible in the form of traveller's cheques.

Leave documents in the hotel safe, and keep what you take, including credit cards, in an inside pocket or a pouch inside your clothes.

Don't carry your handbag slung loosely over your street-side shoulder; it could be ripped off by thieves on motorbikes or in cars.

Make photocopies of your tickets, driving licence, passport, and other vital documents to facilitate reporting a theft and obtaining replacements.

Never leave anything of value in your car when parked, not even in the boot (trunk), particularly in urban areas.

Any loss or theft should be reported at once to the nearest police station—for insurance purposes.

I want to report a theft.	***Voglio denunciare un furto.***
My ticket/wallet/passport/handbag/ credit card has been stolen.	***Mi hanno rubato il mio biglietto/ porta foglio/passaporto/la mia borsetta/carta di credito.***

CUSTOMS *(dogana)* and ENTRY REGULATIONS

Visitors from EU countries, Austria, Liechtenstein, Malta, and Switzerland need only a national identity card to enter Italy. For nationals of other Western European countries, North America, Australia, New Zealand, and Japan, a passport is required. Visitors from other countries may need a visa: check with your travel agent or nearest Italian consulate before you leave home.

The chart below shows what main items you can take into Italy duty free (note that allowances are subject to change at short notice).

For what you can bring back home, ask before your departure for the customs notice setting out allowances.

	Cigarettes		Cigars		Tobacco	Spirits		Wine
1)	200	or	150	or	250 grams	2 liters	or	2 liters
2)	200	or	50	or	250 grams	2 liters	or	2 liters

1) Residents of non-European countries.
2) Residents of Europe, entering from a non-EU country.
Gifts: L. 1) and 2) L.67,000.

Currency restrictions. You may import unlimited amounts in foreign currencies or lire, but to take the equivalent of more than L. 20,000,000 in or out of the country, you must complete a V2 declaration form at the point of entry.

I've nothing to declare.	***Non ho nullo da dichiarare.***
It's for my personal use.	***È per mio uso personale.***

D

DRIVING

To take a car into Italy, you should have:
- a valid national driving licence accompanied by a translation (free from automobile associations) or an International Driving Permit. The pink EU licence, without translation, is accepted in Italy
- car registration papers
- Green Card (an extension to your regular insurance policy, making it valid specifically for Italy); if you plan to stay in Italy for more than 45 days, you must take out Italian insurance
- a red warning triangle (to be placed at least 30 metres (100 feet) behind the car)
- a national identity sticker for both cars and caravans (trailers).

You must be at least 18 years old to drive a car in Italy. Drivers of motorcycles need the same documents as car drivers. A driving licence for motorcycles is required for two-wheelers over 49 cc.

Drivers entering Italy in a car not their own must have the owner's written permission. One-axle caravans may be no wider than 2.3 metres (7.5 feet) and no longer than 6 metres (19.6 feet), including the tow hook, while for two-axle caravans, the maximum width allowed is 2.5 metres (8.2 feet) and the maximum length 7.5 metres (24.6 feet). The maximum height is 3 metres (9.8 feet).

Fuel and oil (*benzina; olio*). Before leaving home, check with your automobile association about the latest regulations concerning petrol (gasoline) coupons giving tourists driving foreign-registered cars the right to buy fuel at a discount in Italy.

Petrol stations—most have a self-service pump—generally provide full service from 7 a.m. to 12:30 p.m. and from 3 to 7:30 p.m. in summer, closing half an hour earlier in winter. Many close on Sundays. Stations along the motorways are open 24 hours a day. Attendants expect a tip for special attention.

Speed limits in Italy are currently as follows (in km/h): Cars towing caravans (trailers) : 80 km/h on main roads, 100 km/h on motorways. Motorcycles: Less than 100 cc, 80 km/h maximum speed, not allowed on motorways; 100 to 149 cc, 90 km/h maximum speed, not allowed on motorways; more than 150 cc, as for cars.

Rules of the road. Drive on the right, overtake (pass) on the left. When overtaking or remaining in the left-hand lane, keep your directional indicator flashing. Where roads of similar importance intersect, the car on the right has priority.

Road conditions. The ACI (Automobile Club d'Italia) operates a 24-hour telephone assistance centre staffed with multi-lingual personnel who give information on road and weather conditions, petrol coupons, hotels, and so on. Dial 4477 (preceded by area code 06 if you call from outside Rome).

The *autostrada* network covers approximately 6,000 km (3,700 miles). Access signposts are green. A toll, varying according to vehicle size and distance travelled, is charged on most stretches except on sections near the largest cities and in certain areas in the south.

Accidents and breakdowns. To report an accident, dial the all-purpose emergency number 113. There are emergency telephones on the motorways. Some have separate buttons for technical problems (indicated by a monkey wrench) and injuries (a red cross); press the button until a lamp lights up and wait for help.

If you break down on any road in Italy, you can dial 116 for ACI assistance. You will, however, be charged, so it's a good idea to take out international breakdown insurance before leaving home.

Parking. In cities, the wisest course is to find a supervised parking place (*parcheggio custodito*) near your hotel and leave your car there for the duration of your stay. There are authorized parking areas (*parcheggio a pagamento*), often near the main railway station, where you pay by the hour, as well as car parks (parking lots) outside the centre with bus connections into town. Many larger towns have multi-level parking garages (*autorimessa* or *garage*). In a "Zona Disco," you need a parking disc (*disco di sosta*), obtainable from service stations. Set it to show the time you arrived and it will indicate when you have to leave. Then display it in the car, visible through the windscreen. Don't leave your car in places marked by yellow-and-black stripes, or where it says "Zona Rimozione" (removal zone), "Zona Verde" (green zone), or "Zona Pedonale" (pedestrian zone), or in a "Sosta Vietata" (no parking) or "Divieto di Sosta" (no stopping) zone; if you park there, it may be towed away.

Never leave valuables in a parked car and never leave the glove compartment open.

Road signs. Most road signs used in Italy are international pictographs. Below are some written ones you may come across:

Accendere le luci/i fari (in galleria)	*Use headlights (in tunnel)*
Deviazione	*Diversion (Detour)*
Pedaggio	*Toll*
Pericolo	*Danger*
Rallentare	*Slow down*
Senso unico	*One-way street*
Senso vietato/Vietato l'ingresso	*No entry*
Uscita	*Exit*

E

ELECTRIC CURRENT

In general, it is 220-volt, 50-cycle A.C., but 125-volt outlets still exist. The voltage might be indicated on the socket in hotels, but it is best to ask. Voltage transformers can be purchased in electrical appliance shops in Italy, but it is probably easier to obtain one before leaving home. Italian plugs are round, so you may also need an adaptor plug.

What's the voltage —125 or 220?	***Qual è il voltaggio —centoventicinque o duecentoventi?***
an adaptor plug	***una presa multipla***
a voltage transformer	***un trasformatore***

Italy

EMBASSIES and CONSULATES *(ambasciata; consolato)*

Contact the embassy or consulate of your home country when in trouble (loss of passport, problems with the police, serious accidents). All embassies are in Rome, while many countries also maintain consulates in other Italian cities. Embassies in Rome (prefix 06):

Australia	Via Alessandria 21/5; tel. 852 721
Canada	Via G. Battista de Rossi 27; tel. 445 981
Eire	Largo Nazareno 3; tel. 67 82 541
New Zealand	Via Zara 28; tel. 440 29 28
South Africa	Via Tanaro 14; tel. 841 97 94
U.K.	Via XX Settembre 80a; tel. 482 544 411
U.S.A.	Via Vittorio Veneto 119; tel. 487 02 35

EMERGENCIES

Unless you are dialling 116, a multilingual service, enlist the help of someone who speaks Italian, as you have to give your name and whereabouts.

Can you place an emergency call for me to the...?	***Può fare per me una telefonata d'emergenza...?***
fire brigade	***ai pompieri***
hospital	***all'ospedale***
police	***alla polizia***

G

GETTING TO ITALY

By Air

Scheduled flights. Rome's Leonardo da Vinci (Fiumicino) and Milan's Linate and Malpensa airports (see page 221) are the main gateways to Italy, though certain direct, scheduled international flights operate into Bologna, Genoa, Naples, Pisa , Turin, Venice, Sardinia, and Sicily. From Milan and Rome there are regular scheduled flights to some 30 destinations within Italy.

The most economical ticket on scheduled flights is the Super APEX midweek (limited length of stay), which must be booked two to four weeks before departure.

Package tours are offered by a wide range of tour operators and travel agents. The majority of package tours from overseas start out in Rome and include a choice of guided tours throughout the country. If you book a charter fare and plan to tour Italy independently, look into fly-drive possibilities with flight and car hire included. The Italian National Tourist Office (see page 242) distributes lists of tour operators offering package tours and special-interest holidays, including language, art, and architecture courses.

By Road (See also DRIVING)

The main access roads from France to Italy lead via the Mont Blanc (Monte Bianco) Tunnel (12 km/7.5 miles), Fréjus Tunnel (13 km/8 miles, between Grenoble and Turin), and Côte d'Azur (French Riviera) motorway to Genoa. Alpine border passes between France and Italy are the Little St. Bernard Pass (Col du Petit St.-Bernard/ Colle del Piccolo San Bernardo), c. 2,100 metres/6,890 feet, between Bourg St-Maurice and Aosta, the Col du Mont Cenis (Colle del Moncenisio), c. 2,000 metres/6,562 feet, between Lanslebourg and Susa, Col du Montgenèvre (Colle del Monginevro), c. 1,900 metres/6,234 feet, between Briançon and Cesana, Col de Larche (Colle della Maddalena), c. 2,000 metres/6,562 feet, between Larche and Vinadio, and Col de Tende (Colle di Tenda), c. 1,900 metres/6,234 feet, between the French Riviera and Cuneo.

From Switzerland to Italy, you could take one of the following tunnels: Great St. Bernard *(Grand St. Bernard/Gran San Bernardo)* 7 km/4.5 miles, St. Gotthard *(San Gottardo)* c. 16 km/10 miles or San Bernardino c. 7 km/4.5 miles, continuing down to Lake Como. Or cross one of the border passes: Great St. Bernard (c. 2,500 metres/ 8,202 feet), Simplon (Sempione; c. 2,000 metres/ 6,562 feet), Splügen (Spluga; c. 1,800 metres/5,906 feet), or Bernina (c. 2,300 metres/7,546 feet).

If you are driving through Austria, the main access road crosses the Brenner *(Brennero)* Pass (c. 1,300 metres/4,265 feet) between Innsbruck and Vipiteno. There is also the Reschen *(Resia)* Pass (c. 1,500 metres/4,921 feet) between Landeck and Merano, and the Plöcken *(Monte Croce Carnico)* Pass (c. 1,300 metres/4,265 feet) between Oberdrauburg and Tolmezzo, or the Number 100/S49/S51 road from Lienz to Cortina d'Ampezzo.

Italy

From the U.K. and Eire, the shortest Channel crossings are the Dover-Calais/Boulogne and Folkestone-Calais/Boulogne routes. If you'd prefer to drive through Belgium, Germany, and Switzerland or Austria, take the ferry from Dover to Ostend or Zeebrugge. From Boulogne, Paris, and Cologne, you can put your car on a train to Milan. If you drive across the Continent yourself, you will find that the excellent motorway network takes you to the toe of Italy without your ever leaving a motorway.

Car ferries connect Italy with France (Porto Torres, Sardinia-Toulon), Malta, Tunisia, Yugoslavia, Greece, Turkey, and Egypt.

Regular coach services operate from major cities on the Continent, as well as from London, to a number of destinations in Italy.

By Rail (See also TRANSPORT)

Ferrovie dello Stato (FS), Italian State Railways, offices will help tourists travelling by rail to plan an itinerary:

Canada—2055 Peel Street, Montreal, Que. H3A IV4, tel. (514) 845 91 01; 111 Avenue Road, Concourse Level, Toronto, Ont. M5R 3J8, tel. (416) 927 7712

U.K.—50, Conduit Street, London WIR 9FB, tel. (01) 434 3844

U.S.A.—500 North Michigan Avenue, Suite 1310, Chicago, IL 60611, tel. (312) 644 09 90; 6033 West Century Boulevard, Suite 1090, Los Angeles, CA 90045, tel. (213) 215 98 14; 342 Madison Avenue, Suite 207, New York, NY 10173, tel. (212) 697-1482 or (800) 248-7245. Travellers from countries where the FS is not represented should contact their national railways or a travel agency.

The European national railways offer a wide range of bargain tickets. Many of the railpasses mentioned below must be obtained before leaving home.

The *Eurailpass,* an individual ticket available to people residing outside Europe, is valid for first-class unlimited rail travel in 16 European countries (Austria, Belgium, Denmark, Eire, Finland, France, West Germany, Greece, Italy, Luxembourg, the Netherlands, Norway, Portugal, Spain, Sweden, and Switzerland), including travel on some private railways, buses, and many ferry boats and steamers. The *Eurail Saverpass* is a special first-class ticket for two or more people travelling (two or more between October 1 and March 31), while the *Eurail Flexipass,* for North Americans, Mexicans, Australians, and New Zealanders (also for first class), offers more flexibility for ten days' travel within a two-month period. The *Eurail Youthpass* for those under 26 years of age allows one or two months of unlimited second-class rail travel. Surcharges are imposed on fast trains like EuroCity (EC), Intercity (IC), Rapido (R) and TGV, and for certain ferry crossings during high season.

For residents of European countries, there's the *Rail Europ S* (RES) ticket, which entitles senior citizens to purchase train tickets at reduced prices. A family of at least three people can buy a *Rail Europ F* card; the holder pays full fare, the rest of the family obtains a 50% reduction. The whole family is also entitled to a 30% reduction on Sealink and Hoverspeed Channel crossings. Europeans under 26 years of age can purchase an *Inter-Rail* card, good for one month of unlimited second-class travel.

Anyone permanently residing outside Italy can buy the *Biglietto Turistico di Libera Circolazione* (BTLC) for unlimited first- or second-class rail travel during 8, 15, 21, or 30 days. With this ticket there are no supplements on Intercity or Rapido trains, and no extra charge is made for seat reservations. The *Biglietto Chilometrico* is valid for two months of first- or second-class travel. It can be used by as many as five people, even if not related, for 20 trips totalling a maximum of 3,000 km (1,864 miles), with supplements for Rapido and Intercity trains.

GUIDES and TOURS

Local tourist offices and major hotels can help you find qualified guides and give you a list of guided tours.

The Italian tourist agency CIT and many private firms offer morning, afternoon, half- and full-day city sightseeing tours, plus excursions to many points of interest.

Can you recommend a sightseeing tour/an excursion?	***Può consigliare un giro turistico/una gita?***
We'd like an English-speaking guide.	***Desideriamo una guida che parla inglese***

H

HEALTH and MEDICAL CARE

If your health-insurance policy does not cover you while abroad, take out a short-term policy with your insurance company, automobile association, or travel agency before leaving home. Visitors from EU countries with corresponding health-insurance facilities are entitled to medical and

Italy

hospital treatment under the Italian social security system. Before leaving home, ensure that you are eligible and have the appropriate forms.

If you need medical care, ask your hotel receptionist to help you find a doctor (or dentist) who speaks English. Throughout Italy, in an emergency you can telephone 113 (the national police) for an ambulance.

Tap water is safe to drink unless there is a sign reading "Acqua Non Potabile."

Pharmacies. The Italian farmacia is generally open from 8:30 a.m. to 1 p.m. and from 4 to 8 p.m. At least one in each district or locality operates on a rotating basis during the afternoon break, at night, and at weekends. The addresses and opening hours of pharmacies on duty appear on every pharmacy door and in the local papers.

Bring to Italy an adequate supply of any prescribed medication.

Where's the nearest (all-night) pharmacy?	*Dov'è la farmacia (di turno) più vicina?*
I need a doctor/dentist.	*Ho bisogno di un medico/dentista.*

L

LANGUAGE

Standard Italian is understood by most Italians, though many different dialects are spoken. Some, like Venetian, show Slavic and Illyrian influences, while others have affinities with French. Sardinian is so different it's virtually a separate language.

Staff at the major hotels and shops in the big cities and resort areas usually speak some English. Most Italians appreciate foreigners making an effort to communicate in their language, even if it's only a few words.

Just bear in mind the following tips on pronunciation:

"c" is pronounced like "ch" in change when it is followed by an "e" or an "i"

"ch" together sounds like the "c" in cat

"g" followed by an "e" or an "i" is pronounced like "j" in jet

"gh" together sounds like the "g" in gap

"gl" together sounds like "lli" in million

"gn" is pronounced like "ni" in onion.

The Berlitz phrase book ITALIAN FOR TRAVELLERS covers almost all the situations you're likely to encounter in your travels in Italy. Also useful is the Berlitz Italian-English/English-Italian Pocket Dictionary, which contains the basic vocabulary a tourist will need, plus a menu-reader supplement.

LOST PROPERTY

Cynics say anything lost in Italy is lost forever, but that's not necessarily true. Restaurants more often than not will have the briefcase, guide book, or camera you left behind waiting for you at the cashier's desk. If you're not sure where the loss occurred, have your hotel receptionist call the lost-property office *(ufficio oggetti rinvenuti* or *smarriti)*. Report the loss of your passport or identity papers to your embassy or consulate.

In Rome, lost objects usually end up at the Ufficio Oggetti Rinvenuti at Via Bettoni, 1 (tel. 58 16 040).

I've lost my handbag/ passport/wallet.	***Ho perso la mia borsetta/il mio passaporto/il mio portafoglio.***

MAPS

Tourist offices give away basic street plans featuring a selection of local information. More detailed maps are on sale at newsstands.

I'd like a street plan of ... a road map of this region	***Vorrei una pianta della città una carta stradale di questa regione.***

MONEY MATTERS

Currency. Italy's monetary unit is the lira (plural lire, abbreviated L. or Lit.).

Coins: L. 5, 10, 20, 50, 100, 200, 500.
Banknotes: L. 1,000, 2,000, 5,000, 10,000, 50,000, 100,000.

For currency restrictions, see CUSTOMS AND ENTRY REGULATIONS.

Banks and currency exchange. Most banks are open from 8:30 a.m. to 1:30 p.m. and from 2:30 to 4 p.m., Monday to Friday, though hours may vary. Money can be changed at currency-exchange offices *(ufficio di cambio)* in main railway stations and airports. However, the rate of exchange tends to be less advantageous than that offered by banks. The same applies to foreign currency or traveller's cheques changed in hotels, shops or restaurants.

Credit cards, traveller's cheques, Eurocheques. Most hotels, many shops, service stations, and restaurants honour the major international credit cards. Traveller's cheques and Eurocheques are accepted in cities and tourist resorts. Outside the towns, it's best to have some cash handy. Take your passport or national identity card along when you go to cash a cheque.

Sales tax. A VAT or sales tax of 9 to 38% is imposed on most goods and services in Italy.

Tax refunds. Foreign visitors residing outside the EU will be refunded the IVA paid on larger purchases made in shops displaying the "Italy Tax Free" symbol—a red package attached to a balloon. Goods valued at L.300,000 or more qualify for the refund. Obtain a receipt from the shop, to show on departure together with the goods to a customs officer. Post the receipt in one of the special boxes to be found past the customs area at most international airports in Italy. Or send it by mail within 50 days of the date of purchase. A small service charge will be deducted from the refund.

Where's the nearest bank/ currency-exchange office?	***Dov'è la banca più vicina/ l'ufficio di cambio più vicino?***
I'd like to change some pounds/ dollars	***Desidero cambiare delle sterline/ dei dollari.***
Do you accept traveller's cheques?	***Accettate i traveller's cheques?***
Can I pay with this credit card?	***Posso pagare con questa carta di credito?***

N

NEWSPAPERS and MAGAZINES *(giornale; rivista)*

A selection of British and continental newspapers and magazines are on sale, sometimes a day late, at the airports and major railway stations, and at newsstands in the big cities. The Paris-based *International Herald Tribune*, printed in Rome, is available early in the morning. Prices are high for all foreign publications. See the local papers for information on events and entertainment. For news about sports, consult the salmon-pink newspaper *Gazzetta dello Sport*.

*Do you have any English-
language newspapers?*　　**Avete giornali in inglese?**

OPENING HOURS *(orari di apertura)*

Banks are generally open from 8:00 a.m. to 1:30 p.m. and from 2:30 to 4 p.m., Monday to Friday. Currency-exchange offices at airports and major railway stations are open till late in the evening and on Saturdays and Sundays.

Churches generally close for sightseeing at lunchtime, approximately noon to 3 p.m. or even later.

Museums and art galleries are usually open from 9 or 9:30 a.m. to 2, 3, or 4 p.m., and in some cases from 5 to 8 p.m., Tuesday to Saturday, and until 1 p.m. on Sundays. Closing day is generally Monday. If Monday is a holiday, some museums and galleries close the following day. Check times locally before you set out.

Post offices normally open from 8:15 or 8:30 a.m. to 1:30 or 2:00 p.m., Monday to Friday, till noon on Saturdays and on the last day of the month. Main post offices in larger cities keep longer hours.

Shops open from 9 a.m. to 12:30 or 1 p.m. and from 3:30 or 4 to 7:30 or 8 p.m. In Milan and Turin, the lunch break is normally shorter and closing time earlier. Most shops close on Monday morning. Food stores generally open earlier, closing on Wednesday or Thursday afternoons. Shops in tourist resorts stay open all day, every day, in high season.

POLICE

The municipal police *(vigili urbani)*, wear navy blue or white uniforms with shiny buttons and white helmets. They direct traffic and handle routine tasks. Some municipal police act as interpreters. Look for the special badge on their uniforms. The *carabinieri,* dressed in brown or black uniforms, maintain law and order throughout the country. Italy's frontiers, ports, airports, and railway stations come under the jurisdiction of the national police *(polizia di stato)*. A branch of the national force, the *polizia stradale* or *polstrada,* patrol the roads.

Italy

In an emergency, dial 112 or 113 for police assistance.

Where's the nearest   **Dov'è il posto di polizia più**
police station?   **vicino?**

PUBLIC HOLIDAYS

Banks, government offices, most shops, and some museums and galleries are closed on the following days:

January 1	*Capodanno or Primo dell'Anno*	New Year's Day
January 6	*Epifania*	Epiphany
April 25	*Festa della Liberazione*	Liberation Day
May 1	*Festa del Lavoro*	Labour Day
August 15	*Ferragosto*	Assumption Day
November 1	*Ognissanti*	All Saint's Day
December 8	*L'Immacolata Concezione*	Immaculate Conception
December 25	*Natale*	Christmas Day
December 26	*Santo Stefano*	St. Stephen's Day
Movable date:	*Lunedi di Pasqua*	Easter Monday

Shops and offices also close on local feast days held in honour of a town's patron saint.

Are you open tomorrow?   **È aperto domani?**

R

RADIO and TV *(radio; televisione)*

During the tourist season, RAI, the Italian state radio and television network, broadcasts news in English from Monday to Saturday at 10 a.m. and on Sundays at 9:30 a.m. Vatican Radio carries foreign-language religious news programmes. British (BBC), American (VOA), and Canadian (CBC) programmes are easily obtained on short-wave radios.

RAI television and private channels broadcast exclusively in Italian.

RELIGIOUS SERVICES

The major religions all have congregations in the cities. Check local newspapers for details, or ask at your hotel or the local tourist office.

Is there a... near here?	*C'è una ... qui vicino?*
Catholic/Protestant church	*chiesa cattolica/protestante*
mosque	*moschea*
synagogue	*sinagoga*
At what time is mass/the service?	*A che ora è la messa/la funzione?*

RESTAURANTS

In theory, an Italian **ristorante** is supposed to be larger and more elaborate than a **trattoria,** but they are both restaurants, as are the less common and simpler **osteria, locanda,** and **taverna.** A **rosticceria,** originally a shop specializing in grilled dishes, now provides tables for guests to eat on the premises. A **trattoria-pizzeria** serves pizza in addition to other simple meals. For a quick lunch-time snack, choose a **tavola calda** ("hot table"), a stand-up bar serving a variety of hot and cold dishes throughout the day, to take away or eat on the spot. A **gelateria** specializes in rich, creamy Italian ice-cream. If you just want an espresso, soft drink, beer, or aperitif, head for a **caffè** or **bar.**

A service charge (*servizio*) is added to all restaurant bills, but it is customary to leave an additional 5 to 10% tip for the waiter. In cafés and bars, it usually costs much more to sit at a table, rather than stand at the counter.

When eating out, you are required by law to obtain a *fattura fiscale*, an official receipt indicating the sales tax (IVA). In theory, you can be stopped by the police as you leave the restaurant and fined if you are unable to present the receipt.

To help you order...

Waiter!/Waitress!	*Cameriere!/Cameriera!*
May I have the menu, please?	*Posso avere il menù?*
Do you have a set menu?	*Avete un menù a prezzo fisso?*

Italy

I'd like to pay.	***Vorrei pagare.***
I'd like a/an/some…	***Vorrei …***
beer	***una birra***
fruit	***della frutta***
ice-cream	***un gelato***
(mineral) water	***dell'acqua (minerale)***

… and read the menu

acciughe	anchovies	**legumi, verdure**	vegetables
agnello	lamb	**lepre**	hare
anguilla	eel	**macedonia di frutta**	fruit salad
anitra	duck	**maiale**	pork
aragosta	spiny lobster	**manzo**	beef
aringhe	herrings	**melanzane**	aubergine (eggplant)
arrosto	roast		
bisteca (di filetto)	(rib) steak	**merluzzo**	cod
cacciagione	game	**una minestra**	soup
carciofi	artichokes	**delle patate**	potato
casalinga	homemade	**del pesce**	fish
cavolfiore	cauliflower	**oca**	goose
cinolle	onions	**ostriche**	oysters
coniglio	rabbit	**patate**	potatoes
costoletta	cutlet	**peperoni**	sweet peppers
cozze	mussels	**pesce**	fish
crudo	raw	**pesce spada**	swordfish
dolce	sweet (dessert)	**piccata**	veal cutlet
fagioli	beans	**piselli**	peas
fegato	liver	**pollame**	poultry
formaggio	cheese	**pollo**	chicken
frittata	omelette	**polpette**	meatballs
frutti di mare	seafood	**pomodori**	tomatoes
funghi	mushrooms	**riglia**	red mullet
gamberetti	shrimps	**riso**	rice
granchio	crab	**salsiccia**	sausage

scaloppina	breaded veal cutlet	*tonno*	tunny (tuna)
		trotat	trout
sogliola	sole	*vitello*	veal
suovo	egg	*vongole*	clams
tacchino	turkey		

SPAS *(terme)*

Italy has some 200 spas and health resorts—institutions using thermal waters for rest, recreation, or treatment.

For information on individual spas, contact:

Assoterme, Via Margutta 19, 00187 Rome; tel. (06) 36 14 044

TIME DIFFERENCES

Italy follows Central European Time (GMT + 1). From the last Sunday in March to the last Sunday in September, clocks are put ahead one hour (GMT + 2).

New York	London	Rome	Sydney	Auckland
6 a.m.	11 a.m.	noon	8 p.m.	10 p.m.

What time is it?   ***Che ore sono?***

TIPPING *(mancia)*

A service charge of approximately 15% is added to hotel and restaurant bills. If prices are quoted as all-inclusive, *tutto compreso*, the service charge is included, but not necessarily the IVA (VAT/sales tax); ask if you're not sure. In addition to the service charge, it is customary to give the waiter something extra. Bellboys, doormen, bartenders, and service-station attendants all expect a tip.

Thank you, this is for you   ***Grazie, questo è per lei.***

Keep the change.   ***Tenga il resto.***

Italy

TOILETS

Toilets may be labelled with a symbol of a man or a woman or the initials W.C. Sometimes the wording will be in Italian, but beware, as you might be misled: *Uomini* is for men, *Donne* is for women. Equally, *Signori*—with a final *i*—is for men, *Signore*—with an *e*—is for women.

Where are the toilets?   ***Dove sono i gabinetti?***

TOURIST INFORMATION OFFICES

The Italian National Tourist Office (ENIT, *Ente Nazionale Italiano per il Turismo*) is represented in Italy and abroad. The organization publishes detailed brochures with up-to-date information on accommodation, means of transport, general tips, and useful addresses for the whole country.

Australia and New Zealand—Correspondent: c/o Alitalia, Orient Overseas Building, Suite 202, 32 Bridge Street, Sydney, NSW 2000; tel. (2) 271-308

Canada—Italian Government Travel Office/Office National Italien de Tourisme, 1 Place Ville-Marie, Suite 1914, Montreal, Que. H3B 3M9; tel. (514) 866-7667

Eire—Italian State Tourist Office, 47 Merrion Square, Dublin 2; tel. (01) 766-397

South Africa—Italian State Tourist Office, London House, 21 Loveday Street, P.O. Box 6507, Johannesburg 2000; tel. (11) 838-3247

U.K.—Italian State Tourist Board, 1 Princes Street, London W1R 88AY; tel. (01) 408 1254

U.S.A.—Italian Government Travel Office, 630 Fifth Avenue, Suite 1565, New York, NY 10111; tel. (212) 245-4822; Italian Government Travel Office, 500 North Michigan Avenue, Suite 401, Chicago, IL 60611; tel. (312) 644-0990,6; Italian Government Travel Office, 360 Post Street, Suite 801, San Francisco, CA 94108; tel. (415) 392-6206

Where's the tourist office?   ***Dov'è l'ufficio turistico?***

TRANSPORT

See also CAR RENTAL and DRIVING

By city transport

Taxis (*tassì* or *taxi*) may be hailed in the street, picked up at a taxi rank or ordered by telephone. Make sure that the meter is running. Extra charges for luggage and for trips at night, on holidays, and to airports are posted inside every cab. Taxi drivers expect a 10 to 15% tip.

In addition to **bus** *(autobus)* services, some big cities operate **trams/streetcars** (called *tram* in Italian). Naples has four **funicular** *(funicolare)* routes. Rome, Milan, and Naples are also served by **underground/subway** *(metropolitana,* abbreviated *metrò)* systems. In Venice, of course, there's no way to move on wheels; instead, there are diesel-powered **water buses**, as well as **water taxis** and **gondolas.**

At bus stops *(fermata),* signs indicate the numbers of the buses stopping there and the routes they serve. Buy tickets for buses and trams in advance at tobacconists, newsstands, or bars. Board buses through the door marked "Salita"; the exit is indicated by the word "Uscita." *Metrò* tickets can be purchased from machines at the stations.

Rome's orange buses are crowded on certain routes and at rush hours, but they are an inexpensive means of transport. Tickets can be purchased in books of ten; one-day, three-day, and weekly tickets are sold at the ATAC (Rome's transport authority) booth in Piazza dei Cinquecento, in front of the Stazione Termini, the central railway station.

Rome's *metrò* railway Line A runs from Via Ottaviano, near the Vatican, southeast to Via Anagnina, stopping at more than 20 stations and passing in reach of the city's popular tourist sights. The intersecting Line B runs from Stazione Termini, with stops at the Colosseum, EUR, Ostia Antica, and Ostia Lido.

Rome's horse-drawn cabs have been a familiar sight in the capital for centuries. Fares are not fixed, so it's best to agree on a price with the driver before setting off.

Florence has about 40 main city and suburban bus routes. For information and a free bus map, go to the ATAF office at Piazza del Duomo 57r. Board buses at the rear and punch your ticket in the red machine.

Milan is served by ATM buses and trains. The city's *metrò* system is *Metropolitana Milanese,* of which Line 1 is of most interest to visitors. Information and tourist tickets are available at the ATM office on the mezzanine floor of the Duomo *metrò* station.

In **Naples,** buses can get crowded, but they are the only means of transport in certain areas of the city. The convenient *metrò* connects the Stazione Centrale in the east with the Stazione Mergellina in the west.

Venice's water buses *(vaporetto* and the smaller and faster *motoscafo)* ply the Grand Canal and shuttle between the islands. Tickets can be bought from bars and kiosks and at most stops. Apart from ordinary single tickets (buy one and get it punched before boarding or you'll have to pay a surcharge), there are passes valid for 24 hours. Venice has about six water-taxi *(motoscafo di nolo)* stations. Although theoretically the rates are fixed, they tend to vary; agree on the fare in advance. This also applies to trips by gondola.

By coach

Italy has a vast network of coaches (long-distance buses)—called *pullman* or *corriera*—and each province has its own coach companies. Information on destinations and timetables are posted at coach terminals, usually situated near the town's railway station, and can be obtained from local or regional tourist offices (see page 242).

By train

Children under the age of 4 travel free (unless individual accommodation is required); aged 4 to 12 inclusive, they pay half fare. Apart from providing one of Europe's lowest regular fares, the Italian State Railways offer several reduced rates—see GETTING TO ITALY, page 230. Tickets can be purchased and reservations made at travel agencies and railway stations.

Italian trains are classified according to speed. Best and fastest are the *Intercity (IC;* first and second class; some require supplementary fare and seat reservations) and the *Rapido (R;* some are first class only; supplementary charge compulsory). *Espresso (EXP)* is an ordinary express train, usually with both first- and second-class cars, but a few are second-class only; no supplementary charge is made. The *Diretto (D)* is a fast train making a number of local stops, while the *Local (L;* sometimes termed *Accelerato, A)* is a slow local train which stops at every station. *Littorina* is the name of a small diesel train used on short runs.

By boat

There are regular, daily car-ferry connections between Reggio di Calabria and Sicily, Villa San Giovanni and Sicily, Naples and Sicily; between Civitavecchia and Sardinia, Livorno and Sardinia; and between Naples and the islands of Capri and Ischia, as well as regular boat services linking Genoa, Sardinia, Naples, and Sicily and in general connecting the mainland with Italy's many smaller islands. Ferries and hydrofoils also operate between towns and sites on the northern lakes of Como, Garda, and Maggiore. For information on schedules and fares, apply to a travel agency or the regional tourist office, or phone (06) 42 12, ACI's telephone assistance centre.

By plane

Alitalia, Italy's national airline, and ATI and other domestic airlines have regular flights between Rome and/or Milan and some 30 Italian cities and towns and less frequent service to a number of smaller airports. Detailed information is available at travel agencies and Alitalia offices. Reductions on domestic flights include 90% off for children under 2 years of age who do not occupy a seat, 50% for the age group 2 to 11 included, 30% from 12 to 21 included. In addition, there are discounts on night flights and weekend tickets.

When's the next bus/train/boat/plane for...?	*A che ora parte il prossimo autobus/treno/battello/aereo per...?*
What's the fare to...?	*Quanto costa il biglietto per...?*
I want a ticket to...	*Vorrei un biglietto per...*
single (one-way)/	*andata/andata e*
return (round-trip)	*ritorno*
first/second class	*prima/seconda classe*
I'd like to make seat reservations.	*Vorrei prenotare un posto.*

USEFUL VOCABULARY

please/thank you	*per favore/grazie*
where/when/how	*dove/quando/come*
how long/how far	*quanto tempo/quanto dista*
what/why/who	*che (che cosa)/perchè/chi*
yesterday/today/tomorrow	*ieri/oggi/domani*
day/week/month/year	*giorno/settimana/mese/anno*
near/far	*vicino/lontano*
good/bad	*buono/cattivo*
big/small	*grande/piccolo*
more/less	*più/meno*
full/empty	*pieno/vuoto*
cheap/expensive	*buon mercato/caro*
hot/cold	*caldo/freddo*
open/closed	*aperto/chiuso*
free (vacant)/occupied	*libero/occupato*

Italy

old/new	***vecchio/nuovo***
Monday	***lunedì***
Tuesday	***martedì***
Wednesday	***mercoledì***
Thursday	***giovedì***
Friday	***venerdì***
Saturday	***sabato***
Sunday	***domenica***

W

WEIGHTS and MEASURES

Italy uses the metric system.

Length

Weight

Temperature

ABOUT BERLITZ

In 1878 Professor Maximilian Berlitz had a revolutionary idea about making language learning accessible and enjoyable. One hundred and twenty years later these same principles are still successfully at work.

For language instruction, translation and interpretation services, cross-cultural training, study abroad programs, and an array of publishing products and additional services, visit any one of our more than 350 Berlitz Centers in over 40 countries.

Please consult your local telephone directory for the Berlitz Center nearest you or visit our web site at http://www.berlitz.com.

Helping the World Communicate